THE LOST TOMB
of
ALEXANDER
THE GREAT

Richmond Editions

ISBN: 1-902699-62-9

Publisher: Danièle Juncqua Naveau

Managing Editor: Nick Easterbrook

Academic Editor: Dr Mark Merrony

Assistant Editors: Jenny Finch, Christelle Yeyet-Jacquot

Production Manager: Sophie Chéry

Production Assistant: Arvind Shah

Rights Manager: Jane Lowry

Picture research: Aline da Silva Cerqueira

Reprographics: Periplus Publishing London Ltd

Printed in Italy by L.E.G.O. S.p.A.

THE LOST TOMB

of

ALEXANDER
THE GREAT

ANDREW MICHAEL CHUGG

Acknowledgements

I would like to express my particular gratitude to the following for their assistance in the preparation of this book:

The staff of Bristol Central Library;

The staff of Bristol University Arts and Social Sciences Library;

Dr David Jeffreys for his help concerning Memphis;

Dr Poul Pedersen of the Danish Halikarnassos Project;

Dr José Antonio Peña of the University of Granada for a Spanish reference;

Dr Richard L. and Penelope W. Betz, Hemispheres Antique Maps and Prints;

Dr Jean-Yves Empereur, Director of the Centre for Alexandrian Studies, for his encouragement;

Mrs Gulgun Kazan of the British Institute of Archaeology at Ankara for providing an elusive reference;

Dr Judith McKenzie for a new and precious ancient reference;

Dr Sean Kingsley, Managing Editor of *Minerva: The International Review of Ancient Art and Archaeology*, for his advice, enthusiasm and support;

Dr Mark Merrony, the principal editor of this book, for his dedication.

Contents

Prologue: Alexander's Afterlife

The conquests of Alexander the Great loom among the towering events of world history. The story has launched more than a thousand books in over a hundred languages. Yet one aspect of Alexander's biography has languished in a state of sad neglect, for virtually all the existing works close with Alexander's death or provide a mere outline of subsequent events. The only previous book in English dedicated to the subject of his tomb was published nearly two centuries ago (E. D. Clarke, *The Tomb of Alexander*, 1805). Not only has it now become a rarity, but it is also out of date. It is the purpose of this account to correct this deficit and to show that a detailed knowledge of Alexander's afterlife is integral to a proper appreciation of his impact on history.

This book takes up the tale where others abandon it with the events surrounding Alexander's death in Babylon late in the evening of 10 June 323 BC. It describes the preparation of the catafalque (funeral carriage) meant to return his body to his homeland, but diverted to Egypt by Ptolemy, who was most likely acting to fulfil Alexander's wishes. It is contended that Ptolemy's hijacking of the corpse was probably the direct cause of the attack on Egypt by Perdiccas, the Regent, who was assassinated there by his own men, having twice failed to force the crossing of the Nile.

The initial entombment of Alexander at the old Egyptian capital of Memphis is analysed in terms of the iconography and possible location of this sepulchre and it is demonstrated that, contrary to received opinion, the Memphite tomb probably existed for three or four decades. This was eventually relocated to Alexandria by Ptolemy's son. There, Alexander achieved the apotheosis he had consciously pursued in life. An enormous temple precinct was constructed in the heart of the city and a high priest was appointed annually to orchestrate his worship.

The tomb returned to the centre-stage of world history in the time of Cleopatra in the 1st century BC as the Romans sought to complete their nascent empire with the conquest of Egypt. Alexander became an icon for Caesar's faction and the tomb a place of pilgrimage, reviled by his Republican opponents. Cleopatra dreamt of re-establishing Alexander's empire, through the pliable medium of Mark Antony and his military prowess, but Rome would not brook a rival near her throne, so the lovers perished in defeat.

The Roman emperors saw in Alexander an exemplar for their autocratic rule, so the tomb basked in their patronage for several centuries more. However, in the late 3rd and 4th centuries AD Alexandria suffered a series of violent upheavals, in one of which the mausoleum overlying the tomb was destroyed. A case is made that almost the last of these shocks, a devastating earthquake followed by a tidal wave in AD 365, was most likely culpable. Any restoration of the tomb was precluded by the growing political power of the Christian Church, which could only see in the deified Alexander a potent pagan rival. The once famous tomb vanished mysteriously from history.

The forces of Islam captured Alexandria in AD 642 and ushered in a lingering decline of the greatest of Greek cities. For nearly a millennium almost nothing was said of the tomb in the ancient texts. By the late medieval period the area of the city had shrunk to less than a third of its extent in the time of Cleopatra and almost all that remained lay in ruins. However, from the early 16th century visitors began once again to report the existence of a tomb of Alexander amidst the wasted vestiges of antiquity. Evidence is presented here for the first time, which firmly links this medieval tomb with a sarcophagus now in the British Museum. There are also intriguing connections between this relic and the Memphite tomb and also with the Late Roman period when the Alexandrian tomb was destroyed.

In the modern era the search for the tomb is inextricably connected with the archaeologists' struggle to reconstruct ancient Alexandria from fragments in the dust. Progress is seriously hampered by the fact that the modern city has spread to encompass the entire ancient ruin field. Some of the best evidence was gathered in the mid–19th century just before the developers sealed over the deeply buried remains of the Roman and Ptolemaic cities. By integrating the archaeological material with information from written and cartographic sources, a new hypothesis for the nature and location of the Alexandrian tomb has been formulated. If this fresh theory is correct, not only may it provide the key to comprehending the detailed layout of the ancient city, but it also implies that a substantial fragment of the wall that surrounded the precinct of Alexander's tomb has survived unrecognised into the present day.

The history of Alexander's tombs is a complex and intricate tapestry, for the threads of evidence are fragmentary, diverse and interwoven through 25 centuries. But to unravel the mystery is a thrilling experience, offering as it does glimpses of the vanished glories of the ancient world together with telling insights into the minds of Alexander, the people who followed him and those who succeeded to the kingdoms of his empire. Some admired and worshipped him, whilst others detested and denounced everything he stood for. The polarity and strength of opinion many centuries after his death are the most impressive testament to the enduring potency of his influence. What though, we might wonder, would Alexander himself have made of the reactions he stirred?

I should like, Onesicritus, to come back to life for a little while after my death to see how men read these present events then. If now they praise and welcome them, do not be surprised, for they think, every one of them, that this is a fine bait to catch my goodwill.

Alexander quoted by Lucian, *How to Write History*, 40.

Dramatis Personae: **our sources**

P art of the special fascination of this story is that it extends across 25 centuries and weaves together ancient Egyptian, Greek, Roman, Arab and modern European cultures. A consequence of this diversity and longevity is that the reader will meet a kaleidoscopic cast of characters on their journey through these pages. It has, therefore, seemed appropriate to devote this chapter to a concise but informative introduction to the principal persons on whose testimony this fresh account relies. These have loosely been subdivided into ancient and modern sources and they are listed in alphabetical order, so that these pages also serve as a type of glossary for occasional reference.

This book mainly concerns itself with Alexander's death and his afterlife with its focus on his famous tomb. Alexander himself, of course, is undoubtedly the most important figure of all, and the chapter will fittingly conclude with a summary of his astonishing career.

Ancient texts

Achilles Tatius: Greek erotic novelist most probably of the 2nd–3rd century AD, though his date is still disputed. His surviving work *Leucippe and Cleitophon* includes a brief but remarkable description of ancient Alexandria. A partial papyrus manuscript has been found in Egypt.

Aelian (Claudius Aelianus): Greek writer who taught rhetoric in Rome *c.* AD 220.

Alexander Romance: a semi-legendary account of Alexander's career, compiled by a native Egyptian editor from older stories and fables in the early 3rd century AD. Although hopelessly disjointed and inaccurate as a work of history, it is nevertheless valuable in that it preserves some traditions lost from the more authoritative ancient accounts. It is also good on Alexandria, since its creator was probably a resident of the ancient city. The compiler is known as Pseudo-Callisthenes, because some of its manuscripts falsely attributed it to Alexander's court historian Callisthenes. It survives today in several versions, of which the oldest and most faithful to the original are a Greek manuscript of the 3rd century AD, the Armenian translation and the Latin edition of Julius Valerius.

Ammianus Marcellinus: born in Antioch and active in the second half of the 4th century AD, he was virtually the last of the secular Latin historians of Rome. His accounts of Alexandria are particularly valuable, since he seems to have visited the city in the aftermath of the great earthquake of AD 365.

Aristobulus: accompanied Alexander in his campaigns, perhaps in the capacity of an engineer or architect. Subsequently penned an influential but lost history of Alexander's reign, which was a major source for Arrian, Plutarch and Strabo.

Arius Didymus: prolific and respected Alexandrian scholar of the 1st century BC. He was a close friend of Octavian/Augustus and probably accompanied him during his visit to Alexander's tomb in 30 BC. Likely to be the source for the construction of a new mausoleum for Alexander by Ptolemy IV Philopator (r. *c.* 221–205 BC).

Arrian (Flavius Arrianus Xenophon): rose to become Governor of Cappadocia under the Emperor Hadrian (r. AD 117–38) in the early 2nd century AD. An experienced military commander, he wrote his *Campaigns of Alexander* to rescue the king's reputation as a general and a conqueror from a morass of misconceptions and inaccuracies then current in Roman literature. In doing so, he tended to suppress biographical details and anecdotes in favour of troop dispositions, military logistics and strategic intent. His lost *History of Events after Alexander*, which survives only in fragments and a partial epitome, probably contained the most authoritative account of the movements of Alexander's remains after his death.

Caesar (Gaius Julius Caesar): author of *The Civil War* and purported to have written *The Alexandrine War* – describing a military campaign in Alexandria in 48 BC, although the latter was most likely ghostwritten by Aulus Hirtius. A recorded visitor to Alexander's tomb in the same year. Also dictator of Rome.

Curtius (Quintus Curtius Rufus): the most important Latin historian of Alexander's reign. His date is uncertain but the era of the Emperor Claudius in the 1st century AD seems likely, when a man of the same name was proconsul of Africa. The work is highly rhetorical and struggles to project a progressive deterioration on to Alexander's character, reminiscent of that exhibited by Gaius Caligula. Curtius' facts are usually reliable, but his interpretations of the facts are hopelessly distorted by his preconceptions.

Dio Cassius (Cassius Dio Cocceianus): born in Nicaea *c.* AD 155, he was an eminent Greek politician and governor under the Severan emperors. He was twice raised to the consulship and died *c.* AD 235. Author of an important *History of Rome*, some of which only survives in an epitome.

Diodorus Siculus: a Sicilian Greek of the 1st century BC, he wrote a universal history incorporating a volume dedicated to Alexander. He visited Alexandria and the precinct of Alexander's tomb, probably during the reign of Cleopatra VII (r. 51–30 BC).

Ephemerides (Alexander's *Royal Journal*): our main source for the course of Alexander's fatal illness. Some have tried to show that it is a forgery, but similar official diaries were kept by earlier Macedonian kings and by the Ptolemies. Aelian attributed the *Ephemerides* to Eumenes of Cardia, Alexander's Chief Secretary (and co-written by Diodotus of Erythrae).

Ibn Abdel Hakim: Arab writer of the mid-9th century AD. He knew Alexandria just before the so-called medieval walls were finalised by the Sultan Ahmed Ibn Tulun and he provides tantalising hints of its topography and a medieval mosque of Alexander.

Herodian: a Greek historian of the 3rd century AD, he wrote some time around the year AD 240.

John Chrysostom (St): pupil of Libanius and subsequently Archbishop of Constantinople around AD 400. Among his sermons is a passage believed to be the earliest assertion that Alexander's tomb had disappeared.

Josephus (Flavius Josephus): Jewish historian of the 1st century AD. He makes frequent mention of Alexandria due to the large Jewish community in the city in his time.

Justin: the 4th-century AD epitomiser of a history of the world by a 1st-century BC Latin writer called Pompeius Trogus. Trogus was a dedicated Republican and therefore highly antagonistic to absolute monarchy, a prejudice which he makes little attempt to conceal in his account of Alexander's career.

Libanius: Greek sophist and rhetorician of Antioch (lived AD 314–*c.* 94). Though of pagan sympathies and a friend of Julian the Apostate (r. AD 361–3), he also taught St John Chrysostom and received an honorary Praetorian Prefecture from the Christian emperor Theodosius I (r. AD 379–95).

Lucan (Marcus Annaeus Lucanus): the nephew of Seneca (tutor of Nero (r. AD 54–68) and the author of a book about Egypt). Recalled from Athens to join the court of the emperor, Lucan's innately republican sentiments were stimulated by the spectacle of Nero's descent into cruelty and debauchery. In AD 65, at the age of 25, he was implicated in Calpurnius Piso's plot to assassinate the emperor. When the conspiracy failed, Nero required him to commit suicide. His legacy was the *Pharsalia*, an unfinished poem recounting the civil war between Caesar and Pompey and recognised as a jewel of Latin literature. It contains two passages which provide the most detailed description of Alexander's tomb.

Lucian: Syrian Greek writer and satirist of the second half of the 2nd century AD.

Nearchus: admiral of Alexander's fleet for the voyage through the Indian Ocean and the Persian Gulf. Author of a lost history concentrating on India and his famous voyage, which was the principal source for Arrian's *Indica*.

Onesicritus (of Astypalaea): a pupil of Diogenes the Cynic, he was Alexander's helmsman on the voyage down the Indus. He wrote a biography of Alexander, now lost, which teemed with anecdotes and local colour. His work was an influential source for Plutarch, Strabo and perhaps parts of the *Alexander Romance*.

Parian Marble (*Marmor Parium*): a Greek inscription carved in about 263/2 BC found on the Aegean island of Paros and giving a chronology of events. The last surviving entry is for 299/8 BC, but there are major lacunae. However, the last fragment is complete until 309 BC. It was found in 1897 and is now in the Paros museum. Paros was part of the Ptolemaic Empire, ruled by Ptolemy II Philadelphus (r. 285–246 BC), when the marble was set up.

Pausanius: Greek travel writer of the mid-2nd century AD, perhaps from Lydia. His principal work is the *Description of Greece*.

Plutarch: Greek essayist and scholar of the 1st to early 2nd century AD. His *Life of Alexander* is the most biographical of surviving texts and drew upon the widest range of primary sources. His earlier essays *On the Virtue or Fortune of Alexander* are also important biographical sources on the king.

Pseudo–Callisthenes: see *Alexander Romance*.

Ptolemy I Soter (r. 323-282 BC): author of the most detailed and accurate contemporary history of Alexander's campaigns. Though now lost, this work was the most important source for Arrian's *Campaigns of Alexander*. It is believed by some that his accuracy and detail rely upon his acquisition of Alexander's *Ephemerides (Royal Journal)*, when he took possession of Alexander's body. At least three ancient sources independently assert that he was Alexander's illegitimate half-brother. Also one of Alexander's most senior officers and later pharaoh of Egypt.

Strabo: Greek geographer of the late 1st century BC and early 1st century AD. He lived in Alexandria for around five years and in his 17th book gave the most important description of the city as it was in about 20 BC.

Suetonius (Gaius Suetonius Tranquillus): author of *The Twelve Caesars*, which is a scandalous but accurate set of biographies of the first 12 Roman princes from Julius Caesar to Domitian. He wrote when they were safely dead, in the early 2nd century AD.

Zenobius: Greek sophist who taught rhetoric in Rome under Hadrian and compiled a book of 'proverbs' by Lucillus of Tarrha in Crete and Arius Didymus of Alexandria.

Modern texts

Achille Adriani: director of the Graeco-Roman Museum in Alexandria from 1932–40 and again from 1948–52. Author of the theory that the Alabaster Tomb in Alexandria is the antechamber of a tomb of Alexander the Great.

Leo Africanus: Moorish traveller in Africa, who was captured by pirates in 1520 and ended up in the service of Pope Leo X, who converted him to Christianity. His *Description of Africa* remained the best general account of the continent for centuries, and it included a description of Alexandria, which he probably visited several times between *c.* 1515 and 1520.

Napoleon Bonaparte: instigator of the *Description de l'Égypte*, the greatest work on ancient and medieval Egypt ever published. Also Emperor of France (r. 1804-15).

Giuseppe Botti: founder of the Graeco-Roman Museum in Alexandria and its director from 1892–1904. Author of numerous archaeological works on Alexandria including a reconstructed map of the ancient city.

Georg Braun and Frans Hogenberg: cartographers of Cologne, who sought to emulate the success of Ortelius' *Theatre of the World* by publishing an atlas of plans of *Cities of the World*. They included a beautiful chart of Alexandria, which, despite some distortions, contains much valid information on the early 16th-century city.

Evaristo Breccia: director of the Graeco-Roman Museum in Alexandria from 1904–32. Author of *Alexandrea ad Aegyptum*, an important guide book to the ancient city and the remains in the Museum.

Louis-François Cassas: French artist and traveller. Visited Alexandria and drew many important vistas and a map in 1785.

Edward Daniel Clarke: English scholar and traveller. Commissioned by Lord Hutchinson to retrieve the antiquities garnered by the French in 1801, he discovered an ancient sarcophagus in the hold of the French hospital ship, *La Cause*, and established that there was a local tradition that it had once contained Alexander's corpse. Author of *The Tomb of Alexander*.

Dominique Vivant Denon: associate of Napoleon and foremost among the scholars who accompanied the French expedition to Egypt in 1798. Author of *Travels in Egypt*. Later director of the Louvre.

Jean-Yves Empereur: founder in 1990 and director of the Centre d'Études Alexandrines (CEA). Author of numerous books and scholarly articles on Alexandria including *Alexandria Rediscovered* and *Hoi Taphoi Tou Megalou Alexandrou*.

Mahmoud Bey el-Falaki: sent by Mohammed Ali to train as an engineer in France, in 1865 he was commissioned by the Khedive Ismaïl, as a favour to Napoleon III (r. 1852–70) of France, to determine the layout of ancient Alexandria. He succeeded brilliantly in defining the basic street grid and outline of the Roman metropolis, but argued ineffectually for the Nabi Daniel Mosque as the site of Alexander's tomb.

P. M. Fraser: Author of *Ptolemaic Alexandria*, 1972; a mine of information on the ancient city.

David George Hogarth: English archaeologist of the late 19th and early 20th century. Author of an influential report in 1895, which concluded that archaeological resources were better directed elsewhere than Alexandria.

Jean-Philippe Lauer: leading French Egyptologist of the 20th century and a specialist in the Memphite necropolis of Saqqara.

Auguste Mariette: discoverer and excavator of the Serapeum at Saqqara. First Head of the Egyptian Antiquities Commission and the greatest Egyptologist of the 19th century.

Luigi Mayer: artist employed in 1792 by Sir Robert Ainslie, British Ambassador in Constantinople, for a project to draw a large collection of scenes from around the Ottoman Empire. The fruits of the expedition were published between about 1801 and 1804 as a magnificent series of aquatint engravings, including many views of Alexandria.

Richard Pococke: early 18th-century English antiquarian and traveller. Author of the *Description of the East* published in 1743, he had paced around the walls of Alexandria in 1737.

Alan John Bayard Wace: English professor of archaeology, who published an obscure article on 'The Sarcophagus of Alexander the Great' in the *Bulletin of the Faculty of Arts of Farouk I University in Alexandria* in 1948.

Alexandre-Max de Zogheb: member of a prominent Alexandrian family, who published his *Études sur l'ancienne Alexandrie,* containing a chapter on Alexander's tomb, in 1909. The main source for Ambroise Schilizzi's implausible tale of the discovery of Alexander's tomb beneath the modern Nabi Daniel Mosque.

Alexander's exploits in life

Alexander was born the son of King Philip II (r. 359–36 BC) of Macedon and his Molossian queen Olympias in July of 356 BC. During Alexander's childhood and youth Philip gradually established Macedon as the dominant power in Greece. In 338 BC Philip destroyed opposition to his authority from Athens and Thebes at the Battle of Chaeronea, where Prince Alexander led a dashing cavalry charge and annihilated the Theban Sacred Band, who had been considered the finest soldiers in Greece. When his father was assassinated by Pausanius in 336 BC, Alexander succeeded to the throne. He crushed insurrections among the tribes to the north, marching as far as the Danube. Thebes and Athens took advantage of his absence to stir up a rebellion among the city-states, but he retaliated with lightning speed, bringing his army south by forced marches through the mountains. Thebes was besieged, captured and razed to the ground in accordance with a vote of Alexander's allies.

In 334 BC Alexander led a Greek coalition in an attack upon the Persian Empire with the initial aim of freeing the Greek cities of the Ionian coast. In May he decisively defeated the Persian armies of the region of modern Turkey at the River Granicus. By the summer of the following year all the Greek states had been duly liberated, but Alexander continued to pursue the war by marching towards the heart of the Persian Empire. Darius (r. 336–30), the 'Great King', had gathered an enormous Persian host and the armies clashed on the shores of the Gulf of Issus, highway into Syria. Alexander routed his opponent's forces by a combined assault with his cavalry and the ferocious Macedonian phalanx, and Darius fled back to Persia to raise a further army. Alexander marched down the Levantine coast, besieging and capturing Tyre and Gaza and closing all the Mediterranean ports to the Persian fleet, which was eventually compelled to surrender. In Egypt, where Persian rule had been particularly oppressive since its conquest 10 years earlier, Alexander was welcomed as a deliverer.

Having founded Alexandria near the westernmost mouth of the Nile, Alexander took his army north again for the final showdown with Darius. The climactic battle of the war was fought on the wide, flat plain of Gaugamela in October 331 BC. For a third time Alexander triumphed through a perfectly executed stratagem to weaken the Persian centre. Once again Darius fled the field, whilst Alexander proceeded to capture Babylon and the palaces of Susa and Persepolis, declaring himself 'King of Asia'.

Alexander resumed the pursuit of Darius in the summer of 330 BC, heading north towards the Caspian Sea. Darius' entourage panicked and executed the deposed Great King. Alexander pressed the pursuit of the dregs of Persian resistance into the region of modern Afghanistan, successively defeating Bessus and Spitamenes. After a series of hard-fought campaigns stretching over two years, the ancient nations of Bactria and Sogdiana were finally pacified. In the summer of 327 BC Alexander crossed the Hindu Kush and commenced the invasion of India. At the Battle of the Hydaspes Alexander defeated the army of the Rajah Porus, despite his deployment of a large number of war elephants against the Macedonians.

Alexander marched ever eastwards, towards the Ganges, but continual drenching by the Indian monsoon and rumours of vast armies with thousands of elephants on the road ahead combined to sap the morale of his troops. Beside the River Beas, the army refused to advance further, forcing Alexander to agree to turn back. Nevertheless, he refused to retrace his steps, but instead led his forces down the Indus to the Indian Ocean, attacking and conquering several large native kingdoms on the way. Nearchus was appointed to command a fleet, which was to sail back to the heart of the empire via the Straits of Hormuz and the Persian Gulf, whilst Craterus was appointed to lead a large fraction of the army and baggage train back via a circuitous but safe northern route. Alexander attempted to lead a third contingent directly back to Persia by crossing the near-waterless Gedrosian Desert. Owing partly to a noble but misguided effort to stay in touch with his fleet, Alexander's force suffered grievous losses to the harshness of the terrain. In the event discipline did not falter, and the king was able to lead the survivors in a triumphant, Dionysiac procession through Carmania in the autumn of 325 BC. Spirits were lifted further when contact was finally re-established with Nearchus' fleet.

In 324 BC Alexander held court in Susa, where he arranged his own marriage to a daughter of Darius. Around 100 of the most senior Macedonians and Greeks were also given Persian noblewomen as brides in the same ceremony. But clouds were gathering. In the autumn at Ecbatana, Alexander's friend and deputy Hephaistion died suddenly of a feverish illness. Alexander was devastated, but found solace in a campaign against bandit tribes in the mountains. In the spring of 323 BC he returned to Babylon to organise a campaign to conquer the Arabian Peninsula, but fell ill with a raging fever at the end of May and expired less than two weeks later.

Embracing the full range of the ancient sources Alexander emerges as an almost Hamlet-like figure, more sinned against than sinning. In a sense Alexander, too, was haunted and motivated by his father's ghost. Arrian comments particularly that his unique attribute was the expression of genuine conscience and remorse for misdeeds that appear rather slight relative to those of other Graeco-Roman kings. He may well have saved more lives than he destroyed and rarely used violence without just cause. Dying young, he left his surviving family dreadfully exposed to the machinations of his enemies, such that virtually all his immediate relations, including both his sons, had been murdered within 15 years of his death. Nevertheless, his legacy is enormous. He was the founder of the Hellenistic Age, which in turn has bequeathed us the foundations of our modern art, science and culture.

1. Death in Babylon

Grecian galleons, The Sack of Troy, to the Gardens of Babylon
A play of millions roared along
The gigantic dreams of Alexander the Great
Civil wars where brothers fought and killed their friendship in hate
All seen by Zeus performing scenes of the magical way
The day the circus came to town

Circus of Heaven, Yes (lyrics by Jon Anderson)

In the spring of the year 323 BC, Alexander the Great, in the company of Ptolemy and a task-force of several crack regiments, descended from the cool of the Zagros Mountains of western Persia into the sweltering Mesopotamian plains (fig. 1.1). He had recently concluded a successful winter campaign against the Cossaeans, a tribe of mountain bandits, in the habit of preying on travellers whenever unrestrained by royal bribes. His route probably passed through Susa, where he had established his Persian queen, Stateira, and the rest of the family of Darius, the former Great King, in the palace. Now he was heading for his capital at Babylon straddling the River Euphrates, where the Tower of Babel, the fabled seven-storey ziggurat, loomed beside the river (fig. 1.2) and the Hanging Gardens still bloomed on terraces above an artificial lake fed from the Euphrates.[1]

Between Susa and the River Tigris he was met by embassies from cities, nations and regions beyond his empire in the west including Ethiopia, North Africa, Spain, Rome and lands north of the Danube. They congratulated him upon his victories, presented him with golden crowns, and invited his arbitration in various disputes. Following his spectacular and triumphal return from India a little over a year before, there was a

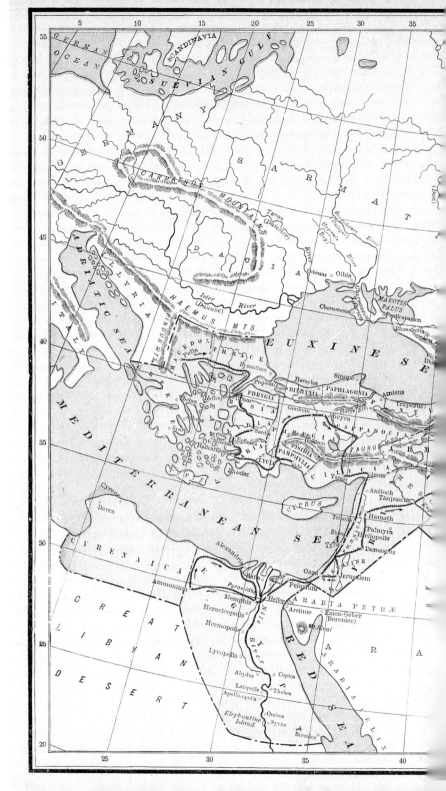

Figure 1.1. Map of Alexander's empire at its greatest extent, from Standard Atlas & Gazetteer.

© A. M. Chugg

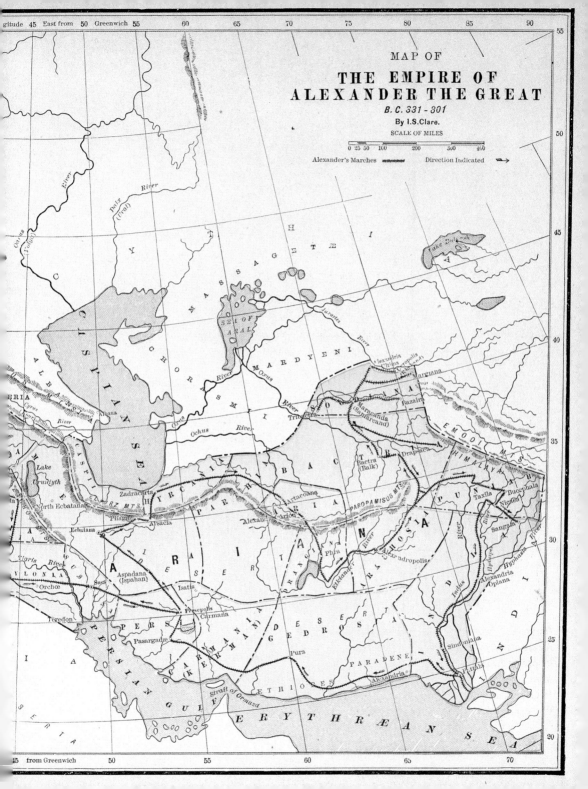

MAP OF

THE EMPIRE OF
ALEXANDER THE GREAT

B. C. 331 - 301

By I.S.Clare.

SCALE OF MILES

0 25 50   100   200   300   400

Alexander's Marches ⌇⌇⌇⌇⌇⌇   Direction Indicated →

burgeoning anticipation that Alexander would soon be moving west, so seeking intelligence on his precise intentions would have been the covert mission of these envoys.[2]

After crossing the River Tigris, about 65km away from Babylon, Alexander was met by a deputation of Chaldaean astrologers from the temple of the god Marduk in the city. Their leader, Belephantes, reported an oracle from the god to Nearchus, Alexander's admiral, who relayed their warning to the king. The Chaldaeans had divined from the inauspicious configuration of the heavens that Alexander's entry into Babylon would be fatal to him, particularly if he entered the city from the west. Alexander was suspicious of their motives, quoting them a cynical line from a lost play by Euripides, 'Prophets are best, who make the truest guess'.[3]

The basis of Alexander's scepticism was the failure of the Chaldaeans to make significant progress on the restoration of the Esagila (shrine of Marduk), which Alexander had ordered on his first visit to Babylon over seven years earlier. Greek propaganda claimed this shrine had been razed by the Persian king, Xerxes, in the early 5th century BC, but it was probably just suffering from the ravages of time. Alexander's new plan was to use his army to clear the foundations in preparation for the reconstruction. He suspected that the Chaldaeans might be attempting to delay this project further by averting his entry into the city, because they benefited from the revenues of the temple estates, and were reluctant to divert a large proportion of this for the upkeep of the shrine. Nevertheless, the king was initially willing to accept the second part of the priests' advice: to enter the city from the east. This route proved impassable because of swamps, so he failed to assuage the god in this respect also.[4]

There was some sense in the Chaldaeans' warning, since Babylon was on the verge of its stifling summer, when the combination of heat and the diseases of a crowded populace posed a considerable danger to visitors, in particular, owing to their lesser natural immunity. Alexander was especially anxious to enter the city at this time, partly to oversee the final preparations

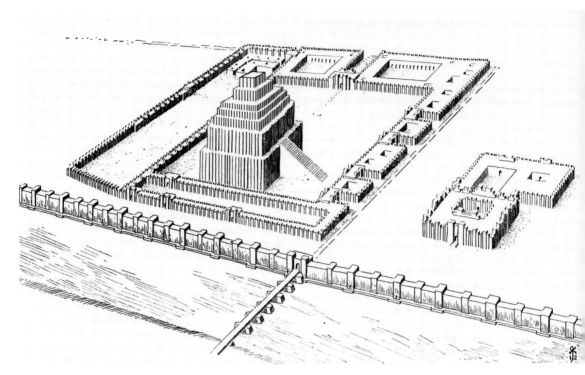

Figure 1.2. Reconstruction of the temple of Marduk and the ziggurat in Babylon at the time of Alexander's death in 323 BC, adapted from R. Koldewey, Das wieder erstehende Babylon, *Leipzig, 1913, Fig. 119.*

for his Arabian campaign. He planned to sail around the Arabian Peninsula with his fleet, accompanied by an army marching along the coast. A massive harbour was under construction and a fleet of triremes was being fabricated from the cypresses of Babylonia. It was mid-April and the departure was scheduled for early June.

Of greater significance was the massive funeral pyre for Hephaistion, Alexander's former deputy, closest friend and probable lover, nearing completion across a levelled section of the city walls. Alexander's lieutenant, Perdiccas, had brought the body and the main army down from Ecbatana in the mountains, where Hephaistion had died of a fever late in the autumn.[5]

At Babylon Alexander held court in the Palace of Nebuchadnezzar in the northern sector of the city, not far from the Ishtar Gate on the eastern bank of the Euphrates (figs 1.3 and 1.4). In the second half of April his time was divided between planning for the Arabian expedition, holding audiences with embassies from Greece and preparing for the funeral (table 1.1). In these final months Alexander seems to have planned everything on a breathtaking scale, and Hephaistion's funeral rites and solemnities were no exception.

The pyre was designed by Alexander's court architect, Deinocrates, who seems to have been inspired by the step-pyramid of the Tower of Babel. Although constructed in wood, rather than brick, it was of comparable size to the ziggurat (about 70m high and 180m wide) and comprised seven stages.

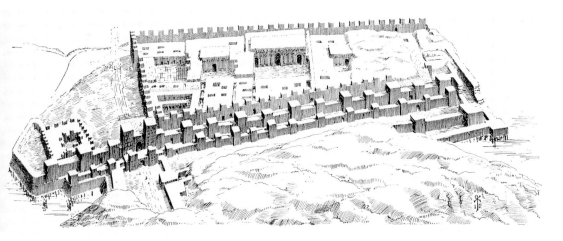

Figure 1.3. Reconstruction of the Ishtar Gate and the Palace of Nebuchadnezzar at Babylon by Robert Koldewey. The chamber with three arched portals off the courtyard in the upper centre is the throne room; adapted from R. Koldewey, op. cit., Fig. 43.

A. ZIGGURAT

B. TEMPLE OF MARDUK

C. ISHTAR GATE

D. PALACE OF NEBUCHADNEZZAR

E. RIVER EUPHRATES

F. SOUTHERN FORTRESS

G. NORTHERN FORTRESS

H. PROBABLE SITE OF HANGING GARDENS

I. POSSIBLE SITE OF HEPHAISTION'S PYRE

walls & buildings
roads
water courses

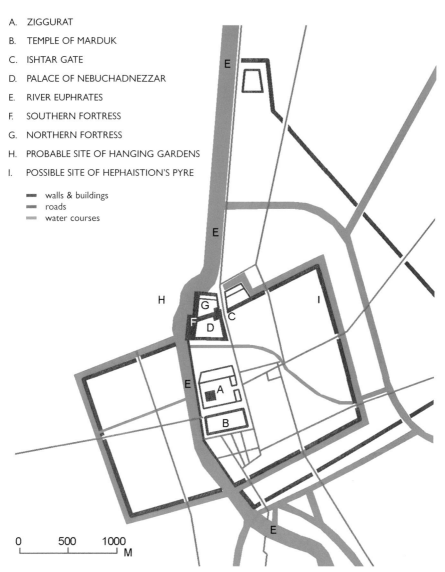

Figure 1.4. Plan of Babylon around the time of Alexander's death in 323 BC.
© A. M. Chugg

Figure 1.5. Reconstruction of Hephaistion's funeral pyre constructed in Babylon with ziggurat in the background, by F. Jaffé in the 19th century, Berlin, Plate XVIII.13.
© A. M. Chugg

Stage one was adorned with the prows of 240 galleys, each with five banks of oars, two kneeling archers, a pair of hoplites and red felt banners billowing between each vessel; stage two featured flaming torches decorated with eagles and serpents; stages three and four displayed royal hunting scenes and a war of the centaurs; stage five was decorated with lions and bulls; and stage six, panoplies of Greek and Persian arms. Most splendid of all, on the apex stood the mythical Sirens of Homer's *Odyssey*, each hollowed out to accommodate a living singer keening out rhapsodic laments.[6]

A large section of the city wall had been torn down to form a baked tile foundation for this gleaming edifice (fig. 1.5), and it cost a reputed 12,000 talents, equivalent to about 25 tonnes of gold. It remains the most lavish funerary monument in history and a testament to the profundity of Alexander's grief. A poignant detail is related by Diodorus, how during the period of mourning Alexander ordered that the sacred fires should be extinguished in the temples. This rite was normally only performed upon the death of the king, so the Persians considered it a grim omen. In Greek terms, however, this recalls the definition of a friend as a second self and also the king's most famous quote concerning Hephaistion, 'He too is Alexander'.[7]

In the aftermath of the funeral, around the beginning of May, Alexander was probably finding the atmosphere both physically and mentally oppressive at Babylon. He had been made aware of a problem with the canal system built by the Assyrian kings to divert the annual flood of the Euphrates. This occurred in the spring as the snows melted in the Armenian mountains, threatening to burst the river's banks. A little way upstream of Babylon a canal called the Pollacopas had been dug to redirect the flood south from the river towards an area of lakes and marshes bordering on the Arabian Desert 160km from the city. The flaw in this system lay in the sogginess of the soil at the junction of the canal with the river. This made it easy to open up the channel in the spring, but it required two months of effort from a vast work force to close it up again in the autumn.

Alexander set off on an engineering expedition with a small section of the fleet in an attempt to solve this problem. He sailed up the Euphrates and down the Pollacopas to the marshes and lakes. On the way he spotted an area of stonier ground, where a new channel might be dug. Among the lakes the king located a suitable spot and began the establishment of a new city, the last of around 30 such foundations undertaken by Alexander.

On returning to Babylon through the marshes several vessels of his flotilla went astray in the narrows, but were eventually found by a pilot sent to rescue them. Alexander's flagship must have dawdled among the reeds as menacing clouds of mosquitoes whined about in the sultry air.

In an area of the marshlands where some of the tombs of the Assyrian kings were located, Alexander had taken the helm when a gust of wind flipped his cap from his head and on to some reeds near a tomb. The royal diadem was bound about this cap, so its association with a royal grave was considered a bad omen. A Phoenician oarsman dived into the water to recover the diadem and placed the cap on his head to keep it dry for the king.

Subjects who wore the royal insignia for whatever reason were always executed under Religious Law. Nevertheless, Aristobulus, one of Alexander's engineers and probably an eyewitness, attests that the sailor was merely flogged to avert the omen, then rewarded with the gift of a talent (about 26kg of silver).[8]

By the time of Alexander's return to Babylon in the second half of May, several army groups had arrived to reinforce the Arabian expedition, including 20,000 Persians under Peucestas. Sacred envoys from the Greeks were also waiting to present Alexander with golden crowns. Athens and Sparta had voted to award 'divine honours' to Alexander the previous year, probably as a placatory gesture, since these states were considered to be the most antagonistic to Alexander's rule in Greece. Precedents for this exalted form of recognition had included the worship of Lysander as a god in many Greek cities after the Spartan victory over the Athenians at Aegospotami in 404 BC and heroic honours for Dion, Plato's protégé, upon his triumphant return to Syracuse in 357 BC. Paradoxically, his own Macedonians seem to have refused Alexander these honours, although they had been accorded to his father, Philip II (r. 359–36 BC) during his lifetime. The mission of the envoys may have been formally to confer these honours upon Alexander.[9]

Emissaries from the god Ammon in Egypt had also arrived to deliver a verdict on the king's enquiry as to how the spirit of Hephaistion might be honoured. The god had determined that Hephaistion might be offered sacrifice as a hero, so Alexander began to plan the establishment of his cult.

Shortly afterwards another ominous incident transpired. Alexander and his companions had left the throne room to play ball according to Plutarch, to be rubbed down with oil in Diodorus' account or simply because they were thirsty in Arrian's version. During his absence a deranged prisoner from Messenia called Dionysius approached the throne, sat in it and wore the royal diadem and robes.[10] When questioned, the man was unable to offer any explanation for his behaviour, which only made the omen worse. In accordance with the law Alexander had him executed. All this was recorded by the Greek writers. It is interesting to note that this scenario bears a striking resemblance to the ancient ritual of having a criminal play-act the role of the king in times of ill omen. This custom traditionally ended with the execution of the substitute, thus diverting the bad luck.[11]

Most of the details known of Alexander's final illness are summarised in table 1.2. In particular, there are edited extracts from the *Ephemerides*, Alexander's *Royal Journal*. Both Arrian and Plutarch cite this source for their versions of the king's fatal illness. Some scholars question the authenticity of this document, since it mentions the god Serapis, supposed to have been invented by Ptolemy in Alexandria after Alexander's death. Yet the Greeks commonly renamed foreign deities with the nearest familiar equivalent, and it is likely that, when transcribing the scrolls, a scholar in Alexandria changed the name of a particular Babylonian deity, such as Marduk, to be more recognisable to his readership. There is a second instance of this apparent anachronism in Plutarch's account, where Serapis appears to the prisoner who sat on the throne. In any case, it is known that Alexander's successors in Egypt as well as other kings of Macedon kept similar diaries of their affairs. Several factors suggest the *Journal* is a reliable source, such as the banality of many details, the consistency of its medical case history, and the concordance of Babylonian topography with modern excavations.[12]

The 30 May was a day of celebration culminating in a formal banquet in honour of Nearchus. After the festivities the king bathed and then attended a private drinking party organised by his friend, Medius of Larissa. On leaving this symposium he again bathed, then seems to have slept until the following evening when he dined with Medius, who afterwards hosted a second drinking party deep into the night in the company of 20 or so leading Macedonians. More probably on this occasion than the previous evening, Alexander drank undiluted wine from a large cup in commemoration of the death of Heracles, whereupon Arrian, Diodorus, Justin and Plutarch all mention that the king felt a sharp pain as though pierced by a dagger or spear. Plutarch locates the pain in Alexander's back, whilst dismissing the story as a fiction. Justin writes melodramatically that the king 'was carried half-dead from the table. He was wracked with such agony that he asked for a sword to put an end to it and felt pain at the touch of his attendants as if he were all over wounds'. The *Journal* records that Alexander bathed and ate lightly after this party, then slept in the bathroom as he was starting to feel feverish.[13]

On 1 June the king was carried on a couch to perform the daily sacrifices. Afterwards he lay in the men's apartments of Nebuchadnezzar's palace until dark, whilst playing dice with Medius and issuing instructions to his officers: the land army was to depart for Arabia in three days and the fleet would sail in four. In the evening he had himself ferried across the river to the gardens, where he bathed and rested. These probably lay just north of the inner walls on the west bank of the Euphrates opposite Nebuchadnezzar's palace and may have been the famous terraced Hanging Gardens, which Strabo placed on the banks of the Euphrates and which were probably constructed by Nebuchadnezzar for his queen (fig. 1.6). Plutarch mentions that Alexander had his bed set beside a 'great plunge-bath' in the gardens, which may refer to the pool at the base of the terraces from which water was drawn up to irrigate the foliage. The next day the king bathed and sacrificed as usual, then lay down in his canopied bed, chatted with Medius and was entertained by listening to tales of Nearchus' voyage back from India.

After instructing his officers to meet him at dawn, he dined lightly and was carried back to the canopied bed, but lay in a high fever all night.

On 3 June, after bathing and sacrificing, he explained his plans for the Arabian voyage to Nearchus and to the other officers, but his fever grew more intense towards evening and he had a bad night. The following day, after bathing and sacrificing, he 'no longer had any rest from the fever', although he summoned his officers to discuss the filling of vacant army commands and ordered them to complete the preparations for the voyage.

After bathing in the evening he was very ill, although the next morning he was again carried to the house near the pool, where he offered sacrifices and gave further instructions for the voyage to his most senior officers. On 6 June he barely managed to offer the sacrifices, yet persisted in planning the voyage, but his fever grew worse. That evening, or possibly the next day, Alexander ordered his generals to wait in the courtyard of the palace and the battalion and company commanders to remain outside the gates. On 7 June he was carried back from the gardens to the palace. Now extremely ill, though still recognising his officers, he was voiceless.

His fever burned high over the next few days, fuelling speculation among the troops that he may have died. In their grief and suspicion they yearned to see him one last time and thronged the gates of the palace shouting threats at the king's Companions, who relented and admitted them to file past his bedside (fig. 1.7). He acknowledged them by raising his head or signing with his eyes. Curtius quotes the king asking, 'After my death will you find a king who deserves such men?' and says that Alexander collapsed in exhaustion after everyone had passed. He then took his ring off his finger and handed it to Perdiccas. Curtius and Justin claim he commanded that his body be taken to Ammon, the Egyptian god. When his Companions asked him to whom he bequeathed his kingdom, he replied, 'To the strongest', and some of the sources add that he foresaw great funeral games (table 1.2). When, finally, Perdiccas asked him at what times he wished his divine honours to be paid to him, he answered, 'When you are happy'.

Five of the king's Companions, Pithon, Seleucus, Attalus, Peucestas and Menidas, together with the seers Demophon and Cleomenes, held an overnight vigil in the temple of Serapis, enquiring whether it would be desirable for Alexander to be brought there to be cared for by the god, but the shrine's oracle indicated that he should remain where he was. Aristobulus has written that Alexander, made thirsty by his fever, became delirious after drinking some wine, and this detail might be fitted to around 9 June. On the evening of the next day Alexander was pronounced dead. He was not quite 33 years old.[14]

> *At first the sounds of lamentation, weeping and the beating of breasts echoed throughout the royal quarters. Then a sad hush fell, enveloping all in a still silence like that of desert wastes, as from grief they turned to considering what would happen now. The young noblemen who formed his customary Bodyguard could neither suppress their bitter anguish nor confine themselves to the vestibule of the royal canopy. They wandered around like madmen, filling the whole city with the sound of their mournful grieving, foregoing no kind of lament that sorrow suggests in such circumstances. Accordingly, those who had been standing outside the royal quarters rushed to the spot, barbarians and Macedonians alike, and in the general grief conqueror and conquered were indistinguishable. The Persians recalled a master of great justice and clemency, the Macedonians a peerless king of outstanding valour; together they indulged in a kind of contest in mourning.*[15]

Quintus Curtius Rufus

After Alexander's death, the sincerity of the shocked grief is epitomised by the reaction of Darius' mother, Sisygambis, who, upon hearing the news, turned to face the wall and starved herself until she died five days later.[16]

On 16 June, when Egyptian and Chaldaean embalmers arrived to treat Alexander's corpse, they found it uncorrupted and retaining a lifelike

Figure 1.6. A reconstruction of the Hanging Gardens of Babylon, one of the Seven Wonders of the Ancient World, from L. de Colange, ed., Voyages and Travels or Scenes in Many Lands, *c. 1887, 153.*

complexion despite the summer heat. At first they did not dare touch him, but after praying to gain the gods' consent they cleaned out his body and laid it in a golden sarcophagus crammed with exotic spices and perfumes.[17]

What was the cause of Alexander's death? Unfortunately, we lack sufficient details to make a certain diagnosis, but assuming the *Journal* account is authentic, it is possible to argue that one diagnosis fits the case history significantly better than any other.

At the time of the king's death there was no suspicion of poisoning. After all, the account given by the *Journal* is a classic case history for death through disease. However, within a year or two at most (and probably sooner) the story emerged that Alexander had been poisoned by order of Antipater, his regent in Macedon. A certain Hagnothemis, who is otherwise unknown, is supposed to have heard the tale from Antigonus, Alexander's governor of Phrygia. Alexander had ordered in 324 BC that Craterus should take over the regency of Macedon, thus providing Antipater with a motive.

The poison is described as having been provided by Aristotle, Alexander's former tutor, or as taking the form of water collected from the River Styx. This was considered deadly because of its extreme coldness and was transported to Babylon in a mule's hoof, the only vessel capable of withstanding its legendary caustic properties. Cassander, Antipater's son, was the supposed emissary and he had indeed joined Alexander late in 324 BC or early in 323. A story relates that, being new to the court, he was foolish enough to laugh at a Persian performing *proskynesis* (an expression of respect) before the king. Alexander was furious and dashed his head against the wall. Plutarch says that when Cassander caught sight of a statue of Alexander at Delphi many years later he shook uncontrollably.[18]

The poison was supposedly administered at Medius' party by Iollas, Alexander's cup-bearer, Cassander's younger brother and reputedly Medius' lover. On the strength of this rumour, Hypereides, the Athenian orator and a bitter enemy of Macedon, proposed a vote of thanks to Iollas not very long after Alexander's death and Olympias, Alexander's mother, had Iollas' ashes exhumed and scattered to the winds in 317 BC.[19]

One problem with this story is that it contains fictitious elements, such as the river water and the mule's hoof. If some parts of it are an invention, then the rest must also be suspect. Arrian was aware of several fantastical versions of the tale, one of which survives in the *Alexander Romance*, and both he and Plutarch were deeply sceptical (although Justin accepted the story and extended the plot by implicating Alexander's officers).

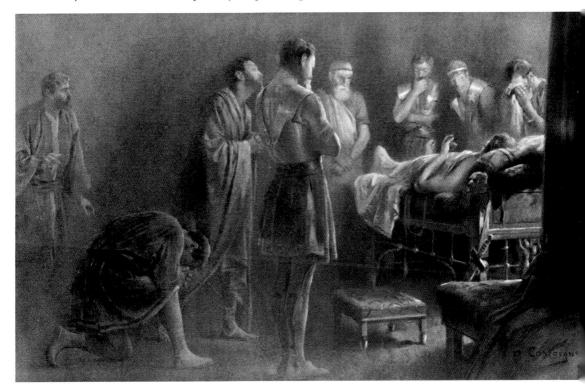

Figure 1.7. Imaginative reconstruction of the death of Alexander by André Castaigne, Century Magazine, 1899.

This story is also questionable because it emerged at a time of warfare between the Diadochi, Alexander's successors, among whom Antipater, and later Cassander, were leaders. Any scandal that would have helped weaken the loyalty of their Macedonian troops would have suited their opponents. In other words, even if Alexander had not been poisoned this story may well have been fabricated. Moreover, it is very difficult to make any sensible poisoning scenario fit the case history from the *Journal* account. For this reason those who favour the poisoning theory have traditionally been leading critics of the *Journal*'s authenticity. Interestingly, the testimony of Justin, who treated the poisoning story as fact, recorded that Alexander's illness lasted for more than six days. Medically, any poison potent enough to produce sharp and incapacitating pains should have been promptly fatal.[20]

Slow strychnine poisoning has also been proposed, but the risks associated with such a complex and protracted plan seem prohibitive given that Alexander had a knowledge of herbal medicine. Engels has also pointed out that the lethal variety of strychnine has an extremely bitter taste and that Alexander's reported symptoms do not fit the physiological effects of either slow or fast administration of strychnine.[21] Moreover, Antipater on his deathbed showed considerable loyalty to Alexander's wife and son by placing them in the care of Polyperchon, rather than his son Cassander. In short, while poisoning cannot be excluded as a possibility, it is very unlikely.[22]

Did Alexander drink himself into an early grave? There is no dispute that the king sometimes drank heavily, but this was usual among high-ranking Greeks of the period. Ephippus, a hostile and indiscriminate gossip, attributed Alexander's death to the anger of Dionysus, the god of wine, who was also associated with the city of Thebes, which had been destroyed by Alexander's allies.[23] This may, therefore, be a wishful case of poetic justice. Aelian gives another edited extract from the *Royal Journal* detailing various drinking parties attended by Alexander in a three-week period around October 324 BC. The extract appears to have been selected with the purpose of demonstrating that Alexander drank excessively, yet it reports drinking bouts confined to just four evenings in the period – hardly intemperate in the circumstances. Aristobulus, who will have been an eyewitness, wrote that Alexander only sat long over his wine for the sake of conversation with his Companions.[24]

Alcoholic hepatitis may sometimes be associated with fever and can terminate in coma, but it would almost invariably be accompanied by jaundice and evidence of profound malnutrition, neither of which was observed. The possibility of incidental contamination of Alexander's wine with lead or methanol has also been raised, but neither would be expected to produce a raging fever. It is therefore unlikely that Alexander's drinking was the direct cause of his demise, though alcohol may possibly have exacerbated another disease.[25]

Other popular diagnoses include the suggestion of leukaemia, though the king's illness seems to have been too short and sudden for this to be likely. In all probability, Alexander's death was the genuine consequence of infection by a biological disease. Typhus is an old favourite, transmitted by fleas, lice, mites and ticks and frequently epidemic in crowded and unsanitary living conditions. It manifests as fever, back and muscle pain, severe headache, a cough and a prominent rash. Some districts of Babylon were probably densely populated, but Alexander's personal living conditions were obviously spacious and he was in the habit of bathing at least once a day, and there is no evidence of any rash. On the contrary, his corpse is described as pure and fresh by Plutarch.[26]

In 2003 a television documentary raised the possibility that there had been an outbreak of West Nile fever at Babylon, but this disease is comparatively rare in humans and the mortality is less than one case in 1,000. Another of the experts in this programme suggested that Alexander had poisoned himself by overdosing on hellebore, but this is a noxious purgative medicine and there seems to be no case in history of anyone killing themselves in this fashion.[27]

Oldach and Richards have recently proposed a diagnosis of typhoid fever with the rare complication of ascending paralysis and coma. Unfortunately, their case rests heavily upon a supposition that abdominal pain 'in the right upper quadrant' was a key symptom. The only evidence for this comes from the dubious *Alexander Romance*, which states that Alexander 'suddenly shouted with pain as if struck through the liver with an arrow.' It should be stressed that the Greeks considered the liver to be the seat of the passions. So being struck through the liver has similar poetical overtones in the original Greek of the *Romance* to being 'pierced through the heart' in English, and it should not be taken literally. The credibility of the *Romance* is also undermined by episodes such as Alexander's conversation with talking trees.[28]

Another problem with the typhoid theory is that the Persian kings had their drinking water boiled and there is no reason to suppose that this practice was discontinued at the royal palaces following Alexander's accession. Furthermore, the marshes he sailed through in May seem to have been fed by the Pollacopas Canal, believed to have branched from the Euphrates upstream of Babylon; so there are no grounds to suppose that the king was exposed to Babylonian sewage effluent. While the typhoid hypothesis cannot be ruled out, a water–borne disease does not appear to fit well with the evidence.[29]

Early in 325 BC Alexander had suffered an arrow wound to his chest while leading the storming of a Mallian town, possibly Multan, in India. Ptolemy stated that air was seen to escape from the wound as well as blood when the arrow was withdrawn, implying perforation of the lung. On the strength of this, and Alexander's voicelessness in the late stages of his final illness, pleurisy has been considered a likely complication. Ptolemy was not an eyewitness at this siege and the rest of the ancient accounts suggest the arrow actually lodged in Alexander's breast-bone, which would be more medically consistent with the reported speed and completeness of the king's recovery from the wound. Pleurisy is therefore less likely than is sometimes portrayed.[30]

Malaria provides a perfect fit to virtually every known feature of Alexander's final illness. It was first suggested as long ago as the 19th century and is endorsed by many modern writers, but it never seems to have been put forward with quite as much force and detail as it merits. We can be confident that Alexander would have been exposed to malaria-carrying mosquitoes in the swamps south of Babylon some time around the middle of May, since malaria has been endemic to Mesopotamia since very ancient times. There are four species of malaria parasite, but only one of these, *Plasmodium falciparum*, commonly leads to a prompt death. The nature of the illness produced by *P. falciparum* malaria is summarised in the following extracts from articles on this subject:[31]

Malaria is a parasitic disease endemic in many tropical and sub-tropical parts of the world. It is usually transmitted by the bites of infected anopheline mosquitoes. Falciparum malaria… is associated with the highest levels of parasites in the blood and is the most severe form of malaria, sometimes fatal. The incubation period of falciparum malaria is usually nine to fourteen days during which the parasites develop silently in the liver before they mature, multiply and invade the red blood cells… According to an expert consulted by the Medical Protection Society in a recent case, one of the chief characteristics of infection is the extreme variability of signs and symptoms of the attack. Classical symptoms of malaria such as cold and rigors followed by high fever and sweating repeated at regular intervals are rare. The early symptoms of malaria include tiredness, depression, headache, pains in the back and limbs, loss of appetite and nausea. In about thirty per cent of patients the illness starts with a rigor; mild diarrhoea, perhaps accompanied by slight jaundice or cough. Although the spleen is often enlarged it is often not palpable. The development of severe malaria is variable. Most often the patient is not very ill during the first three or four days of the illness but deteriorates rapidly towards the end of the first week and this deterioration can occur over the course of a few hours…. The symptoms of severe malaria vary depending on which of the patient's organs are damaged by the dividing form of the parasite, which situates itself in small blood vessels within the organs. The brain, kidneys and lung are often involved. Cerebral malaria may develop slowly or rapidly. Headache, agitation or drowsiness, abnormal behaviour or coma can ensue. Temperature is usually high but may be subnormal. In such cases death is likely to be the outcome unless there is skilled intervention in hospital at an early stage.[32]

…in practice the characteristic periodicity is not in fact observed in many cases, owing to infections with multiple generations of parasites whose development cycles are not synchronized. Experiments… were carried out for many years at Horton Hospital in Epsom in England. These experiments proved that in malaria caused by P. falciparum, the most dangerous species of malaria, most attacks take the form of subcontinuous or quotidian (peaking every twenty-four hours) fevers.[33]

It is worthwhile listing the parallels between the circumstances and symptoms of Alexander's illness and a typical case history for *P. falciparum* malaria:

1. Alexander was in a malaria-infested area two weeks before his illness, a period consistent with the incubation of the disease.

2. The *Journal* hints at fatigue and lethargy at the onset of illness, typical of *P. falciparum* malaria.

3. Plutarch describes back pain and Justin describes pain in different areas; pains in the back and limb joints are a common precursor of the disease.

4. Sources hint at a light appetite, a symptom of the early days of the illness.

5. Arrian implies an initially intermittent fever with peaks each night, because he says that after the fourth day Alexander 'no longer had any rest from the fever'. This is a quotidian fever becoming subcontinuous and is highly characteristic of *P. falciparum* malaria.

6. Alexander was not very ill during the first three or four days of his illness, but he deteriorated rapidly towards the end of the first week – the classic pattern of *P. falciparum* malaria.

7. *P. falciparum* malaria provides two possible causes for the reported voicelessness: a pulmonary complication or the beginning of neurological effects. In severe cases the brain and the lungs are the most commonly affected organs.

8. Aristobulus says the king became delirious, probably towards the end. This would fit with the agitation, confusion and fitting which typify the onset of cerebral malaria.

9. The lack of deterioration in Alexander's body days after his supposed death may well be explained by a terminal coma from cerebral malaria, a common complication of *P. falciparum* malaria.

10. A diagnosis of *P. falciparum* malaria does not require any exacerbating circumstance for it to prove fatal, such as heavy drinking and a debilitating chest wound. *P. falciparum* malaria could have killed Alexander even if he had been fit and healthy before his illness, as is suggested by his exploits against the Cossaeans.

It would not be surprising if so mundane an explanation as malaria should prove unpopular with those sensationalists who prefer to portray Alexander's career as some kind of theatrical tragedy and with those moralists who like to see the great undone by their personal weaknesses, but we are dealing with real life here rather than romantic fiction.

In the course of his reign Alexander made mistakes. On balance he should have intervened to save Thebes from the retribution of his allies, even though the city had twice broken peace treaties with him and had murdered members of the Macedonian party at the start of the revolt. In retrospect it was an over-reaction to attack the camp of the Indian mercenaries at Massaga, even though they may have been attempting to desert and could have posed a threat to him in the future. Alexander should have tailored his policies to the fanaticism of the Brahmins on the lower Indus to have avoided much unnecessary bloodshed. Crossing the Gedrosian Desert with so large a force was an excessive risk, which led to the unnecessary deaths of many of his followers. Above all, the killing of Cleitus the Black following a drunken argument at a party in Samarkand was reprehensible, despite the fact that Cleitus had insulted him. This is not just because Cleitus was a senior officer and the king's friend, but also because he was the brother of Alexander's nurse and had saved the king's life during the battle at the Granicus.[34]

These failings should be weighed against Alexander's achievements and legacy. In contrast to the insular prejudice of most Greeks at the time, which labelled all foreigners and their cultures as barbarous, Alexander operated a relatively enlightened multiracial policy. This included the regular reinstatement of local rulers, adoption of some Persian, Egyptian and Indian customs, marriage to Bactrian and Persian princesses, friendship with Indian philosophers and recruitment of many thousands of Persian youths, the so-called *epigoni* (afterborn), into his army.

Alexander was largely responsible for the spread of Greek culture across the Middle East and beyond as far as India, where its influence is still discernible today. He saw money and treasure as commodities to be utilised rather than hoarded and sought to open up trade routes between the Mediterranean and the Far East, especially by founding many new cities and the exploration of sea-lanes in the Gulfs of Persia and Oman.

Collectively, these policies engendered a huge economic boom in the eastern Mediterranean in the decades following his death. They resulted in significant rises in the standard of living of millions and financed the construction of spacious and gleaming Hellenistic cities all around the Mediterranean seaboard. During the next few centuries these cities fostered a great flowering of art, literature and science, much of which survived to stimulate the flourishing Renaissance in medieval Europe. The greatest of these cities was Alexandria, which had been founded by Alexander at the western end of the Nile delta in 331 BC. Its lighthouse, the Pharos, became one of the Seven Wonders of the Ancient World, while its Great Library housed the knowledge of mankind, but there was a third building of equal fame which stood at the heart of the city for at least five centuries. It was known as the *Soma* – the Greek word for a body, since it contained Alexander's embalmed corpse.

Above all Alexander deserves to be judged in terms of the ideals of his own culture and times. It is anachronistic to analyse his career in terms of modern moral and ethical codes, that would have been ridiculed in his own society. His personal ideals are epitomised by Xenophon's *Cyropaedia* and Homer's *Iliad*; a copy of which he kept beneath his pillow. These books provide parables lauding the heroism of combat, the immortality of fame and the chivalry of befriending worthy enemies after their defeat. Alexander was not always a perfect exemplar of these virtues, but on the whole he came close enough to deserve his epithet of greatness.[35]

Table 1.1. Outline of Alexander's final months.

DATE IN 323 BC	EVENTS	SOURCES
February–March	Conclusion of campaign against Cossaeans in the Zagros Mountains	Arrian 7.15.1-3, Diodorus 17.111. 4-6 – campaign lasted 40 days
Mid-April	Arrival at Babylon	Strabo 16.1.5 – two months to clear temple site, work unfinished at Alexander's death
Mid- to late April	Receives embassies from the Greeks	Arrian 7.19.1
Late April–early May	Funeral of Hephaistion	Diodorus 17.114-115
May	Expedition to Pollacopas marshes, foundation of a new city	Arrian 7.21, Diodorus 17.116.5
3rd or 4th week of May	Return to Babylon, passed tombs of Assyrian kings	Arrian 7.22, Diodorus 17.116.6-7
Late May	Receives word that Hephaistion may be worshipped as a Hero, deranged prisoner sits on Alexander's throne	Arrian 7.23.6-24.3, Plutarch 73.3-4, Diodorus 17.115.6
30 May	Comus in honour of Nearchus	Plutarch 75.3
Evening of 31 May	Alexander begins to feel feverish after 2nd symposium of Medius	Arrian 25.1 and Plutarch 75.3, quoting *Ephemerides* by Eumenes of Cardia
Evening of 10 June	Death of Alexander	Aristobulus in Plutarch 75.4 and Plutarch 76.4, Arrian 7.26.3, *Ephemerides*, Babylonian records (Samuel, Ptolemaic Chronology, 1962, 47)
16 June	Embalming of corpse begun	Curtius 10.10.9-13, Plutarch 77.3

Table 1.2. Alexander's illness (A = Arrian, D = Diodorus, C = Curtius, J = Justin, L = Lucian, N = Nepos, P=Plutarch).

DATE IN 323 BC	EVENTS	SYMPTOMS
30 May	Banquet in honour of Nearchus followed by a bath (J, P)	
Night	Medius' drinking party (A, D, P) Rose, bathed and slept (A)	
31 May, 18 Daesios	Dined with Medius after rising (A)	Implies slept until evening (A)
Night	Drank till late (A, J, P), bathed, ate a little (A), slept in bathroom (A, P)	Sharp pain in back drinking cup of Heracles (A, D, J, contradicted by P) Began to feel feverish (A, P)
1 June, 19 Daesios	Carried to sacrifices on couch, lay in men's apartments, instructed officers on Arabian voyage (A) Bath, moved to bedchamber, dice with Medius (P)	
Night	Carried on couch across river to garden, bathed and rested (A) Bathed, sacrificed, dined (P)	Feverish throughout night (P)
2 June, 20 Daesios	Bathed, offered sacrifices (A, P), went into canopied bed, conversed with Medius (A), entertained by listening to Nearchus' account of his voyage lying down in bathroom (P)	
Night	Instructed officers to meet him at dawn, dined lightly, carried to canopied bed (A)	High fever (A)
3 June, 21 Daesios	Bathed, sacrificed, explained plans for Arabian voyage to Nearchus and other officers (A): entertained by listening to Nearchus' account of his voyage lying down in bathroom (P)	Fever grew more intense (P)
Night		Bad night (P)
4 June, 22 Daesios	Arabian expedition: planned departure of fleet (A). Bathed, sacrificed, summoned officers and ordered them to see that all was ready for the voyage (A) Bed moved to be beside great plunge-bath, discussed filling vacant posts in the army with his officers (P)	No longer any respite from fever (A) Fever high all through day (P)

Table 1.2. continued

Night	Bathed	Very ill after bathing (A)
5 June, 23 Daesios	Arabian expedition: planned departure of fleet (A) Carried to house near diving place, sacrificed, summoned most senior officers and gave instructions for the voyage (A)	
6 June, 24 Daesios	Carried to offer sacrifices (A, P), continued to instruct officers (A)	Fever still worse (P)
Night	Ordered generals to wait in the courtyard and officers outside (P)	
7 June, 25 Daesios	Continued to offer sacrifices, ordered generals to wait in the courtyard and commanders of brigades and battalions to wait before the gates, carried (through them) from garden to palace (A) Moved back to palace across river, slept a little (P)	Very ill, then extremely ill (A) Knew officers, but said no more, now speechless (A, P) Fever did not abate (P)
Night		High fever
8 June, 26 Daesios		High fever (A), speechless (P)
9 June, 27 Daesios	Troops file past (A, C, D, J, P) 'After my death will you find a king who deserves such men?' (C, J) Handed ring to Perdiccas (C, D, J, N, L) Instructed that his body be transported to Ammon (C, J, L) 'To whom do you leave your kingdom?'–'To the best' (A, C, D, J) Foresaw great funeral games (A, C, D, J, P) Perdiccas asked him when he wished divine honours paid him – 'When you are happy' (C)	Speechless (A) Voice failing (C, J) Collapsed from exhaustion when troops left (C) Delirious after drinking wine to quench thirst (P)

Night	Pithon, Attalus, Demophon, Peucestus, Cleomenes, Menidas, Seleucus spent night in temple of Serapis, enquiring whether Alexander should be moved, god replied no (A, P)	
10 June, 28 Daesios	Died (A), died towards evening (P), died 10/11 June according to a Babylonian tablet	
11 June, 30 Daesios	Died according to Aristobulus (P) – note that Daesios had no 29th day, so there is little real disagreement here: late on 10 June might be 11 June	
16 June	Embalmers arrived, no decay of corpse despite heat, did not dare touch him at first, due to lifelike appearance (C) Body uncorrupted for days (P)	Coma (?)

1 Arrian, *Anabasis Alexandri*, 7.15; Plutarch, *Alexander*, 72; Diodorus Siculus, 17.111.4.

2 Arrian, 7.15.5; Pliny, *Natural History*, 3.57; Arrian, *Anabasis Alexandri*, 7.15.

3 Diodorus Siculus, 17.112.3.

4 M. Wood, *In The Footsteps of Alexander The Great*, London, 1997, 95; Strabo, *Geography*, 16.1.5.

5 Strabo, *Geography*, 16.1.5; Diodorus Siculus, 17.112.

6 Diodorus Siculus, 17.115; for possible archaeological evidence of this site, R. Koldewey, 1913, 301-2; J. Oates, 1979, 159.

7 Diogenes Laertius, Zeno, 124; Plutarch, *Moralia*, 93E; Achilles of Patroclus, 'The companion whom I valued above all others and as much as my life', *Iliad*, 18.81 (paraphrased by Alexander in Arrian, *Anabasis Alexandri*, 7.14.6).

8 Other historians seem to have accentuated the dramatic irony of the story by claiming the sailor was rewarded with a talent then executed.

9 A. B. Bosworth, 1988, 280; Curtius, *History of Alexander*, 10.5.11.

10 Plutarch, *Alexander*, 73.

11 Wood, 1997, 225.

12 For these extracts, Aelian, *Varia Historia*, 3.23; Athenaeus, *Deipnosophistae*, x. 434b. The authenticity of the *Journal* has been generally accepted by N. G. L. Hammond, 1981; although doubts have been expressed by Bosworth, 1988. Tacitus, *Histories*, 4.83.4: it is probable that Serapis was derived by Ptolemy from Egyptian traditions. The sacred Apis bulls at Memphis were identified with Osiris after their death and worshipped as 'Osor-Hapi', perhaps 'Serapis' in Greek. It has been suggested that there was an Egyptian shrine of this nature in Babylon, but this is an intricate hypothesis. For the reliability of the *Journal* as a source, Hammond, 1981, 1; P.A. Brunt, 1976, xxiv; U. Wilcken, 1894, 84-126, esp. 117.

13 L. Pearson, 1960, 67; Plutarch, *Alexander*, 75; Justin, *Epitome of the Philippic History of Pompeius Trogus*, 12.13.9.

14 Plutarch, *Alexander*, 75.4. For the date of Alexander's death, Plutarch, *Alexander*, 75.4 and 76.4; A. E. Samuel, *Ptolemaic Chronology*, 1962. The *Alexander Romance* (Armenian Version, 286) gives an erroneous date for Alexander's death. The chronology of Alexander's death is also examined by B. Welles, 8, 1963, 467, note 5; and Samuel, 1962, 46.

15 Curtius, *History of Alexander*, 10.5.7.

16 Curtius, 10.5.19-25.

17 Curtius, 10.10.9 and Plutarch, *Alexander*, 77.

18 This version of the poisoning story is mainly derived from Plutarch, *Alexander*, 77, who was skeptical, as was Arrian 7.27, whilst Curtius 10.10.14 and Diodorus 17.118 were more neutral, and Justin 12.14 accepted the story as fact.

19 Plutarch, *Moralia*, 848.

20 Justin, *Epitome of the Philippic History*, 12.15.1 and 12.15.12.

21 D. W. Engels, 1978, 73, 224-8.

22 R. D. Milns, 1968, 257. Plutarch, *Alexander*, 8. Diodorus, XVIII.48.4.

23 Pearson, 1960, 62.

24 Aelian, *Varia Historia*, 3.23; Arrian, *Anabasis Alexandri*, 7.29.4.

25 D. W. Oldach and R. E. Richard, 338.24, 1998. The case for alcohol as an exacerbating cause of Alexander's death, rather than a root cause, is presented by J. Maxwell O'Brien, 1992.

26 Falciparum as well as leukemia is also suggested by F. Schachermeyr, 1973, 563.

27 UK Channel 5, 22.10.2003.

28 D. W. Oldach and R. E. Richard, 338.24, 1998; R. Lane Fox, 1973, 463; Stoneman, 1991, 31.

29 M. Renault, 1975, 228; Brunt, I, 1976, map.

30 Bosworth, 1996, 62; Plutarch, *De Alexandri Magni Fortuna Aut Virtute*, 2.9 in Moralia, 341C .

31 For *P. falciparum* malaria as a cause of Alexander's death, E. Littré, 1872, 406-415; Engels, 1978, 224-8.

32 P. D. Clarke and A. Bryceson, 1994.

33 R. Sallares, 2002, 11.

34 Arrian, *Anabasis Alexandri*, 1.9.9; Arrian, *Anabasis Alexandri*, 4.27; Plutarch, *Alexander*, 50-52; Curtius, 8.1.22.

35 Plutarch, *Alexander*, 8.

2. Funeral Games

Bedford: *Hung be the heavens with black, yield day to night!*
Comets, importing change of times and states,
Brandish your crystal tresses in the sky,
And with them scourge the bad revolting stars
That have consented unto Henry's death!
King Henry the Fifth, too famous to live long!
England ne'er lost a king of so much worth.

Gloucester: *England ne'er had a king until his time.*
Virtue he had, deserving to command:
His brandish'd sword did blind men with
    his beams;
His arms spread wider than a dragon's wings;
His sparkling eyes, replete with wrathful fire,
More dazzled and drove back his enemies
Than mid-day sun fierce bent against their faces.
What should I say? his deeds exceed all speech:
He ne'er lift up his hand but conquered.

Exeter: *We mourn in black: why mourn we not in blood?*

William Shakespeare, *Henry VI,* Part 1, Act 1, Scene 1

Shakespeare foreshadowed the Wars of the Roses with three royal dukes lamenting the demise of Henry V. So, too, the Wars of the Successors began in Babylon with Alexander's passing. His Macedonian marshals mourned their king in blood.

On 11 June 323 BC Perdiccas called an emergency meeting of senior officers to discuss the succession. Many troops of lower rank also crowded into the hall and the event escalated into an *ad hoc* session of the Assembly of the Macedonians. The atmosphere was tense and fractious, and Curtius gives a near-verbatim account of the spiralling arguments, which led to a schism between the infantry, led by an officer called Meleager, and the cavalry, commanded by Perdiccas and Alexander's Bodyguards.[1]

The appeals of Perdiccas and the Bodyguards to await the birth of Alexander's child by his queen Roxane, who was six months pregnant, were met with antagonism and hostility. The infantry were loath to risk electing a child monarch of half-barbarian blood. Instead, they proclaimed Arrhidaeus, Alexander's mentally impaired half-brother, as their new king under the regnal name of Philip III.

There was fierce fighting around Alexander's deathbed. Outnumbered, the cavalry withdrew from Babylon to camp out in the surrounding plains, where they instigated a siege by cutting all supplies to the city. Meleager was forced to negotiate and settled for the position of Perdiccas' deputy. Perdiccas tricked him by persuading Philip-Arrhidaeus to denounce Meleager's supporters, who were then trampled to death by the elephants. Meleager was assassinated shortly afterwards.[2]

Alexander's body seems to have been left virtually unattended until Perdiccas reasserted his authority. Aelian says, 'While his followers argued about the succession … he was left unburied for thirty days', but the more detailed and plausible account of Curtius states that the embalmers treated the corpse about a week after the pronouncement of death. By that time the body should have putrified in Babylon's summer heat, but the embalmers found the corpse to be remarkably pure, fresh and lifelike. The ancient stories remembered this as a sign of Alexander's divinity, but medically speaking it is a strong indication that death occurred much later than was thought at the time. It was emphasised at some length in the previous chapter that Alexander had probably entered a deep, terminal coma due to the onset of cerebral malaria, and may not have expired until shortly before the embalmers began their work.[3]

Perdiccas called upon the Assembly of the Macedonians to endorse a string of key decisions. Justin writes that Alexander's body was placed in their midst whilst they deliberated. The Assembly voted for the abandonment of Alexander's Last Plans and approved the division of the kingdoms of the empire among his Bodyguards and Companions. Ptolemy was awarded the governorship of Egypt, probably at his own instigation. Diodorus and Justin state that a decision was made to transport Alexander's corpse to a temple of the Egyptian god Ammon. They and Arrian name the officer appointed to take charge of the preparation and escort of the catafalque as Arrhidaeus, although Justin confuses him with Philip-Arrhidaeus.[4]

The main historical text relating events after Alexander's death was the history of Hieronymus of Cardia, who was a friend and countryman of Eumenes, Alexander's Secretary. His work has not survived except for a few fragments, but seems to have been quite reliable. It is likely that Diodorus, and possibly also Trogus (Justin's source), derived their information about the decision to send the body to Ammon from Hieronymus. This is particularly interesting since Curtius and Justin state that Alexander's last request was to take his body to Ammon and are probably using a different source for this (probably Cleitarchus). If this is the case, then Alexander's request to be taken to Ammon must be true.[5]

Alexander's request is thoroughly consistent with our knowledge of his personality and beliefs. He seems to have considered himself to be the 'Son of Ammon' in a religious (but probably not a literal) sense and he deferred to Ammon's authority in such matters as Hephaistion's worship. Above all, he knew that in Egypt he stood to achieve the apotheosis, which was perhaps the driving force for his pursuit of superhuman achievements. In this vein Lucian puts the following words into Alexander's mouth:[6]

I have lain in Babylon for three whole days now, but Ptolemy of the Guards is pledged, as soon as he can get a moment's respite from present disturbances, to take and bury me in Egypt, there to be reckoned among the Gods.[7]

It is therefore plausible that Alexander really did ask to be buried with Ammon in Egypt and that the Assembly of the Macedonians acquiesced to this request in the emotive atmosphere shortly after his death.

Roxane gave birth to a son in the late summer, who was named Alexander IV after his father. He shared in a joint kingship with Philip-Arrhidaeus, whilst Perdiccas administered the empire as their regent. A serious rebellion broke out in Greece, and the Greeks settled in the eastern satrapies by Alexander revolted. Contingents of Alexander's Bodyguards set out to counter these threats. Ptolemy left to take up the governorship of Egypt, while Perdiccas, accompanied by the kings, led the Grand Army against the king of Cappadocia, who had refused to acknowledge Macedonian supremacy.

Remaining at Babylon, Arrhidaeus spent over a year preparing a splendid catafalque for Alexander. Diodorus records that Arrhidaeus 'spent nearly two years in making ready this work', but this seems unlikely. It probably reached Syria in the winter of 322/21 BC and cannot have travelled much further than a few miles per day, despite being 'accompanied by a crowd of road-menders and mechanics'. It may, therefore, have left Babylon as early as the summer of 322 BC. Diodorus gives an exceptionally detailed description of the carriage and its contents, deriving from an eyewitness account, and believed to be a surviving fragment of Hieronymus.[8]

Diodorus begins by describing the coffin of 'hammered gold' and 'fitted to the body', which suggests a shape like an Egyptian mummy-case. The space around the body was packed with preservative spices to keep it sweet and uncorrupted and the coffin was draped with a pall of gold-embroidered purple, about which were stacked the panoplies and arms of the deceased in the traditional fashion. This coffin was destined to survive for over 240 years after Alexander's death and is mentioned by several other ancient authors including Strabo and Curtius, who confirm it was crammed with perfumes and that Alexander was crowned with the royal diadem. The *Alexander Romance* also has a reference to the coffin:[9]

> *I command the administrators of the kingdom to build a golden sarcophagus, weighing 200 talents, to hold the body of Alexander, the King of Macedonia.*

Figure 2.1. Nike, winged goddess of Victory, holding out a wreath on the reverse of a gold stater of Philip-Arrhidaeus minted around the time Alexander's catafalque was under construction in 323/2 BC. © Peter A. Clayton

Much of this section is an obvious forgery, probably by a Rhodian pen, and it is badly corrupted in surviving versions. Nevertheless, it contains some striking references, which suggest that it was originally composed within a generation or two of Alexander's death.

The carriage took the form of an Ionic temple about 6m long and 4m wide with a colonnade supporting a pediment and a roof fashioned from fish-scale tiles of gem-encrusted gold. Golden acanthus plants wound up the length of each column and water-spouts were spaced around the pediment to drain the roof, taking the form of goat-stag masks, from which were suspended brightly coloured garlands. From each corner of the pediment rose a statue of the winged goddess of victory, Nike, displaying a trophy (fig. 2.1) and beneath these statues large golden bells suspended by tassels tolled mournfully to announce from afar the approach of the cortège. Within the colonnade nets of thick golden cords curtained the space beneath the vault where the coffin lay, and the bottom edges of these were weighed down by sculpted and painted tablets running around the carriage. The front, side and rear panels depicted: Alexander riding in a chariot and wielding a sceptre surrounded by Macedonian and Persian bodyguards and a vanguard of his troops; the Macedonian cavalry; a herd of war elephants; and a flotilla of warships. Guarding the entrance a pair of golden lions glared out imperiously over the backs of 64 mules hitched to four poles in the Persian fashion. Even these beasts were each richly arrayed with a gilded crown, a bejewelled collar and a pair of golden bells.

The temple rumbled along on four gilded wheels borne by two axles, coupled to an ingenious suspension system supporting the carriage and protecting its precious cargo from the jolts of the unmetalled road. As a finishing touch a mast jutted skywards from the centre of the roof bearing a banner of royal purple with a huge golden olive wreath that glinted vibrantly in the sunlight, each flash seeming from a distance like a thunderbolt cast by Zeus.

…[The catafalque] *appeared more magnificent when seen than when described. Because of its widespread fame it drew together many spectators; for from every city into which it came the whole population went out to meet it and again escorted it on its departure, never becoming sated with the pleasure of beholding it.*[10]

Some modern reconstructions of the carriage depict it with a barrel-vaulted roof (fig. 2.2) because the term used by Diodorus may be translated to mean 'a vehicle with a vaulted roof' or simply 'a covered carriage'. It has been proposed that its architects were imitating the barrel-vaulting used in the funeral chambers of Macedonian tumulus tombs, a form used to provide the strength required to support the weight of the overlying earth. The rest of Diodorus' description is reminiscent of a classical Greek temple of the Ionic order, so a roof with a squat Λ cross-section would perhaps have been more likely.[11]

The sequence of events involving the transportation of Alexander's body on this carriage from Babylon to Egypt is shrouded in a fog of apparent contradictions in the surviving accounts of ancient writers. The story of these events is like a smashed vase with some shards altogether lost. Had we only a few fragments, then they would be unlikely to share common edges, so they could be arranged to fit many different reconstructions. But in reality we have many pieces, so it is possible to fit many of them back together.

An area of ambiguity is whether Perdiccas intended to bury Alexander in Egypt or in Macedonia. Although there is persuasive evidence of a plan to take the body to Ammon when Arrhidaeus was appointed, Pausanius writes of Ptolemy:[12]

The Macedonians who had been entrusted with the task of carrying the corpse of Alexander to Aegae, he persuaded to hand it over to him.

Aegae was the site of the Royal Cemetery in Macedon, where in 1977 Professor Andronikos discovered the intact tomb of an important king beneath the Great Tumulus. It is now generally accepted that this was the grave of Philip II, Alexander's father, so Aegae was the obvious alternative to Egypt. A summary of a lost history by Arrian[13] bolsters the idea that Perdiccas had some other destination than Egypt in mind:

Figure 2.2. Reconstruction of Alexander's catafalque with a barrel vault, after Antoine Quatremère de Quincy (c. 1780), re-drawn by G. Heck and engraved by Henry Winkles for a book published in 1851. © A. M. Chugg

And Arrhidaeus, who guarded the body of Alexander, led it, against the orders of Perdiccas, from Babylon via Damascus to bring it before Ptolemy, son of Lagus, in Egypt. Despite the opposition of Polemon, an associate of Perdiccas, Arrhidaeus managed to achieve his design.

The *Alexander Romance* also states that the Macedonians wanted to take Alexander's body to Macedonia.[14]

In order to reconcile the two traditions it is necessary to infer that Perdiccas changed his mind at some point. It is easy to understand how

Perdiccas and the Assembly may initially have been swayed by grief, sympathy and respect to honour Alexander's orders and agree to bury him in Egypt. It is equally apparent that practical considerations may have caused the Regent to regret such a decision, since under the Macedonian constitution it was the prerogative of the new monarch to bury his predecessor. Consequently, Perdiccas would have been reluctant to cede this honour to Ptolemy. There also seems to have been a prophecy that the royal line would end when the kings ceased to be buried at Aegae. Perhaps most worryingly of all, Perdiccas stood to bring the full wrath of the baleful Olympias down upon himself should he fail to return her son's remains to her. How, though, might the *volte-face* be presented to the army without losing face?[15]

Perhaps the most colourful account of the journey of Alexander's body to survive from antiquity is the story given by Aelian in *Varia Historia*. This is worth quoting in full:

Alexander, son of Philip and Olympias, lay dead in Babylon – the man who said he was the son of Zeus. While his followers argued about the succession he lay awaiting burial, which even the very poor achieve, since the nature common to all mankind requires a funeral for those no longer living. But he was left unburied for thirty days, until Aristander of Telmissus, whether by divine inspiration or for some other reason, entered the Assembly of the Macedonians and said that of all kings in recorded history Alexander was the most fortunate, both in his life and in his death; the gods had told him that the land which received his body, the former habitation of his soul, would enjoy the greatest good fortune and be unconquered through the ages.

On hearing this they began to quarrel seriously, each man wishing to carry off the prize to his own kingdom, so as to have a relic guaranteeing safety and permanence for his realm. But Ptolemy, if we are to believe the story, stole the body and hurriedly made off with it to Egypt, to the city of Alexander. The other Macedonians did nothing, whereas Perdiccas tried to give chase. He was not so much interested in consideration for Alexander and due respect for his body as fired and incited by Aristander's prediction. When he caught up with Ptolemy, there was quite a violent struggle over the corpse, in some way akin to the one over the phantom at Troy, which Homer [Iliad 5.449] celebrates in his tale, where Apollo puts it down among the heroes to protect Aeneas. Ptolemy checked Perdiccas' attack. He made a likeness of Alexander, clad in royal robes and a shroud of enviable quality. Then he laid it on one of the Persian carriages, and arranged the bier sumptuously with silver, gold and ivory. Alexander's real body was sent ahead without fuss and formality by a secret and little used route. Perdiccas found the imitation corpse with the elaborate carriage, and halted his advance, thinking he had laid hands on the prize. Too late he realised he had been deceived; it was not possible to go in pursuit.

Aristander had been Alexander's principal soothsayer, and features prominently in the extant histories, where his prognostications are normally supportive of the king. In Babylon, a month after Alexander's death, Aristander's prophecy provides a good explanation of how the army might have been swayed to demand that the corpse be returned to Macedonia for burial.

Many of the essential details in Aelian's tale are corroborated elsewhere, but some of his interpretations of the facts are dubious. The story probably reflects an underlying truth which has become distorted.

It is virtually certain that there was a disagreement between Perdiccas and Ptolemy concerning the fate of Alexander's corpse and that Ptolemy arranged for the catafalque to be diverted to Egypt as soon as it reached Syria in defiance of Perdiccas' orders. Strabo agrees with Aelian, Pausanius and Arrian in stating this:[16]

For Ptolemy, the son of Lagus, forestalled Perdiccas by taking the body away from him when he was bringing it down from Babylon and was turning aside towards Egypt, moved by greed and a desire to make that country his own.

Strabo wrongly conflates the hijacking of the corpse with Perdiccas' ensuing attack on Egypt and therefore incorrectly implies that Perdiccas escorted the catafalque.

Diodorus, though silent about the controversy, hints at the potential for conflict by mentioning Ptolemy's army:[17]

> *...Arrhidaeus... brought the body of the King from Babylon to Egypt. Ptolemy, moreover, doing honour to Alexander, went to meet it with an army as far as Syria, and, receiving the body, deemed it worthy of the greatest consideration.*

Evidently Ptolemy arranged for the diversion of the cortège with the collaboration of its commander, Arrhidaeus. Arrian states this explicitly, while Pausanius agrees that Ptolemy suborned the escort. Diodorus and Arrian imply again that Ptolemy and Arrhidaeus were in league since their writings indicate that Ptolemy nominated Arrhidaeus to be one of the two Guardians of the joint kings shortly afterwards. This appears to have been intended as a reward for services rendered.[18]

How did Perdiccas react to the provocation? Fortunately, a more obscure but informative fragment of Arrian's lost account of the hijack has survived:[19]

> *The partisans of Perdiccas, Attalus and Polemon, sent out by him to prevent the departure, returned without succeeding and told him that Arrhidaeus had deliberately given the body of Alexander to Ptolemy and was carrying it to Egypt. Then, even more, he wanted to march to Egypt in order to take away the rule from Ptolemy and put a new man in his place (one of his friends) and retrieve the body of Alexander. With this intention he arrived in Cilicia with the army.*

It seems clear that Polemon and Attalus were ordered to pursue the catafalque by Perdiccas, as soon as he received word of Arrhidaeus' treachery. The arrival of Ptolemy's army perhaps prevented them from obtaining it and there may have been actual skirmishes.

This was the winter of 322-21 BC and Perdiccas and the Grand Army were in Pisidia in modern Turkey (1,100km away). The cortège must have been in northern Syria, where the routes from Babylon to Macedon and to Egypt diverged. Such momentous news probably reached Perdiccas at a gallop, in which case he knew it within a week or two. Arrhidaeus and Ptolemy would have been greatly hampered by the ungainly carriage and its gangling train of mules, and Perdiccas may have calculated that a cavalry force could overtake them before they reached Egypt. In this context Aelian's story of the chase can be seen to make reasonable sense. Hard-pressed by the pursuit, Ptolemy may have decided either to create a decoy or to sacrifice the real carriage in favour of saving its precious cargo. Aelian's description of the decoy carriage and its contents closely resembles Diodorus' more elaborate account of the real catafalque, and may therefore be true.[20]

It is certain that Perdiccas attacked Egypt with the Grand Army in the aftermath of Ptolemy's hijacking of Alexander's corpse, since his invasion is one of the key events of classical history. Diodorus gives the most detailed account, but there are also outlines by Arrian, Justin, Nepos, Pausanius, Plutarch and Strabo. A near-contemporary inscription from the island of Paros dates the offensive to July 321 BC, but it probably began with the opening of the campaign season in the spring. To what extent was this momentous assault triggered by the theft of Alexander's corpse?[21]

The ambiguity of this point stems from the influential but biased account of Diodorus. He ignores the illegality and drama of the hijack and instead treats the event as a stately procession, and Ptolemy's provocation of Perdiccas is overlooked. Diodorus instead claims that his supporters advised him to 'defeat Ptolemy first in order that there might be no obstacle in the way of their Macedonian campaign'. The same explanation is cited by Justin: '…it seemed more to the purpose to begin with Egypt, lest, while they were gone into Macedonia, Asia should be seized by Ptolemy'. This was a risky strategy because, when Perdiccas marched on Egypt, Antipater was on the verge of invading Asia across the Hellespont.[22]

There is a strong implication in Aelian's tale that the attack upon Egypt was the consequence of stealing Alexander's body. Arrian's version makes this explicit, and hints that relations between Perdiccas and Ptolemy had already deteriorated. The account by Pausanius also implicitly supports this version of events: after persuading the escort of the catafalque to hand the corpse over to him, Ptolemy 'proceeded to bury it with Macedonian rites in Memphis, but knowing that Perdiccas would make war, he kept Egypt garrisoned; and Perdiccas took Arrhidaeus, son of Philip, and the boy Alexander, whom Roxane, daughter of Oxyartes, had borne for Alexander, to lend colour to the campaign, but really he was plotting to deprive Ptolemy of his kingdom in Egypt.'[23]

If Perdiccas had been indifferent to the fate of the corpse, his best course would have been to appease Ptolemy in order to concentrate upon the imminent threat from Europe. That he chose instead to assault Egypt suggests that the hijack decisively influenced his plans.

The invasion of Egypt was an abject failure: Perdiccas tried unsuccessfully on two occasions to cross the Nile, losing many troops (many were eaten by crocodiles), and his officers mutinied and stabbed him to death with *sarissas* (long Macedonian pike-spears).[24] The triumphant Ptolemy graciously declined the Army's offer of the Regency. Instead, he nominated Pithon and Arrhidaeus as co-regents for the joint kings. They led the Grand Army back north, and Ptolemy turned his attention to completing Alexander's memorial.

In describing Alexander's entombment in Egypt, Diodorus attributes a sudden change of policy to Ptolemy:[25]

He decided for the present not to send [the body] *to Ammon, but to entomb it in the city that had been founded by Alexander himself, which lacked little of being the most renowned of the cities of the inhabited earth. There he prepared a sacred enclosure worthy of the glory of Alexander in size and construction.*

The reference to Alexandria as the greatest city on Earth is an anachronism, since in 321 BC it was only 10 years old and still mainly a building site. Memphis remained the Egyptian capital and Alexandria's days of glory lay decades into the future. Alexander was indeed entombed in Alexandria within a large enclosure in the time of Cleopatra, when Diodorus visited the city. This appears to be a clumsy attempt to reconcile the statement in his source (Hieronymus?), about Alexander being taken to Ammon, with his personal experience.[26]

Aelian also says that Ptolemy took the body to Alexandria and Strabo asserts that 'the body of Alexander was carried off by Ptolemy and entombed in Alexandria, where it still now lies'. He too is probably drawing on his eyewitness experience, obtained during his residence in the city for several years in the time of Augustus.[27]

There is overwhelming evidence from elsewhere that these writers are not giving an accurate account, for it is virtually certain that Memphis was Alexander's initial resting place and that the body was only transferred to Alexandria some years later. Pausanius maintains that Ptolemy buried Alexander 'with Macedonian rites in Memphis', and Curtius supports this in his history:

Alexander's body was taken to Memphis by Ptolemy, in whose power Egypt had fallen, and transferred thence a few years later (paucis post annis) *to Alexandria, where every mark of respect continues to be paid to his memory and his name.*

The *Alexander Romance* also makes great play of the role of Memphis, blending historical events and fable:[28]

Figure 2.3. Silver tetradrachm showing a portrait of Ptolemy I (r. 305-282 BC).
© Peter A. Clayton

…Then Ptolemy addressed them: 'There is in Babylon an oracle of the Babylonian Zeus. Let us consult the oracle about the body of Alexander; the god will tell us where to lay it to rest.' The god's oracle was as follows: 'I tell you what will be of benefit to us all. There is a city in Egypt named Memphis; let him be enthroned there.' No one spoke against the oracle's pronouncement. They gave Ptolemy the task of transporting the embalmed body to Memphis in a lead coffin. So Ptolemy placed the body on a wagon and began the journey

from Babylon to Egypt. When the people of Memphis heard he was coming, they came out to meet the body of Alexander and escorted it to Memphis. But the chief priest of the temple in Memphis said, 'Do not bury him here but in the city he founded in Rhacotis [Alexandria]. Wherever his body rests, that city will be constantly troubled and shaken with wars and battles.'

None of these statements should be considered decisive. The indisputable evidence comes from the chronology inscribed in Greek upon a slab of marble on the Aegean island of Paros in the year 263-62 BC, when it was part of the empire of the Ptolemies. In its entry for the year 321-20 BC the Parian Marble states clearly that 'Alexander was laid to rest in Memphis'. This near-contemporary public document is a reliable source, since most of the information it contains is verifiably accurate, corroborated by the independent accounts of other ancient historians.[29]

Having established that Ptolemy stole Alexander's body in defiance of Perdiccas, entombed it at Memphis, and readied his defences against an anticipated attack, it is fascinating to enquire why he should knowingly have taken such a tremendous risk in this matter. That it was a perilous risk is shown by the fact that Perdiccas came close to crossing the Nile. Had he succeeded, Ptolemy would certainly have lost his kingdom and most probably his life as well.

There is a suggestion in Diodorus that Ptolemy had been contacted by Antipater with a view to forging an alliance against Perdiccas. This was prompted when Antigonus, the Governor of Phrygia, had fled to Macedon and revealed a plot by Perdiccas to marry Alexander's sister and seize the throne in his own name.[30]

Had Ptolemy behaved less provocatively, it is likely that Perdiccas would have marched against Antipater instead. Ptolemy might easily have spared himself the wrath of Perdiccas at a time when the Regent had just won a minor war in Cappadocia and was supremely powerful in the empire. Significantly, the rashness of the hijacking contrasts sharply with the carefully conceived strategies and alliances, characteristic of Ptolemy thereafter. How have historians sought to explain this conundrum?

A naïve view is that Ptolemy was motivated by the monetary value of the elaborate hearse: he needed its cash value to hire troops to secure his position in Egypt. Yet Diodorus records that Ptolemy had found 8,000 talents in the treasury when he arrived to take control of the country and St Jerome attributed an annual income of over 14,800 talents to Ptolemy's son, Philadelphus. Furthermore, the most valuable item in the funeral cortège was the golden sarcophagus and Strabo notes that this survived intact for another 240 years. In short, the image of Ptolemy as a glorified highwayman is not sustainable.[31]

A more reasonable and commonly expressed opinion is that Ptolemy was seeking to bolster his position through the prestige of obtaining the corpse. Robin Lane Fox refers to the catafalque as 'the spoils that would justify Ptolemy's independence' and Richard Stoneman calls the body a 'symbol of power'. Clearly, the prestige gained from burying the previous monarch in the eyes of the Egyptians and the Macedonians would be uniquely suited to underpinning a claim to the throne.[32]

In 321 BC Ptolemy nurtured no such ambitions, for he refused the role of regent, when offered it after the murder of Perdiccas, and he scrupulously maintained the fiction that he governed Egypt on behalf of Philip-Arrhidaeus and Alexander IV for a further 16 years. Philip Arrhidaeus was murdered by Olympias in 317 BC and Cassander secretly poisoned Alexander IV and his mother Roxane in about 310 BC, but it was not until 305 BC that Ptolemy had himself proclaimed pharaoh and issued the first coins bearing his own distinctive portrait (fig. 2.3). Even then it was only done as a counterblast to the assumption of royalty by Ptolemy's arch-enemies, Antigonus and Demetrius. Evidently, the political aspirations that might have made sense of the hijacking were simply lacking in Ptolemy's plans.

To find a compelling and convincing motive for Ptolemy's actions it is pertinent to examine the ancient texts. Curtius and Justin state that

Alexander commanded that his body be taken to Ammon shortly before he died, while Lucian makes Alexander's ghost claim that Ptolemy had vowed to fulfil this dying wish. Quite simply, we are being told that Ptolemy diverted the catafalque to Egypt in order to keep faith with his dead king.

Historians familiar with the treacherous and cynical behaviour of Alexander's commanders after his death are bound to be sceptical of this touching tale of loyalty beyond the grave. However, there are some special factors in Ptolemy's case, which lend credence to this version of events. Some believe that Ptolemy composed his history of Alexander's campaigns late in life to rescue the king's reputation from the malicious exaggerations and fabrications of earlier accounts. In this behaviour a pattern of fidelity to Alexander's interests is discernible. This demands further explanation.[33]

In an assault upon a town in southern India, Ptolemy received a slight wound to his shoulder, but the swords of the natives had been smeared with poison and he became gravely ill. Curtius, Diodorus and Strabo have recorded Alexander's personal intervention to save his companion. Curtius writes:[34]

Indeed, [the Macedonians'] *concern for Ptolemy was no less than the King's. Exhausted though he was from battle and anxiety, Alexander kept watch at Ptolemy's side and ordered a bed brought in on which he himself might sleep. As soon as he lay upon it, a deep sleep immediately overcame him. On waking, he declared that he had had a dream about a serpent carrying a plant in its mouth, which it had indicated was an antidote to the poison. Alexander also described the colour of the plant claiming that he would recognise it if anyone found it. It was subsequently located – for it was the object of a large-scale search – and Alexander applied it to the wound. Ptolemy's pain immediately ceased and within a short time a scab formed.*

Curious as it may seem to find Alexander acting as his friend's doctor, this is in fact a perfectly sensible story, because we know from elsewhere that the king had studied herbal medicine under Aristotle and regularly prescribed cures for sick members of his entourage.[35] The technique of seeking cures in dreams is also a familiar Greek medical practice.

It may be inferred that Ptolemy felt he owed Alexander his life, a sufficient reason for special loyalty. There was another bond between them, since ancient texts state that Ptolemy may well have been an illegitimate son of Philip II and, therefore, Alexander's half-brother:

> *The Macedonians consider Ptolemy to be the son of Philip, the son of Amyntas, though putatively the son of Lagus, asserting that his mother was with child when she was married to Lagus by Philip.*[36]

> *He* [Ptolemy] *was a blood-relative of Alexander and some believe he was Philip's son (it was known for certain that he was the child of a concubine of Philip's).*[37]

> *And Perdikkas thought that Alexander would leave all his goods to Ptlomeos because he had often spoken to him of Ptlomeos' lucky birth. And Olympias, too, had made it clear that Ptlomeos had been fathered by Philip.*[38]

Modern historians have expressed doubts about this. Fraser speaks of Ptolemy's 'fictitious relationship with Alexander', but Pausanius and Curtius are well informed writers. They should not be dismissed lightly and there does not seem to be any tangible evidence to contradict them. Sceptics argue that Ptolemy encouraged a false rumour of his paternity by Philip to enhance his standing among his followers, but since this would have tarnished the honour of his beloved mother, Arsinoë, this is dubious. Most of Ptolemy's supporters would have been close enough to the Macedonian court to have known the truth anyway. Ptolemy officially claimed a common descent from Heracles with the Macedonian royal family. Theocritus describes Ptolemy as Lagus' son, but also says that Alexander and Ptolemy both 'traced back their line to Heracles'. This was emphasised as part of an *Encomium* (song of praise) to Ptolemy performed at the court of his son Philadelphus.[39]

The clear message from the ancient writers is that Ptolemy found himself obligated by a dual debt of honour to Alexander, of sufficient magnitude to place his kingdom and life in jeopardy through the fulfilment of Alexander's dying wish. If Lucian is correct about his motives then this may help us understand what happened to Alexander's body after it reached Egypt.

Based on information gleaned from historical texts, scholars have erroneously concluded that there was an intention to bury Alexander at the desert oasis of Siwa west of the Nile. Sources in fact specify that the body was to be conveyed to Ammon or the temple of Ammon. It is often assumed that this means Siwa, because the ancient geographers and historians of Alexander called this oasis Ammonium after the god, whose oracle lay there; and because Alexander visited the oracle in 331 BC and consulted it.[40]

There is wide agreement that Alexander's 'voice was failing' or that he was 'voiceless' in his last days. His last words, if correctly documented, cannot have been uttered in anything more than a hoarse whisper, and this is indicated by the brevity of the reported phrases 'to the strongest' and 'when you are happy.' Perhaps, in a rare interval of lucidity, he said something like, 'Take me to Ammon'. The interpretations of such a phrase are various. One possibility would have been an immediate transfer to the temple of a god in Babylon considered to be the local equivalent of Zeus-Ammon, since the Greeks habitually associated foreign gods with their nearest Olympian counterparts. This could explain what prompted the delegation of the king's Companions to ask whether the dying Alexander should be moved to the Babylonian temple of 'Serapis'. Alternatively, Alexander may have intended that his body be taken to Siwa or another temple dedicated to Ammon in Egypt. The name could refer either to the oasis or to the god. In fact, there was a temple of Ammon in most Egyptian cities and the centre of the cult lay at Thebes. It was its high status as an oracular cult centre that made Siwa special, but oracles do not generally feature at funerals.[41]

There are some hints in ancient texts of the form and location of the tomb at Memphis. Apart from Pausanius' mention of burial 'with Macedonian rites', and the involvement of the chief priest of a Memphite temple according to the *Alexander Romance*, the main clue is a plausible link with the worship of Ammon. This corresponds with Alexander's wishes and follows from Ptolemy's determination to implement them.

There is another independent source of evidence for a link between the Memphite tomb and Ammon. Around 319 BC Ptolemy became the first

Figure 2.4 Alexander the Great wearing an elephant scalp and deified with the ram's horns of Zeus-Ammon on the obverse of a silver tetradrachm of Ptolemy I (dating to 310-305 BC). © A. M. Chugg

successor to deviate from Alexander's standard coinage by minting a series of silver tetradrachms with a new obverse design. In place of the famous head of Heracles wearing a lion-scalp headdress, Ptolemy substituted a portrait of Alexander wearing an elephant scalp and the ram's horns of Ammon (fig. 2.4).

This is particularly significant because it is the earliest known depiction of Alexander wearing ram's horns. Ephippus, who may once have served Alexander as an overseer of mercenaries, has described how the king used to dress up in this guise at banquets:[42]

> …*Alexander also used to wear sacred clothing at his dinners, sometimes the purple robe of Ammon and slippers and horns like the god … most of it indeed he wore all the time, the purple chlamys and chiton with a white stripe…*

The ram's horns motif received its most memorable expression in the sensational series of tetradrachms issued by Lysimachus about 298-281 BC in the cities of Ionia (see frontispiece). The elephant-scalp theme also enjoyed enduring popularity, known from surviving fragments of statuettes from Egypt and a portrait head of Alexander, made in North Africa in the 2nd century AD (now in the National Museum, Copenhagen) (fig. 2.5). The most complete statuette was found in the Nile Delta at Athribis, about 65km downstream from Memphis. It represents Alexander on horseback and is believed on stylistic grounds to date from the early Ptolemaic period.[43]

The emergence of these coins immediately after the entombment of Alexander at Memphis, coupled with this evidence, has led Otto Mørkholm to infer the creation of an archetypal funerary statue of Alexander to embellish the Memphite tomb at this time. This attractive theory is consistent with the ancient texts and gives a strong indication of a relationship between Alexander and Ammon at the first tomb. This prompts the question of whether there might have existed a temple dedicated to Ammon at Memphis in 321 BC.[44]

Figure 2.5. Marble head of Alexander (life-size) wearing an elephant's head and ram's horns, from Carthage or Utica in North Africa (Antonine period, AD 138-93), inv. ABb97.

© Department of Classical and Near Eastern Antiquities, National Museum of Denmark

The answer turns out to be an emphatic yes, for there is an early Ptolemaic papyrus which mentions the presence of an 'Imensthotieion' (a temple of Ammon and Thoth) in the Hellenion (Greek quarter) district of Memphis. It is believed that the Hellenion was founded by mercenary troops in the service of a Late Period pharaoh prior to Alexander's conquest. Claire Préaux has plausibly argued that the papyrus cannot be later than the 3rd century BC. It is therefore probable that this temple was available to Ptolemy when he was seeking a sanctuary of Ammon in Memphis, in which to lay Alexander to rest.[45]

Where were the Imensthotieion and the Hellenion? There is only limited evidence available. Memphis was abandoned well over 1,000 years ago and stone robbing has left few remains above ground level. The main New Kingdom cult sites of Ammon-Re at Memphis are connected with Perunefer, the city's port, which may have been at or near the eastern side of the mound district in the heart of the ruin field (fig. 2.6). Greek and Phoenician dedicatory inscriptions were found here in the late 1890s and early 1900s, but Dorothy Thompson, on the basis of the 'Memphis dyke repair papyrus', suggests that the Hellenion is in the north-western quadrant of the site. This may also be consistent with the location of Petrie's 'camp' (a possible barracks) around the Apries palace foundation in the Northern Enclosure. Petrie considered this to have been built to house the king's foreign bodyguard.[46] The most likely location of the Imensthotieion is therefore the district within a few hundred metres to the north-west of the Palace of Apries.[47]

What form might the Memphite tomb have taken? It is possible that Ptolemy created a full-scale Royal Tomb at Memphis, in which case the Royal Tombs at Aegae in Macedon may have provided the best prototypes. The tomb of Alexander's father (Philip II) comprised stone chambers with a painted temple façade and a barrel-vaulted roof to support the tumulus of earth. This would be the best model if Pausanius' mention of burial according to 'Macedonian rites' were taken to refer to the type of tomb in

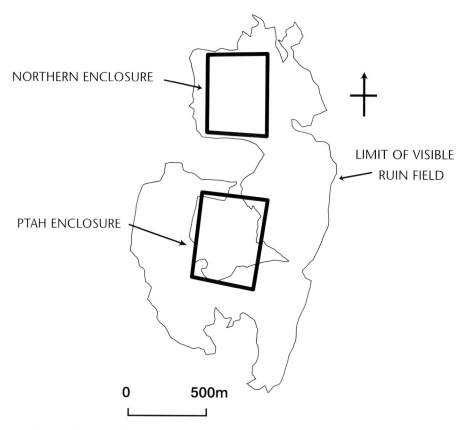

Figure 2.6. Archaeological map of Ptolemaic Memphis, based on a map in David Jeffreys, The Survey of Memphis, *London, 1985, fig. 6.1. Drawn by A. M. Chugg.*

question. However, a Macedonian interment would normally have required the prior incineration of the corpse, which certainly did not happen. The body also seems to have remained in the golden coffin fashioned at Babylon and there are hints that Alexander's remains became the object of religious veneration in a temple context. Pausanius may therefore only be referring to superficial religious ceremonies. Even this soon after his death, Alexander's corpse was probably treated more as a sacred relic than an ordinary human cadaver. His deification had, after all, begun in his lifetime and was perfectly consistent with pharaonic precedent and tradition in Egypt.

The most intriguing possibility regarding the character of the Memphite tomb relates to a surviving antiquity found in Alexandria and now on display in the British Museum. In about 341 BC the last native pharaoh of Egypt, Nectanebo II (r. 360–343 BC), fled to Ethiopia to escape a Persian invasion (Diodorus 16.51). He left behind a magnificent stone sarcophagus, made ready in the traditional fashion for his entombment. Ten years later Alexander ousted the Persians, and a decade after this Ptolemy brought his body back to the city. In all probability the sarcophagus stood empty at that time and there are some circumstantial reasons to suppose that Ptolemy decided to use it for Alexander's sepulchre.

It is most likely that the sarcophagus lay at Memphis at that time, since it was the capital of Nectanebo II (and of the other pharaohs of the 30th Dynasty). He had undertaken an extensive building programme in the Memphite necropolis at Saqqara, which may have related to the intended site of his tomb. Late Period pharaohs were generally buried in the courtyards of major temple complexes, typically in a deep vault beneath a cult chapel. Nectanebo had added temples to the Serapeum and to the Sacred Animal Necropolis, adjoining the Sanctuary of the Mother Cows of the Apis Bulls at Saqqara, the cemetery area in Memphis (figs 2.7a,b). His predecessor, Nectanebo I (r. 380–362 BC), is believed to have decorated the Serapeum approaches with an Avenue of Sphinxes and there was a major cemetery of the 30th Dynasty in its vicinity. Apparently the 30th Dynasty pharaohs identified themselves very closely with the cult of the Apis Bull. This helps to explain the special significance the Egyptians attached to Alexander's act of sacrificing to the Apis Bull when he first reached Memphis.[48]

Interestingly, there is a semi-circle of 11 limestone statues of Greek sages and poets in front of the entrance to the temple of Nectanebo at the Serapeum (figs 2.8a,b). The central figure seems to be Homer, for whom Alexander expressed a passionate appreciation. Another is Pindar, whose

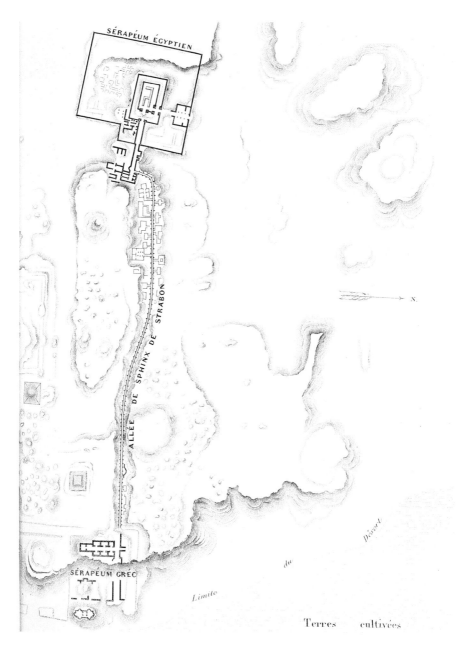

Figure 2.7a. Auguste Mariette's plan of his discoveries at Saqqara. From A. Mariette 1856, Plate II.

house and descendants Alexander saved at Thebes. A third is Plato, the mentor of Alexander's tutor. Jean-Philippe Lauer and Charles Picard have even suggested that a sculpture of Aristotle once stood at the end of the semi-circle closest to the temple.[49]

Opinions as to the date of these sculptures differ: several scholars have favoured the late 3rd or early 2nd century BC, but Lauer and Picard have proposed a date early in the 3rd century under Ptolemy I, which would make them contemporary with Alexander's Memphite tomb. One statue seems to be of Demetrios of Phaleron, the leading philosopher at the court of Ptolemy I. He was exiled to the countryside and probably forced to commit suicide with an asp, when he backed a rival to Ptolemy's successor, Philadelphus, so he is unlikely to have been commemorated by Philadelphus or his descendants. A fragment of an inscription with an artist's signature was

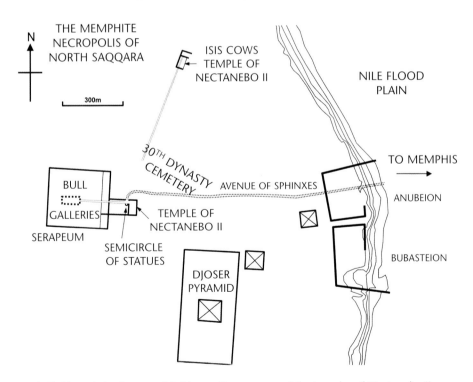

Figure 2.7b Plan of the Avenue of Sphinxes, Serapeum and the temples of Nectanebo II (r. 359/58-42 BC) in the Memphite necropolis at Saqqara. Drawn by A. M. Chugg.

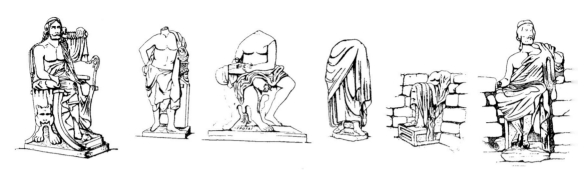

Figure 2.8a Ptolemaic statues of Greek poets and sages (above, left to right, Pindar, Demetrios, Protagoras, Plato, Heraclitus, Homer), adjacent to the temple of Nectanebo II, from sketches published by A. Mariette, in G. Maspero, ed., Le Sérapéum de Memphis *(Appended Atlas), Paris, 1882.*

found in the sand beneath a statue of Cerberus a little further down the Processional Way (*dromos*). This is securely dated to the early 3rd century BC, so most of the Greek statues at the site are likely to be of that era.[50]

Dorothy Thompson has speculated that the semi-circle 'guarded a shrine of some importance – the site once perhaps of Alexander's tomb'. If so, then the shrine in question almost certainly lay within the temple of Nectanebo, as implied by Auguste Mariette's detailed plan (fig. 2.9). This second association between Alexander's tomb and that of Nectanebo II is tantalising.[51]

A cryptic oracle given to Alexander by the god Serapis in the *Alexander Romance* may also be relevant:[52]

You, a callow young man, shall subdue all the races of barbarian nations; and then, by dying and yet not dying, you shall come to me. Then the city of Alexandria… is to be your grave.

Coming to Serapis reads like a euphemism for dying and indeed Serapis

is believed to have derived from Osiris–Apis, a manifestation of Osiris, who was lord of the afterlife. Such prophecies characteristically had double meanings, so this is a further hint that Alexander's first tomb was located at the Memphite temple of Serapis.

The Nectanebo sarcophagus re-enters the story at a much later date, at which point it will be possible to provide a more complete assessment of it and its implications for the location of the Memphite tomb of Alexander.

The duration of the Memphite entombment is disputed by scholars. It is relatively certain that the body was moved to Alexandria some time in the ensuing half century, but it has been argued that Ptolemy made the transfer as soon as two or three years after his defeat of Perdiccas. Careful scrutiny of the evidence does not support this point of view.

The transfer of Alexander's corpse to Egypt has been reconstructed in an unprecedentedly detailed manner that is largely consistent with most of the ancient texts.

The schism between Perdiccas and Ptolemy after Alexander's death from *P. falciparum* malaria resulted in a conflict of interests about the fate of Alexander's corpse. In defiance of Perdiccas, Ptolemy, the new governor of Egypt, hijacked the richly ornamented catafalque, prepared to take Alexander's body back to Aegae in Macedonia and conveyed it to the god Ammon at Memphis out of respect for Alexander's wishes. This may have been done as an act of loyalty as a half-brother, and because Alexander may have once saved his life. Ptolemy completed the entombment of Alexander at Memphis, most likely at the temple of Nectanebo in the Serapeum precinct of North Saqqara. Ptolemy's actions prompted Perdiccas to invade Egypt, but this proved catastrophic for him, resulting in his death. Ptolemy seems to have commissioned a large statue of Alexander adorned with an elephant-skin aegis and deified with the ram's horns of Ammon. Soon afterwards the head of this statue was adopted as the design for the obverse of a new series of coins.

Figure 2.8b Ptolemaic statues of Greek poets and sages situated at the end of the Avenue of Sphinxes, adjacent to the temple of Nectanebo II, photographed by A. Mariette c. 1851. © Bibliothèque Nationale de France

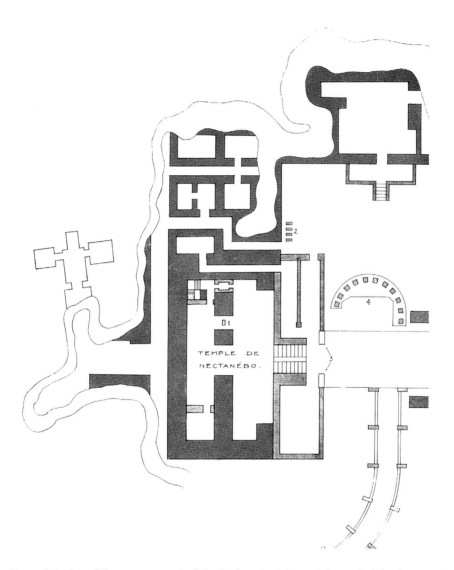

Figure 2.9 Plan of the arrangement of the Ptolemaic statues at the end of the Avenue of Sphinxes (adjacent to the temple of Nectanebo II) by A. Mariette, from J.-P. Lauer and C. Picard, Les statues ptolémaïques du Sarapieion de Memphis, *Paris, 1955, Plate 26.*

1   Alexander's eight most senior army officers at Babylon were: Perdiccas, Ptolemy, Leonnatus, Pithon, Aristonous, Peucestas, Lysimachus and (probably) Seleucus.
2   Curtius, 10.7.16-19.
3   Aelian, *Varia Historia*, 12.64; Curtius, 10.10.9.
4   Diodorus Siculus, 18.3.3; Justin, *Epitome of the Philippic History*, 13.4; Arrian, *History of Events After Alexander* (Photius, 92).
5   M. M. Austin, 1981, 43, note 3.; Hammond, 1983; R. M. Geer, 1947, vii; Pearson, 1960. The *Alexander Romance* 3.33.6 also states that Alexander ordered that his body should be taken to Egypt: G. Kroll, 1926, 139.
6   Plutarch, *Life of Alexander*, 27; Lucian, *Dialogues of the Dead*, XIII.
7   The manuscript read 'three', but Du Soul amended it to 'thirty' on the (very weak) basis of the Aelian story.
8   Diodorus Siculus, 18.28.2. There are serious difficulties with the chronology of the years 321-19BC. This issue is dealt with by H. Hauben, 1977, 85-120; E. Anson, 1985, 303-316. Diodorus Siculus, 18.26-27. F. Jacoby, *Die Fragmente der griechischen Historiker*, Berlin, 1923-30, Leiden, 1940-58 (hereafter abridged to *FGrH*), no. 154, fragment 2.
9   Strabo, *Geography*, 17.1.8; Curtius, 10.10.13. Wolohojian, 1969, section 274, 155; Stoneman, 1991, section 3.32, 154.
10 Diodorus Siculus, 18.28.
11 K. Rhomiopoulou, 1980, 25.
12 Pausanius, 1.6.3.
13 Arrian, *History of Events After Alexander* (Photius, 92).
14 Wolohojian, 1969, section 282, 157-8; Stoneman, 1991, section 3.34, 158.
15 J. B. Bury, S. A. Cook and F. E. Adcock, (eds.), 1927, (article by W. W. Tarn), 482; M. Renault, 1975, 11.
16 Strabo, *Geography*, 17.1.8.
17 Diodorus Siculus, 18.28.2-3.
18 Diodorus Siculus, 18.36.6-7; Arrian, *History of Events After Alexander* (Photius, 92).
19 W. J. Goralski, 1989, 19.
20 Diodorus Siculus, 18.25.6.
21 Diodorus Siculus, 18.33-37; Arrian, *History of Events After Alexander* (Photius, 92); Justin, 13.8; Cornelius Nepos, Eumenes, 3 and 5; Pausanius, 1.6.3; Plutarch, *Life of Eumenes*; Strabo, 17.1.8. Parian Marble, *FGrH* 239, dated 264-263 BC.
22 R. M. Geer, 1947, viii; Diodorus Siculus, 18.25.6; Justin, *Epitome of the Philippic History*, 13.6.
23 Pausanius, 1.6.3.
24 Diodorus Siculus, 18.35.5-36.5; Strabo, 17.1.8.
25 Diodorus Siculus, 18.28.3.
26 The construction of Alexandria's walls is ascribed to Ptolemy by Tacitus, *Histories*, 4.83. Fraser, 1972, vol. 2, 11-12, note 28 to chapter 1; Diodorus Siculus, 17.52.6.
27 Strabo, *Geography*, 17.1.8.
28 Stoneman, 1991, 158, section 3.34.

29 Jacoby, *FGrH*, 239.

30 Diodorus Siculus, 18.25.3-4.

31 Diodorus Siculus, 18.14.1; A. K. Bowman, 1986, 27; Strabo, *Geography*, 17.1.8.

32 Lane Fox, 1973, 478; Stoneman, 1997, 91; J. B. Bury, S. A. Cook and F. E. Adcock, (eds.), 1927, 467.

33 This has been plausibly argued by Hammond, 1983, 83-5, refuting Pearson, 1960, 234.

34 Curtius, 9.8.25-27; Diodorus, 17.103; Strabo, 15.2.7.

35 Plutarch, *Life of Alexander*, 8.

36 Pausanius, 1.6.2.

37 Curtius, 9.8.22.

38 The *Romance of Alexander*, Armenian Version, section 29.

39 Fraser, 1972, vol. 1, 215. Theocritus, *The Idylls*, 17; Satyrus, *FGrH* 631, F 1; W. Dittenberger, ed., *Orientis graeci inscriptions selectae*, Leipzig, 1903-5, (hereafter abridged to *OGIS*), 54, lines 1-5.

40 R. Stoneman, 1997, 91; M. Wood, 1997, 231; R. Lane Fox, 1973, 478. Diodorus, 18.3.5, 18.28.3; Justin, 12.15, 13.4; Curtius, 10.5.4.

41 Renault, 1975, 231 has plausibly suggested that *kratisto* (strongest) might have been Kratero (Alexander's leading general, Craterus) by reason of Alexander's failing voice. 'Zeus-Ammon' is a case of syncretism.

42 Arrian, *Anabasis Alexandri*, 3.5.3. Athenaeus, 12.537E-538B (quoting Ephippus); Curtius, 3.3.17; Diodorus, 17.77.5; for representations of this type of costume: Stewart, 1993, 424-5, fig. 144, the Demetrio Alexander, now in Athens, 422-3, fig. 103, the Alexander Sarcophagus from Sidon, now in Istanbul; Darius wears the royal white stripe in the Alexander Mosaic from the House of the Faun in Pompeii (c. 80 BC).

43 The Search for Alexander: an Exhibition, New York, 1980, exhibit 46.

44 O. Mørkholm, 1991, 63-4.

45 No. 50 in the first volume of the British Museum catalogue. C. Préaux, 1939, 298-9.

46 D. Jeffreys, 1985.

47 Dorothy Thompson, *Memphis under the Ptolemies*, Princeton 1988: 13-16 and 96.

48 The locations of the tombs of the 30th Dynasty are not known, A. Dodson, 2000, 162-3. Examples of the Late Period are the 26th dynasty tombs at Sais and those of the 29th dynasty at Mendes. This type of tomb was one element of a Late Period revival of Old Kingdom styles and traditions, B. G. Trigger, B. J. Kemp, D. O'Connor and A. B. Lloyd, 1983, 321. Arrian, *Anabasis Alexandri*, 3.1.4; Nectanebo II also inaugurated his reign by officiating at the funeral of the Apis Bull at the Serapeum, Nicolas Grimal, 1994, 379.

49 Plutarch, Life of Alexander 8.2 and 26.1. Arrian, Anabasis Alexandri 1.9.10; Plutarch, *Life of Alexander* 11.6; J.-P. Lauer and C. Picard, 1955, 153.

50 F. Matz, 29, 1957, 84-93; Later dates are preferred by other scholars, Fraser, 1972, vol. 2, 404, note 512; D. Thompson, 1988, 116. A date in the reign of Ptolemy I has been argued by J. P. Lauer and C. Picard, 1955.

51 Thompson, 1988, 212; Lauer and Picard, 1955; U. Wilcken, 1917, 149-203.

52 Wolohojian, 1969, sections 93 and 249, 53-55 and 140-1.

3.　The Capital of Memory

In the three centuries before Christ, Alexandria was the largest, most beautiful and most luxurious city in the world. The writer Lawrence Durrell has described Alexandria as 'the capital of memory'. Alexander had wished to provide a port to connect the civilisation of the Nile Valley with the Mediterranean world of the Greeks. A site in the delta was impractical because of the marshy nature of the ground and the annual Nile flood. He therefore chose a location just to the west on a strip of rocky ground about 2km wide sandwiched between the Mediterranean and Lake Mareotis, a freshwater lagoon connected by canals with the Canopic branch of the Nile.

Strabo has provided a detailed account of the layout of the Ptolemaic city, based on his personal observations during a long stay in Egypt beginning in 25 BC. The street plan was a rectangular grid oriented so that the cooling winds that blow from the north-west in the summer flowed down the line of the streets that ran between the sea and the lake (fig. 3.1, fig. 3.2). Two principal streets, twice as wide as the rest and bordered by colonnades of marble and polished granite, intersected at the centre of the city. The longer of these, called 'Canopic Way', ran for some 5km between the Canopic Gate (or Gate of the Sun) in the north-eastern wall and the Gate of the Moon in the south-west. The other probably ran from the

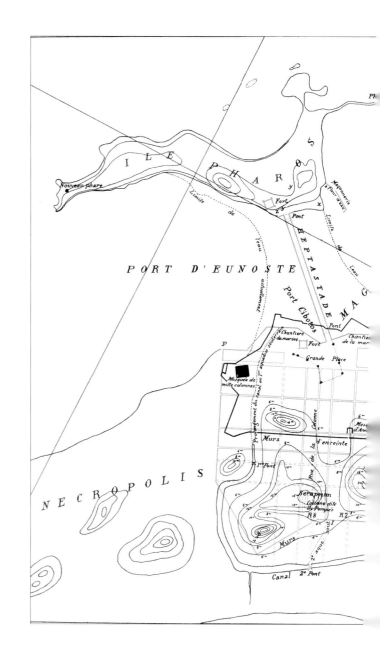

Figure 3.1 Map of Ancient Alexandria by Mahmoud Bey el-Falaki, based on his investigations of 1865-6, originally published in copies of L'Antique Alexandrie by Mahmoud Bey, Copenhagen, 1872.

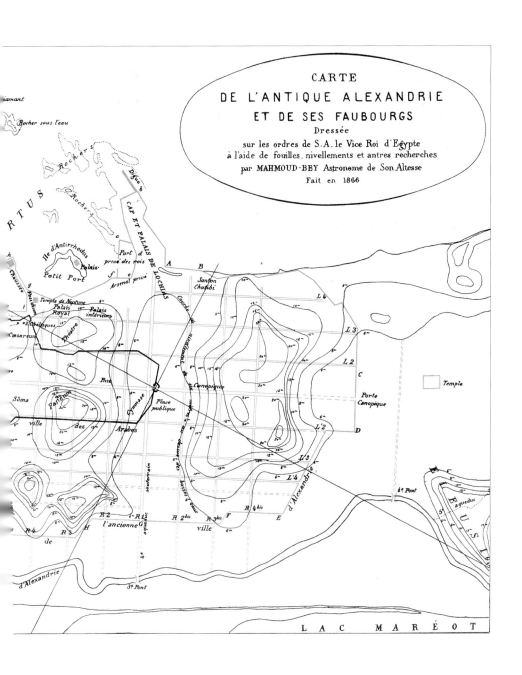

CARTE
DE L'ANTIQUE ALEXANDRIE
ET DE SES FAUBOURGS
Dressée
sur les ordres de S.A. le Vice Roi d'Egypte
à l'aide de fouilles, nivellements et antres recherches
par MAHMOUD-BEY Astronome de Son Altesse
Fait en 1866

Fig. 3.2 Reconstructed view of Alexandria and its harbour in the Hellenistic period looking south. Graphics: Yann Bernard. © *Franck Goddio/Hilti Foundation*

Lochias peninsula on the Mediterranean to the harbour on the lake, although its identification is disputed. A causeway called the Heptastadion, because it was seven stades (about 1.5km) long, connected the city with the nearby island of Pharos. It also separated the eastern 'Great Harbour' (Megas Limen) from the Eunostos (the 'Harbour of Happy Returns'). The famous Pharos lighthouse, the Seventh Wonder of the Ancient World, towered about 120m over the entrance to the Great Harbour at the eastern tip of the island.[1]

Diodorus quotes a census recording the number of free citizens as exceeding 300,000 at the end of the Ptolemaic period. This extrapolates to a total population of around 500,000 when slaves are taken into account. Philo has written that the city comprised five quarters. They were designated Alpha (for 'Alexander'), Beta (for *basileos*, 'king'), Gamma (for *genos*, 'descendant'), Delta (for *dios*, 'Zeus') and Epsilon (for *ektise polin aeimneston*, 'founded an ever-memorable city') according to the *Alexander Romance*, which also asserts that these names were supplied by Alexander. Alpha, the district named after Alexander, lay around the central crossroads. Beta was the royal district containing the palaces of the kings, roughly co-extensive with the district that the Romans later called the Bruchion. It stretched from the Lochias peninsula along the shore as far as the middle of the Great Harbour and as far south as the Canopic Way.[2]

Strabo says the royal district included between a quarter and a third of the whole city (though he may have included some areas that did not strictly lie within Beta). It incorporated a theatre built above a private royal harbour in the lee of the Lochias promontory. There was also an islet in the Great Harbour, called Antirhodos, lying just outside the private harbour's entrance with another palace upon it. The museum and library, the famous centres of learning for the whole Greek world, also lay somewhere in (or near) the royal district, presumably close to the shore, since, when Julius Caesar set fire to a fleet of ships in the harbour, the library accidentally caught alight.

The Egyptian quarter lay either in Gamma or Epsilon. This has also been called Rhakotis, the name, some believe, of the Egyptian port before the foundation of the city under Alexander. Alternatively, this name may originate from 'building site' in Egyptian, perhaps the name given to the new city by the native inhabitants of fishing villages on this shore. The name apparently remained in use by the Egyptian populace throughout the Ptolemaic and Roman periods.[3]

Fig. 3.3 Gold octodrachm *from Ptolemaic Egypt depicting Ptolemy Philadelphus and his sister-wife Arsinoë.* © *The British Museum/Heritage Images*

The Egyptian quarter lay behind the shipyards at the western end of the Great Harbour, perhaps extending from the south-western corner to the Eunostos. There was also a Jewish quarter, almost certainly lying behind the seafront east of Lochias and perhaps within Delta. The final quarter, although unknown, probably bordered the lake south of the Canopic Way, and was perhaps occupied by citizens of predominantly Greek extraction.[4]

Among the great buildings of the Ptolemaic city Strabo records a temple of Poseidon at the centre of the Great Harbour with the emporium, where duties on goods were collected, sited a little further to the west. The principal temple of the city, the Serapeum, was situated partly on rising ground in the south-west corner. Near the middle of the city there was an artificial hill called the Paneum in the shape of a fir cone with a spiral track to a viewpoint at its summit. This used to be identified with the hill of Kom el-Dikka, just south of the mid-point of the Canopic Way, but this has been almost completely removed and overlies Roman levels. A splendid gymnasium with porticoes about 200m long fronted on to the Canopic Way, probably close to the centre of the city. The tribunal (*dicasterion*) and the groves were also situated nearby. Here too within the walls of a large sacred precinct and adjacent to the palace complex lay Alexander's tomb.

The date of the transferral of Alexander's embalmed corpse from Memphis to Alexandria remains uncertain, but various lines of argument tend to converge on 290-280 BC. Pausanius attributes this act to Ptolemy II Philadelphus, the son and heir of the first Ptolemy: '… and [Philadelphus] it was who brought down from Memphis the corpse of Alexander.' The Parian Marble places his birth in 309-8 BC. He reigned jointly with his father from 28 December 285 BC until the death of Ptolemy I Soter in the first half of 282 BC,[5] and later with his sister, Arsinoë (fig. 3.3), whom he married in the incestuous Pharaonic tradition. His reign was long and magnificent, lasting until 246 BC, and presiding over the apex of Ptolemaic power in the eastern Mediterranean.

If Pausanius, established as a reliable source, is correct in making Philadelphus responsible for the transfer to Alexandria, then it would be difficult to date the move much before 290 BC, when Philadelphus was 18. Nevertheless, the authority of a single source is always questionable in the absence of corroboration.

Of the other sources which mention the move from Memphis to Alexandria, Curtius is too vague and the *Alexander Romance* too fantastical to be helpful. On the Parian Marble there is no mention of any transfer of Alexander's corpse up to the last surviving entry in 299-8 BC, but the lost entries must have continued up to the time it was inscribed in 263-2 BC, when Alexander's corpse had reached Alexandria. Since the Parian Marble records the entombment of Alexander's corpse at Memphis in its entry for 321-20 BC, the transfer must surely have been recorded after its last surviving entry. In this negative but persuasive sense, the Marble provides the corroboration of Pausanius' version, and the argument for an early transfer to Alexandria within a decade of Alexander's death is therefore unsustainable on the basis of the evidence.

This merits emphasis, because the mainstream of modern scholarship has often expressed the opposite opinion on this point. In particular, Fraser became embroiled in an argument with Welles[6] in which he sought to prove that Ptolemy transferred the Egyptian capital from Memphis to Alexandria as early as *c.* 320 BC. In pursuit of this theory, he found it convenient also to support an early date for the transfer of Alexander's corpse. He later conceded that the case for an early transfer of the capital cannot be proven, but his opinion on the duration of the Memphite entombment has often been repeated. His reasoning was that Ptolemy should logically have been eager to embellish his new capital with the tomb of its founder. If Ptolemy fulfilled his promise to Alexander by delivering his body to the Egyptian gods, then it is easy to understand why the new pharaoh may have been reluctant to disturb the sacred burial site.[7]

It is feasible that Philadelphus acted while Ptolemy was still alive, since he seems to have progressively taken over the government of the country as his father entered old age. There is also some papyrus evidence suggesting that Menelaos, Ptolemy's brother, became the first high priest of Alexander in Alexandria, probably between 290-85 BC. It would be fitting if this priesthood was established near the date Alexander's body arrived, although Pausanius' words are more in keeping with a move shortly after Ptolemy's death. Free of his father's inhibitions, Philadelphus would have been keen to adorn the new capital with the powerful symbolism of its founder's tomb, so an early transfer date within his reign is likely.[8]

The antechamber of an early Ptolemaic tomb constructed of monumental alabaster blocks was unearthed in the early 20th century by Evaristo Breccia in the Catholic cemetery of Terra Santa. It was more extensively excavated by Achille Adriani, his successor as director of the Graeco-Roman Museum at Alexandria, who confirmed that the main burial chamber was missing. This tomb was built in a style vaguely reminiscent of a Macedonian tumulus tomb of the late 4th century BC. On the basis of the quality of this structure, its date, style and location, Adriani proposed that it might be part of a tomb of Alexander in the city, although several Ptolemies died at this time and it may have been used to entomb one or more of them.[9]

It is known that the Ptolemies established a cult at the royal tombs in Alexandria for the worship of Alexander and their other ancestors. An account by Callixinus of Rhodes describes a procession through Alexandria in 271/70 BC under Ptolemy II Philadelphus, in which statues of Alexander and Ptolemy I Soter were paraded through the streets with images of the gods Dionysus and Priapus and of the goddess Virtue. Even the names of most of the high priests of Alexander have survived thanks to the practice of invoking them in the preambles of certain Ptolemaic decrees and contracts from 272/1 BC onwards. In August 256 BC the priest's name is given as Alexander, son of Leonidas. For 251 BC Neoptolemus, son of Phrixius, had been appointed according to one of the Hibeh papyri, whilst

Figure. 3.4 Gold octodrachm from Ptolemaic Egypt depicting Ptolemy IV Philopator (r. 221-205 BC). © Peter Clayton

an inscription of Ptolemy III Euergetes (r. 246–222 BC) dated 4 March 238 BC names the priest of Alexander as Apollonides, son of Moschion. It is interesting that these documents consistently use the predicate *theos*, meaning 'divine', to sanctify the dead Ptolemies, whereas Alexander seems to have been considered a fully fledged deity who did not need such a careful introduction.[10]

The *Alexander Romance* mentions a 'Grand Altar of Alexander' built by the king 'opposite' the shrine and tomb of Proteus on the island of Pharos.

This could indicate a wide range of locations on the opposite shore in Alexandria. The *Romance* is generally considered quite a reliable source of Alexandrian topography, since Pseudo-Callisthenes almost certainly lived there. Such an altar – which is reminiscent of the contemporary Great Altar at Pergamon – may have been closely associated with Alexander's tomb. The *Romance* also provides details of Alexander's priesthood:[11]

> *There is to be an administrator of the city* [Alexandria], *who will be known as the Priest of Alexander and will attend all the city's great festivals, adorned with a golden crown and a purple cloak; he is to be paid a talent per annum. His person is to be inviolate and he is to be free of all civic obligations; the post shall be the preserve of the man who excels all in nobility of family, and the honour shall remain in his family thereafter.*

Ptolemy IV Philopator (r. 221–205 BC) (fig. 3.4) ascended the throne at about the age of 23 in 221 BC upon the death of his father. He was apparently a hedonist with little interest in the day-to-day business of government. Consequently, much power devolved upon his principal minister, Sosibius. The queen-mother, Berenice II, sought to undermine him, but was poisoned on the minister's orders early in the reign of Ptolemy IV. One of the most important and reliable historical references to the tomb of Alexander was written by Zenobius the Sophist in the first half of the 2nd century AD. This relates to the period after the assassination of Berenice: [12]

> *Ptolemy Philopator… built in the middle of the city* [of Alexandria] *a memorial building, which is now called the Sema, and he laid there all his forefathers together with his mother, and also Alexander the Macedonian.*

Edwyn Bevan in his *History of the Ptolemaic Dynasty* also mentions that the priesthood of the Saviour-Gods, Ptolemy I Soter and his wife Berenice I, became incorporated under the priesthood of Alexander in the year 215–

14 BC, according to a change in the dating formula in papyrus documents. Bevan seems to have been unaware of the Zenobius reference, so he missed the significance of this observation, but his information corroborates Zenobius and probably also dates the commencement or completion of the new Soma mausoleum to this year. The original Alexandrian tomb was therefore vacated at this time and it was Philopator's new edifice that became the famous tomb mentioned by many other ancient writers. Strabo states that this structure was part of the Royal Quarter of the city and describes it as a walled enclosure (*peribolos*) that contained the graves of Alexander and the kings (the Ptolemies):[13]

> *The Soma also, as it is called, is a part of the royal district. This was the walled enclosure which contained the burial-places of the kings and that of Alexander.*

Diodorus also mentions this enclosure, calling it a sacred precinct (*temenos*) 'worthy of the glory of Alexander in size and construction', while Herodian and Dio Cassius simply refer to the 'memorial' of Alexander. The location of the precinct in the middle of the city is supported by Achilles Tatius, an Alexandrian writing before AD 300, who describes a place or district named after Alexander at the main crossroads:[14]

> *After a voyage lasting three days we arrived at Alexandria. I entered by the Sun Gate, as it is called, and was instantly struck by the splendid beauty of the city, which filled my eyes with delight. From the Sun Gate to the Moon Gate – these are the guardian divinities of the entrances – led a straight double row of columns, about the middle of which lies the open part of the town, and in it so many streets that walking in them you would fancy yourself abroad while still at home. Going a few stades further [stade = 165m], I came to the place called after Alexander, where I saw a second town; the splendour of this was cut into squares, for there was a row of columns intersected by another as long at right angles.*

Collectively, these testimonies make it clear that the tombs of Alexander and the Ptolemies were probably contained within one or more mausoleums within a monumental sacred walled precinct. This may have contained one or more temples dedicated to their worship, together with the Grand Altar of Alexander. If the accounts of Strabo, Zenobius and Achilles Tatius are all true then the enclosure was probably situated near the central crossroads or adjacent to them on the northern side of the Canopic Way.

Another intriguing issue raised by these sources is the name of Alexander's tomb. Zenobius says it was called the *Sema*, a Greek word meaning 'tomb', although in Strabo's *Geography* it is called the *Soma*, which means 'body' or 'corpse', though this has been 'corrected' to Sema in many modern editions. The *Alexander Romance* declares: 'And Ptolemy made a tomb in the holy place called "Body of Alexander", and there he laid the body, or remains, of Alexander,' but the later Syriac version reads: 'and they call that place "The tomb of Alexander" unto this day.' John Chrysostom, Bishop of Constantinople in the late 4th century AD, referred to the '*sema* of Alexander', but he seems to have used the word as an ordinary noun, rather than as a name. Similarly, Dio Cassius refers to the '*soma* of Alexander', but appears literally to mean his corpse. Either Soma is being corrected to Sema or *vice versa* by the ancient scribes and copyists, who transmitted these accounts down the ages. Modern editors of Strabo, the *Alexander Romance* and Zenobius have only ever changed Soma to Sema, so that is the more likely emendation by ancient editors too. Furthermore, the fact that several ancient writers explicitly state the name of the monument favours Soma. For these reasons it is probable that the name was indeed the Soma and that those who have emended the manuscripts are in error. It is of course possible that the enclosure was called the Soma and the mausoleum was known as the Sema.[15]

Two Latin authors have provided important details of the architecture of the Soma. Suetonius, describing a visit to the tomb by Augustus in 30 BC, refers to the sarcophagus and corpse of Alexander being brought out from a *penetrali*, an 'inner sanctum' or 'the innermost or secret parts, depths, recesses'. More important are specific verses by Lucan.[16]

Marcus Annaeus Lucanus was born in AD 39. Seneca the Elder was his grandfather and Seneca the Younger, the mentor and advisor of Nero, was his uncle. He seems to have been a boyhood friend of the emperor, first achieving fame as a poet at Nero's court, but he harboured nostalgic republican sympathies, which were amply nourished by the spectacle of the emperor's descent into despotism and debauchery. In AD 65 he joined Calpurnius Piso's plot against Nero, which was betrayed. In the aftermath Nero required him to commit suicide and his masterpiece, the *Pharsalia*, was left unfinished. Having been composed in the last four years or so of his life, it is imbued with a keen contempt for kings and emperors doubtless inspired by his personal experience of absolute power inexorably evolving into absolute corruption.

It is unknown whether Lucan visited Alexandria, but the city figures prominently in his poetry and Suetonius mentions that he was recalled to Rome from Athens by Nero. Even if he had not visited the city himself, his uncle, Seneca, had certainly been there and could have provided detailed information. Two passages in Lucan's *Pharsalia* constitute the only detailed description of the Soma that survives from the ancient world:[17]

Cum tibi sacrato Macedon servitur in antro
Et regem cineres exstructo monte quiescant,
Cum Ptolemaeorum manes seriemque pudendam
Pyramides claudant indignaque Mausolea,...

Though you preserve the Macedonian in a consecrated grotto
and the ashes of the Pharaohs rest beneath a loftily constructed edifice,
though the dead Ptolemies and their unworthy dynasty
are covered by indignant pyramids and Mausoleums,...

...Tum voltu semper celante pavorem
Intrepidus superum sedes et templa vetusti
Numinis antiquas Macetum testantia vires
Circumit, et nulla captus dulcedine rerum,
Non auro cultuque deum, non moenibus urbis,
Effossum tumulis cupide descendit in antrum.
Illic Pellaei proles vaesana Philippi,...

...Then, with looks that ever masked his fears,
Undaunted, he [Caesar] visited the temples of the gods
        and the ancient shrines
of divinity, which attest the former might of Macedon.
No thing of beauty attracted him,
neither the gold and ornaments of the gods, nor the city walls;
but in eager haste he went down into the grotto hewn out for a tomb.
There lies the mad son of Philip of Pella [Alexander],...

The first passage exerts a seductive temptation to formulate the equation: pyramids plus tombs plus Egypt equals Giza. It initially appears that the Ptolemies had been emulating the pharaohs of the Old Kingdom, and the use of the Latin word for a mountain (*monte*) in describing the buildings tends to reinforce this prejudice in modern readers. Furthermore, according to his Last Plans, Alexander intended to bury Philip, his father, in 'a tomb comparable with the Great Pyramid [of Cheops at Giza]' and the mausoleum of Cestius built at Rome under Augustus, where Egyptian influence was felt, is a small pyramid. Nevertheless, first impressions are often deceptive and there is an alternative model for the architecture of the Soma, more compatible with Lucan but unrelated to the monuments of earlier pharaohs. The Great Pyramid at Giza was counted among the Seven Wonders of the World by the Greeks, but they also included another funerary monument in their list, the tomb of King Mausolus of Caria (r. 377-53 BC) at Halicarnassus on the Ionian coast of the Aegean.[18]

Mausolus' sepulchre was an architectural and sculptural *tour de force* largely built after his death by Artemisia, his disconsolate queen, around 352-50 BC. It became known as the Mausoleum and it is the ancestor, in name at least, of all mausoleums. Coincidentally, Alexander besieged and captured Halicarnassus in 334 BC and, intriguingly, Halicarnassus was among the Aegean possessions of the Ptolemies at the time the Soma was built.

The Mausoleum survived largely intact until an earthquake damaged its roof and part of its colonnade some time between the 12th and 15th centuries AD. Unfortunately, the ruins of the building were largely eradicated in the late 15th century by the Knights of St John, who robbed its masonry to construct their nearby castle. Detailed ancient descriptions of its architecture exist and Sir Charles Newton identified the foundations in 1857 and recovered some of its sculptures on behalf of the British Museum, where they may be presently viewed. A reasonably accurate reconstruction of the Mausoleum is therefore possible (fig. 3.5).

Its rectangular podium measured about 36m by 30m and was decorated with bands of sculpture by the leading artists of the age. It was surmounted by a colonnade of 36 Ionic columns, supporting a stepped, pyramidal roof. A statue group of Mausolus and Artemisia in a four-horse chariot was placed on its 42m apex. Beneath the structure lay the only trace of the Mausoleum that survives, a burial chamber about 7m x 7m (fig. 3.6). This edifice stood near the north-east corner of a walled enclosure measuring about 240m x 100m.[19]

It is likely that the Mausoleum inspired the design of the Ptolemies' funerary monuments in the 3rd century BC by virtue of its size, beauty and renown and also because it lay in the middle of another city within their empire. There are some striking parallels between the Mausoleum and Lucan's description of the Soma:[20]

i) Both the Soma and the Mausoleum had a pyramidal superstructure.

ii) A 'hewn-out tomb' into which Caesar 'descended' suggests a subterranean chamber of similar character to the Mausoleum. Suetonius' use of the word '*penetrali*' is also consistent with an underground burial chamber. This would have maintained a cool and constant temperature all year, essential for the preservation of an embalmed corpse.[21]

iii) The Latin '*extructo monte*' at first sight reads as a 'loftily constructed mountain'. This is the line taken by some translators and it would seem to pose a problem for the Mausoleum prototype, although Cicero (whose works Lucan was probably familiar with) uses '*montem*' to mean a tall and splendid villa: '… *ad hunc Tusculani montem extruendum*', which translates as, 'in order to raise that edifice at Tusculum' (Cicero, *In Pisonem* 48). It is therefore appropriate to interpret Lucan as meaning a 'lofty edifice', which fits the Mausoleum model well.

iv) Lucan uses the word 'Mausolea' (with a capital M) to describe the buildings, which provides a direct allusion to Mausolus' tomb.

v) In the line, 'Enclosed by indignant pyramids and Mausoleums', the Latin does not seem to indicate that the pyramids *are* the mausoleums. Just possibly some kings are in pyramids and others in mausoleums, but what Lucan may mean is that the tombs have both a pyramidal superstructure *and* an additional mausoleum part. This makes perfect sense if the Mausoleum of Halicarnassus is their model, but it is difficult to explain, if the tombs were Egyptian-style pyramids. The last line perhaps reads as though Lucan is suggesting that the tombs have their noses in the air out of indignation and contempt that they house the despised Ptolemies and the 'mad son of Philip'.

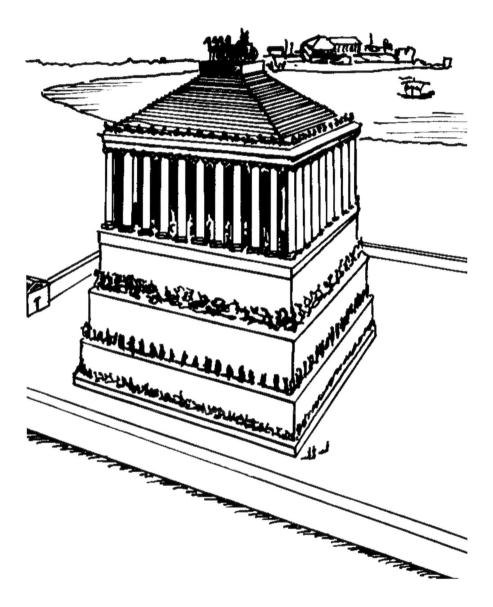

Figure 3.5 Reconstruction of the Mausoleum of Halicarnassus in modern Turkey – one of the Seven Wonders of the Ancient World, the tomb of King Mausolus (r. 377-53 BC), and a plausible model for the design of Alexander's tomb (drawn by A. M. Chugg); based on K. Jeppesen, 1992, 59-02, Plate 25 (attributed to G. Waywells).

The *Pharsalia* references seem to agree in five distinct ways with a Mausoleum prototype and less readily with an Egyptian pyramid model. It should be added that both the Mausoleum and the Soma stood within a large, walled enclosure. An Egyptian-style solid pyramid sufficiently tall as to impress Lucan would have been extremely rugged so its later sudden disappearance would be more difficult to explain by war or earthquake. Conversely, had it been both large and hollow, then the support of its faces would have posed considerable structural engineering problems. In any

Figure 3.6 The preserved subterranean funerary chamber of the Mausoleum at Halicarnassus. © Peter A. Clayton

case, on the balance of the scanty available evidence, the Soma was most probably a close architectural relative of the Mausoleum at Halicarnassus.

There exists one other tantalising line of evidence in the form of several funerary monuments (2m and 3m in height) from the Chatby necropolis in an eastern district of ancient Alexandria and a very similar, larger Ptolemaic tomb found in Cyrene and another mausoleum from Kalat Fakra in Lebanon (figs 3.7a, b, c and d). The designs of these memorials appear to have been influenced by the Mausoleum at Halicarnassus, but they are more readily explained if they echo the design of a royal tomb in Alexandria. At the very least, the Chatby monuments provide a precedent for the introduction of the form of the Mausoleum into the architecture of Alexandrian tombs of the Ptolemaic era.[22]

A single, accurate representation of ancient Alexandria might prove invaluable in helping to interpret descriptions that have survived in the ancient sources. Unfortunately, the few stylised ancient representations identified as possible depictions of the city are problematic.

Many Roman lamps of an apparent 1st century AD date depict similar harbour scenes (fig. 3.8). Among the tall buildings in the background of the harbour, one structure has a pyramidal roof and has been proposed as a possible representation of the Soma. Both the date and location of the scene have been questioned by Bailey, who argues that they are early 3rd century AD views of other North African (Carthage) or Italian (Ostia) ports or are forgeries.[23]

The sculpted cover of the 4th-century sarcophagus of Julius Philosyrius of Ostia (the ancient port of Rome) appears to depict a Pharos-style lighthouse tower and a column similar to 'Pompey's Pillar', a monument erected in Alexandria by the Emperor Diocletian (r. AD 284-305) in AD 298 and still standing today (fig. 3.9). There is also a tower with a pointed roof, possibly representing the Soma. There was a lighthouse designed to resemble the Pharos at Ostia itself, which may suggest that Ostia is represented, especially given its provenance.

Figures 3.7a and b. Ptolemaic funerary monument from the Chatby necropolis in an eastern district of Alexandria. © A. M. Chugg

There are several hints that the sculptor, who had probably never seen Alexandria, intended to evoke the Egyptian port. The date-palm tree on the far left is used as part of the symbolism for Alexandria in a 6th-century AD mosaic in the Church of St John the Baptist at Jerash (fig. 3.10). A palm forest outside the eastern gateway remained a captioned feature of the 16th-century maps of Alexandria by Pierre Belon, and Georg Braun and Frans Hogenberg, although it should be borne in mind that palms also appear outside the gates of cities in other mosaics. Two Tritons are shown blowing conch shells on top of the triple-arched monument.[24] Interestingly, the most famous ancient reference to these mythical sons of Poseidon is in the sculptural ornaments on the first stage of the Pharos lighthouse and Strabo mentions a temple of Poseidon at the centre of the Alexandrian harbour front.

Figures 3.7c and d Ptolemaic tomb from Cyrene in Turkey and a mausoleum at Kalat Fakra in Lebanon dated to the same period. The design of both monuments was probably inspired by the Mausoleum of Halicarnassus. © A. M. Chugg

The name of the deceased alludes to a connection with the eastern Mediterranean and finally, the monuments appear in approximately the correct order (left–right corresponding to east–west). If it is supposed that the tower with the pointed roof is a highly schematic representation of the Soma, then this sarcophagus provides tenuous evidence for the survival of the mausoleum into the early 4th century AD. In any case, it is clear that the sculptor imbued his work with a strong flavour of Ostia, presumably because his knowledge of Alexandria was gleaned verbally rather than pictorially.

There are several mosaics of Byzantine date which show named representations of Alexandria. In particular, the pavement from Jerash (fig. 3.10) depicts a walled city with the inscription 'Alexandria' accompanied by

Figure 3.8 Roman oil lamp in terracotta depicting a harbour scene which may represent Alexandria (1st century BC – 1st century AD), Haifa National Museum, Israel. © *Photo: akg-images/Erich Lessing*

a separate tower (the Pharos). A building on the left with a cupola might be the old Church of St Mark, and another near the centre with a domed roof allegedly represents the Soma, although this is at odds with Lucan's description. There is other evidence indicating that the parts of the Soma above the ground had been destroyed some two centuries before this mosaic was laid.

Perhaps most enigmatically, two images of the Soma have been proposed by the Spanish scholar Alberto Balil. A fragment of a glass cup of the 3rd or 4th century AD (fig. 3.11) found in the 19th century at Carthage has an image of a prominent monument with a portico in the background of a harbour scene with a fisherman and his basket of fish. A portico is a colonnade supporting the roof or other structural elements of a building, and may be used to describe the colonnade of the Mausoleum at Halicarnassus. In 1962 Balil proposed that this image might be a representation of the Soma, but his arguments were mainly based on style.[25]

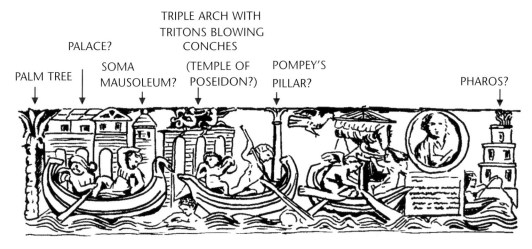

Figure 3.9 Harbour scene depicted on the cover of the sarcophagus of Julius Philosyrius (4th century AD), based on a drawing published by G. Luigi and G. Filibeck, 1931, 39, Fig. 23; and C. Picard, 1952, 61-95. *Drawn by A. M. Chugg*

Figure 3.10 Mosaic pavement in the Church of St John the Baptist in Jerash, Jordan, depicting the urban landscape of Alexandria (6ᵗʰ century AD), Jerash Archaeological Museum, Jordan.

© akg-images/Erich Lessing

In 1984, Balil presented an analysis of a 3rd-century AD Roman mosaic from Toledo in Spain (fig. 3.12). He argued that many of its elements, such as cane fishermen and harbours, are reminiscent of other possible depictions of the port of Alexandria. Of most relevance is the depiction of a multi-stage lighthouse linked with the mainland by an arched causeway, recalling the Pharos accessed via the Heptastadion. Several tall, temple-like buildings are represented with domed or pointed roofs, one of which Balil contended might be a representation of the tomb of Alexander.[26]

In the 1,000-year history of ancient Alexandria almost everything about the city changes, but one theme recurs throughout the period: the rampages of the Alexandrian mob regularly exerted a decisive influence in religious and political disputes. It was generally indiscriminate in its choice of victim, sometimes overthrowing a bloodstained monarch or a poisonous minister, but on other occasions tearing to pieces a venerable scholar or an architectural masterpiece on some wild religious whim. This menacing rabble first intersected the story of the Soma in 89 BC, when the citizens of Alexandria finally lost patience with the hideous and bloated drunkard who had ruled over them as Ptolemy X Alexander I (r. 107-88 BC) on and off for around 20 years. The rioters won over the army to their cause and Ptolemy X was forcibly expelled. He fled to Syria, where he recruited a mercenary army with promises of plunder and riches and marched straight back to Egypt.

Having retaken Alexandria with little difficulty, Ptolemy was confronted with the trickier problem of making good the compact with his troops. His solution, as recorded by Strabo, was to pillage the Soma and steal Alexander's golden sarcophagus, probably the one hammered out to fit the corpse in Babylon 23 decades earlier. The body was afterwards housed in a substitute of glass or translucent alabaster. In the eyes of the Alexandrians this was sacrilege of a high order and the mob rose again within that year to expel the defiler of their founder's tomb. Ptolemy X fled once more towards Myra in Lycia, but Alexandrian naval squadrons pursued him and he was drowned in a sea fight as he was attempting to land at Cyprus.[27]

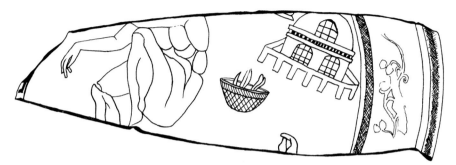

Figure 3.11 Drawing of a fragment of a Roman glass cup depicting a harbour scene with a fisherman and a peristyle monument in the background, perhaps the Soma (3rd or 4th century AD). From Un Fragment de Verre Gravé, Cahiers de Byrsa VIII, 1958-59, 103- 109, Plates I and II, Musée Lavigerie, Imprimerie Nationale, Paris. *Drawn by A. M. Chugg*

Writing 80 years after these events, Strabo continued to reflect the unrelenting contempt of the Alexandrians for the desecrator of the Soma by omitting both Ptolemy X Alexander I and his son Ptolemy XI Alexander II from his dynastic list.

There is little doubt that Ptolemy II Philadelphus relocated Alexander's tomb from Memphis to Alexandria in the early 3rd century BC. In Egypt Alexander was worshipped as a god and his body became a sacred relic. Ptolemy IV Philopator built a new tomb for Alexander in a grandiose mausoleum in about 215 BC. Ptolemy X substituted a glass coffin for Alexander's original gold mummy-case in about 89 BC.

Alexander's tomb in Alexandria took the form of a magnificent mausoleum standing within an even more impressive walled enclosure known as the Soma. There are sufficient hints regarding the appearance of the mausoleum to conclude that it was either based on a simple pyramid structure or, more probably, it resembled the Mausoleum of Halicarnassus, one of the Seven Wonders of the Ancient World. Ancient texts indicate that the enclosure lay at or near the central crossroads and extended northwards towards the royal palaces along the shore of the Great Harbour.

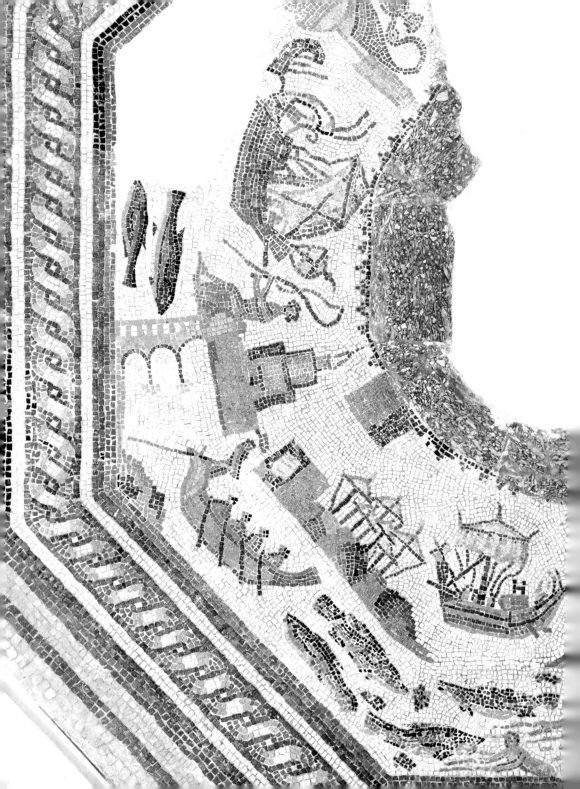

1   The identification of the N-S road has been disputed, notably by F. Noack, 1900, 215-279. Strabo, *Geography*, 17.1.6-10, gives by far the most detailed description of the ancient city, which is the basis of the account given here, except where otherwise indicated. The 'etesian winds', Diodorus, 17.52. Also, Mahmoud Bey El-Falaki, *Mémoire sur l'antique Alexandrie, ses faubourgs et environs découverts*, Copenhagen, 1872.

2   Philo of Alexandria, *In Flaccum*, 55; Fraser, 1951, 103-108; Diodorus, 17.52. Kroll, 1926, 32; Achilles Tatius, *Clitophon and Leucippe*, 5.1.

3   M. Chauveau, 1997, 77; Stoneman, 1991, 63 and 158.

4   Josephus, *Contra Apion*, 2.33, places the Jewish quarter near the Royal Palaces on a harbourless stretch of the coast; he also speaks of the Jews being concentrated in Delta in *The Jewish War*, 2.495. Philo, *In Flaccum*, 55, states that two of the five quarters were predominantly Jewish; there is also a papyrus (BGU 1151, lines 40-41) which apparently asserts that Delta was near the Kibotos harbour, which Strabo places firmly in the west of Alexandria.

5   Pausanius 1.7.1; Bowman, 1986, 235.

6   Fraser, 1972, vol. 2, 11-12.

7   Fraser, 1972, vol. 2, 32.

8   Fraser, 1972, vol. 2, 365.

9   N. Bonacasa, 1991, 5-19.

10 Athenaeus, *Deipnosophistae*, 5.201-203; W. Clarysse and G. van der Veken, 1983; P. Col. (Columbia papyrus) 54; P. Hib. (Hibeh papyrus) 98 (Elsewhere 'son of Kraisis'); W. Dittenberger, Leipzig, 1903-5, 56.

11 Stoneman, 1991, 65, 155.

12 Zenobius, *Proverbia*, 3.94.

13 Bevan, 1927, 231. Strabo, *Geography*, 17.1.8.

14 Diodorus, 18.28; Herodian, *History of the Empire*, 4.8.9; Dio Cassius, *Roman History*, 76.13.2; Achilles Tatius, *Clitophon and Leucippe*, 5.1.

15 The passage from the *Alexander Romance* is absent from manuscript A, but was reconstructed from manuscript B and the Armenian version by G. Kroll, 1926, 145, who then proceeded on his own authority to emend Soma to Sema. For the Syriac *Alexander Romance* see E. A. W. Budge, 1896, 142, but this is much less likely to be authentic. John Chrysostom, *Homily XXVI on the second epistle of St Paul the Apostle to the Corinthians*; Dio Cassius, *Roman History*, 51.16.5;

16 Suetonius, *Lives of the Caesars*, 2.18; the definition is from the Oxford Latin Dictionary.

17 Suetonius, *Lives of Illustrious Men, On Poets, Life of Lucan*; H. Thiersch, 1910, 68-9; Lucan, *Pharsalia*, 8.694-697 and 10.14-20.

18 Diodorus, 18.4.5.

19 K. Jeppesen, 1992, 59-102.

20 Bowman, 1986, 28-9.

21 Suetonius, *Lives of the Caesars*, 2.100-1.

22 A. M. Bisi Ingrassia, 1984, 835-42; Adriani, 1963, 117-118, plate 39; for the Cyrene tomb, J. Fedak, 1990, 385, fig. 168.

23   D.M. Bailey, 1984, 265-72.
24   Picard, 1952, 61-95.
25   J. Ferron and M. Pinard, 1958-9, 103-9; A. Balil, 1962, 102-3.
26   A. Balil, 1984, 433-9.
27   Strabo, *Geography*, 17.1.8.

Previous pages: figure 3.12 Roman mosaic from the villa *of La Vega in Toledo, Spain, depicting what may be Alexandrian port scenes (3rd century AD), Museo de Santa Cruz, Toledo, Spain.* © 1990, Photo Scala, Florence

4.   The Shrine of the Caesars

Like Alexander I will reign,
And I will reign alone;
My thoughts did evermore disdain
A rival on my throne.
He either fears his fate too much,
Or his deserts are small,
That dares not put it to the touch
To gain or lose it all.

James Graham, First Marquis of Montrose,
I'll Never Love Thee More

In the middle of the 1st century BC the tide of world history began to surge dramatically. In the eastern Mediterranean the Hellenistic kingdoms of Alexander's successors had dominated the region almost unchallenged for nearly three centuries. Grown indolent and soft on the prosperity of peace, they made attractive prey for the hawks of the Roman Republic, which had recently emerged triumphant and battle-hardened from the ferocious struggles of the Punic Wars. By 50 BC, Rome stood on the threshold of empire and only Ptolemaic Egypt retained a nominal independence under the juvenile Pharaoh Ptolemy XIII (r. 51-47 BC) and his charismatic elder sister Cleopatra VII (r. 51-30 BC) (fig. 4.1).

It was at this juncture that Julius Caesar (fig. 4.2) chose to cross the Rubicon, sparking a civil war with his rival Pompey. In 48 BC at the Battle of Pharsalus in Thessaly, Pompey was vanquished and fled to his erstwhile friends in Egypt with Caesar in hot pursuit. But Ptolemy's ministers, disdaining to support a lost cause, treacherously murdered the supplicant

Figure 4.1 Portrait head of Cleopatra VII (r. 51-30 BC) in marble, c. 50-30 BC (Berlin State Museum). © *Sandro Vannini/CORBIS*

general. When Caesar arrived in Alexandria a few days later he was greeted in the Great Harbour by Ptolemy's tutor, Theodotus, who presented the signet ring and severed head of Pompey to the Roman dictator. More revolted than appeased by this intended act of friendship, Caesar pursued a policy of guardianship over the youthful Egyptian monarchs appointed to Rome by the will of the late Pharaoh Ptolemy XII Auletes (r. 80-51 BC). This was the occasion of Caesar's visit to the Soma, later celebrated in Lucan's epic poem. Alexander's tomb was at the centre of events again, not just geographically, but also in a deeply political sense, for the scene was set for two epic ideological conflicts, destined to settle the control of the Mediterranean world for the next 500 years: republicanism versus dictatorship, and Roman nationalism versus Graeco-Roman confederation and alliance.[1]

In Rome a great schism was opening between the supporters of the traditional republican constitution and the advocates of dictatorship. Most Romans were aware that their political system was showing signs of strain under the pressures of ruling almost the entire Mediterranean world, but they differed over the best remedy. One faction, of which Caesar was the champion, believed that the new circumstances demanded a decisive central authority, which could only be achieved by resting much of the power of the state in a single person. The opposing faction considered that the problems were a result of compromises already made in the constitution and sought a return to a purer form of republicanism. In this struggle Alexander's career became potently symbolic. As an exemplar of successful absolutist rule he was a propagandist's dream from the perspective of Caesar's party. Conversely, the Republicans found it expedient to revile his memory by emphasising his excesses and supposed megalomania. One of the earliest surviving histories of Alexander was penned in this period by Trogus. It took a relatively hostile line, probably informed by its author's republican sympathies.

Caesar's attitude was demonstrated by his eagerness to grasp the opportunity of a pilgrimage to the tomb of his hero. In his own account he describes how he landed at Alexandria and processed through the city with the full pomp and regalia of a Roman consul. His intention was partly to overawe the fiercely anti-Roman populace, but this elaborate ceremony was probably also inspired by his wish to honour Alexander during his visit to the Soma.[2]

At the time of Caesar's arrival in Egypt, Cleopatra had been evicted from Alexandria in the course of a power struggle with her brother. On learning of the dictator's intention to mediate in the dispute, she returned secretly to the Royal Palaces to seek a favourable judgement. Caesar seems to have been enraptured by the queen and they were soon lovers. Ptolemy's faction responded by besieging the Romans in the palaces, but a few months later Caesar's main army arrived by the long land route. Ptolemy was defeated in a pitched battle and he drowned in the Nile while attempting to flee. When Caesar finally departed from Egypt in the summer of 47 BC, he left the queen as its undisputed monarch. Shortly afterwards she gave birth to his son, whom the facetious Alexandrians nicknamed 'Caesarion' or 'Little Caesar'. Her master plan was to save her dynasty and recover the political fortunes of the Greek world. Accordingly, she intended to persuade Caesar to make Caesarion his heir, thereby cementing a grand alliance of the Greeks and the Romans. The stakes were enormous: success would have meant a realistic possibility of pursuing the elusive dream of recreating Alexander's long-vanished empire; failure might engender the extinction of her dynasty.

The most famous cinematic appearance of the Soma is in Joseph Mankiewicz's epic film *Cleopatra* (1963). In a scene set during his stay in Alexandria, Caesar, played by Rex Harrison, is taunted by the queen, played by Elizabeth Taylor, before an enormous glass sarcophagus. Alexander's embalmed corpse is dimly glimpsed through the misty crystal, as Cleopatra urges the Roman dictator to take up his sword and reconquer Alexander's lost domains. But it was never to be: a few years later Caesar was struck down in the Roman forum, the victim of a Republican conspiracy, and his great-nephew Octavian became the principal

Figure 4.2 Portrait head of Julius Caesar in marble, c. 50 BC, the National Archaeological Museum of Naples. © *akg-images*

Figure 4.3 Bust of Mark Antony in marble, c. 50 BC, the Capitoline Museum, Rome.
© The Art Archive/Museo Capitolino Rome/Dagli Orti

beneficiary of his will. For the time being Cleopatra's ambitions were thwarted.

Octavian formed an alliance with Caesar's former lieutenant, Mark Antony (fig. 4.3), to avenge his uncle's assassins, Cassius and Brutus. Thanks largely to Antony's military prowess, the leaders of the conspiracy were finally defeated and killed at Phillipi in northern Greece in 42 BC. To all intents and purposes the Republican cause died with them. The victors shared the Roman world: Octavian claimed Rome and the West, Antony the alluring East, bringing Egypt within his immediate sphere of influence. Naturally enough he sought a meeting with Cleopatra, who sailed to visit him in a galley of famous splendour. Antony was speedily infatuated, whereas Cleopatra discerned a second chance to fuse an enduring alliance with a foremost Roman general.

For a year they were inseparable, until Antony was reluctantly dragged from the queen's embrace by the pressure of events elsewhere. In the autumn of 40 BC Cleopatra gave birth to twins by Antony. They were named Alexander Helios ('Sun') and Cleopatra Selene ('Moon'), in anticipation of a glorious revival of the Greek empire in the east. It was another three years before their father was to see them for the first time, Antony having married Octavian's sister out of political expediency.

The flame of their romance guttered but could not be extinguished. Antony was drawn back by Cleopatra's magnetism and became committed to the pursuit of her political ambitions. They fought a series of wars in Persia and Armenia with mixed success, although the Greek-speaking nations rallied enthusiastically to their cause, and they became immensely powerful. Rome was seriously antagonised when Antony allowed Cleopatra to divide the eastern provinces among their offspring in 34 BC, declaring, 'Let it be known that the greatness of Rome lies not in what she takes, but in what she gives.' An irrevocable break with Octavian occurred in 32 BC, when Antony divorced his sister. At that point Antony commanded a seasoned army of 30 legions and a fleet of

500 warships. Rome believed he would invade Italy and most considered that this would prove successful.

Antony demurred and the next year Octavian's admiral, Marcus Agrippa, was able to use his superior naval skills to turn the tables on him. By suffering a series of small defeats, Antony and Cleopatra became virtually trapped in the Ambracian Gulf at Actium. Although they were successful in breaking out, three-quarters of their fleet was annihilated. Antony's legions expediently accepted a generous offer of terms from Octavian, and Cleopatra's inspired vision of Graeco-Roman partnership became a lost cause.

Antony and Cleopatra fled back to Egypt as the magnitude of their defeat slowly unfolded. In black despair Antony shut himself away in a tower at the end of a pier in the Great Harbour at Alexandria, which he called the Timoneum, likening himself to the famous misanthrope, Timon of Athens.

Cleopatra continued to pursue feverish plans for the preservation of her kingdom and her dynasty. In particular, according to Dio Cassius, the queen 'proceeded to gather vast wealth from her estates and from various other sources, both profane and sacred, sparing not even the most holy shrines…' The shrines in question are identified by Josephus, a Jewish writer hostile to the queen. He accuses Cleopatra of having 'plundered her country's gods and her ancestors' sepulchres' without offering any further explanation. Presumably, she appropriated part of the gold and valuables stored up in the temples and the tombs of the precinct of the Soma in a desperate attempt to fund a fresh army or fleet.[3]

Octavian meticulously closed in with a large army, still fearing Antony enough to deny him an opportunity to fight back until overwhelming force could be brought to bear. As Octavian approached Alexandria, Antony fell on his sword, dying in Cleopatra's arms, while she was ensconced in her mausoleum in Alexandria. Plutarch refers to the construction programme which included this building:[4]

She had caused to be built, joining to the temple of Isis, several tombs and monuments of wonderful height and remarkable workmanship.

This passage provides further evidence for the hypothesis that tallness was a notable feature of Alexandrian mausoleums and temples. Plutarch adds that these structures were close by the sea, but unfortunately the site of the temple of Isis is unknown. It seems likely the complex was separate from the Soma precinct.[5]

When Caesar was besieged in the palaces at Alexandria, his men set fire to many of the enemy's vessels in the Great Harbour. It is easy to imagine clouds of cinders blown onshore by Alexandria's famous Etesian winds. A stretch of dockside warehouses caught fire and this reportedly engulfed the bookstores of the Great Library. Livy mentions the destruction of 400,000 books or scrolls, although this may be an exaggeration. The most likely location was the central stretch of the Great Harbour, since the ships must have been docked beyond the coastal stretch occupied by the palaces, but near to Caesar's positions for logistical reasons. This general vicinity is also consistent with Strabo's remark that the library and museum adjoined the palaces. It is also known that after the fire Cleopatra began the construction of one of the most opulent of the city's temples, known as the Caesareum or Sebastium, in this location. It is reasonable to infer that an area razed by the fire near the central stretch of the harbour was the main focus of Cleopatra's architectural redevelopments.[6]

Octavian's agents tricked the queen into surrendering and she was taken into captivity. Octavian entered the city in the company of Arius Didymus, an Alexandrian scholar. In the Gymnasium he announced to the crowd that he proposed to spare them all, for the sake of Alexander, their founder, for the beauty of their city, and in response to the pleas for clemency made on their behalf by his friend Arius. He is likely to have accompanied Octavian on his visit to the Soma (fig. 4.4), recorded by Suetonius:[7]

Figure 4.4 Octavian (later proclaimed Augustus) honouring the corpse of Alexander after his victory over Antony and Cleopatra, drawn by J.-H. Fragonard and engraved by L.J. Masquelier after a painting by Sébastien Bourdon c. 1643, Louvre, Paris.

Per idem tempus conditorium et corpus Magni Alexandri, cum prolatum e penetrali subiecisset oculis, corona aurea imposita ac floribus aspersis veneratus est consultusque, num et Ptolemaeum inspicere vellet, regem se voluisse ait videre, non mortuos.

About this time [Octavian] had the sarcophagus and body of Alexander the Great brought forth from its inner sanctum, and, after gazing on it, showed his respect by placing upon it a golden crown and strewing it with flowers; and being then asked whether he wished to see the tomb of the Ptolemies as well, he replied, 'My wish was to see a king, not corpses.'

The same event is also described by Dio Cassius:[8]

He next viewed the body of Alexander, and even touched it in such a fashion that, so it is said, a piece of the nose was broken off. Yet he went not to see the corpses of the Ptolemies, despite the keen desire of the Alexandrians to show them to him, retorting, 'I wished to see a king not dead people.'

Cleopatra was told that Octavian intended to parade her as the main spectacle of his triumph in Rome. This was an intolerable indignity and perhaps Octavian knew this and was therefore complicit in her suicide. The story that she killed herself with asps is likely to be true. Before expiring Cleopatra sent a message to Octavian begging to be buried next to Antony. Perhaps fearing ensnarement by her dying wish, the future emperor sent his men to find her. One of them, seeing the queen already dead, angrily turned on her dying handmaiden: 'Charmion, was this well done?' and she replied, 'Extremely well! And as became the descendant of so many kings.' Her words have become the epitaph of the Ptolemies.

Octavian became the undisputed master of the Mediterranean world. He had Cleopatra's mausoleum finished and entombed her there beside

Antony. In 27 BC the Senate declared him its 'Leader' or 'Prince' (*Princeps Senatus*) and he was awarded the honorary title of 'Augustus' ('revered').[9]

Through a series of skilful administrative changes, the Roman Republic was gradually transformed into the Roman Empire. Even before this in 28 BC Augustus had begun the construction of a monumental mausoleum for his family in the Campus Martius in Rome. The timing suggests that the Alexandrian tombs had been a major source of inspiration, although the essential form of this mausoleum is supposed to have been derived from Etruscan tumulus tombs. A significant part of the supporting structure survives today as do descriptions of it in its heyday. The reconstructed form (fig. 4.5) may be compared with the Mausoleum at Halicarnassus and credible reconstructions suggest an elevated colonnaded rotunda with a large bronze statue of the emperor at the apex of its roof. The earthen in-fill between the concentric, cylindrical walls of the structure and the planting of cypress trees over the top probably reflects Etruscan influence. Augustus' mausoleum also had a more squat profile than its tall, rectangular Greek antecedents. The burial chamber was a cylindrical hall with niches in its walls, forming the innermost ring of masonry. This was above ground level, but, thermally insulated by the surrounding mass of earth, it produced an effect similar to the subterranean funerary vaults of the Greeks.[10]

The civil war between Antony and Octavian triggered the demise of the Republic, the birth of the imperial system of government and the complete subjugation of the Greek kingdoms to the will of Rome. Fortuitously, these outcomes combined to enhance the fame and importance of the Soma in the succeeding centuries. In Alexander the Roman emperors found an exemplar of absolutist rule, in whom their crushing power and extravagant wealth were amply vindicated. His tomb became a regular site of pilgrimage and veneration by the new masters of the East. Before the rise of Christianity his body was perhaps the most important religious relic in the Empire.

In AD 19 the Roman prince Germanicus, a grandson of Antony,

Figure 4.5 Reconstruction of the Mausoleum of Augustus, built in 28 BC partly in the tradition of Etruscan tumulus tombs, but thought to be considerably inspired by the Mausoleums of Alexandria. Drawn by A. M. Chugg

vanquished the king of Armenia and annexed Cappadocia as a Roman province. Shortly after he took a pleasure cruise up the Nile, taking in the sights of Alexandria on the way. It is likely that his wife, Agrippina (daughter of Agrippa) and also their seven-year-old son Gaius accompanied him, since they are known to have been with him in the East. His parents were fond of dressing the child up in a miniature army uniform, which inspired his father's troops to nickname him 'Little Boots', or in Latin 'Caligula', after his military-style footgear. It is an innocent enough origin for a name that became infamous.[11]

Germanicus was rapturously received by the Alexandrians, who harboured fond memories of his grandfather. He addressed them in the Hippodrome: the crowd yelled, 'Bravo! May you live all the longer.' The

Figure 4.6 Bust of Caligula (r. AD 37-41) in marble (AD 161-80), the Capitoline Museum, Rome. © *Charles & Josette Lenars/CORBIS*

Prince replied, 'I am mindful of what is common knowledge and also of the way in which I have found your greetings multiplied through being stored in your prayers.' He is referring, probably with a hint of sarcasm, to the fact that the Alexandrians had exposed him to the wrath of his jealous uncle, the Emperor Tiberius, by offering him worship as a god. Suetonius says of Germanicus that, 'Wherever he came upon the tombs of distinguished men, he always offered sacrifice to their shades.' It is therefore a near certainty that he visited the Soma in the course of his stay and Caligula may well have gone with him, since it would have been regarded as an edifying experience for any Roman princeling.[12]

Germanicus died later the same year, probably by poison, possibly with the emperor's collusion. Although Tiberius subsequently murdered two of his other sons, Caligula (fig. 4.6) became one of his favourites. This vicious old man liked to say that he was nurturing a viper in his bosom that would eventually strike at the Romans after his death.[13]

When Tiberius had grown decrepit, Caligula, with a little help from his ally Macro, the commander of the Praetorian Guard, murdered the emperor by smothering. In this inauspicious fashion Caligula (r. AD 37–41) took the purple. At first the Romans were optimistic at this change of ruler, for Tiberius had been hated as avidly as Caligula's father had been loved, but the symptoms of a murderous strain of insanity were not long in bursting forth.[14]

Many of his traits were relatively harmless. His childhood habit of dressing up and play-acting remained a part of his character, but now he was in a position where the boundaries between fact and fiction might easily become blurred. Of particular relevance is Suetonius' statement: [15]

He frequently wore the dress of a triumphing general, even before his campaign, and sometimes the breast-plate of Alexander the Great, which he had taken from his sarcophagus.

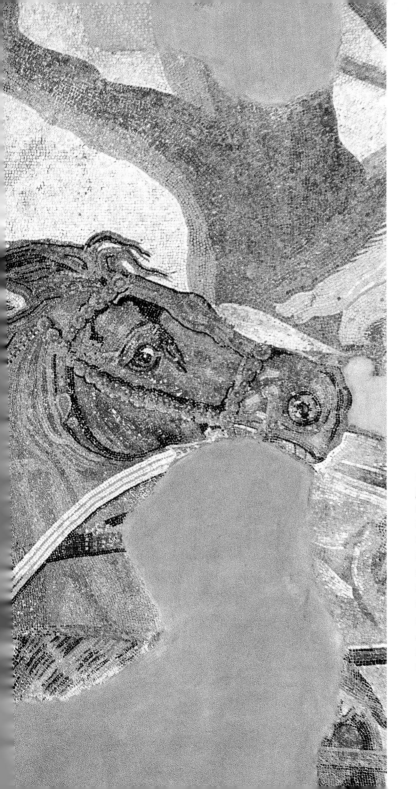

Figure 4.7 Mosaic pavement from the House of the Faun, Pompeii (c. 80 BC), depicting Alexander the Great defeating the Persian king Darius III (r. 336-30) at the Battle of Issus in 333 BC (based on an earlier painting by Philoxenus), the National Archaeological Museum of Naples.

© Mimmo Jodice/CORBIS

This breastplate (cuirass) may have been the same as the one Alexander is shown wearing in the Alexander Mosaic from the House of the Faun at Pompeii (fig. 4.7) or one like it. A similar cuirass was found in the tomb of Alexander's father, Philip. Caligula wore it when he rode across the Bay of Naples on a 5.5km bridge of boats imitating a Roman triumph:[16]

> *Gaius* [Caligula]… *was eager to drive his chariot through the sea, as it were, by bridging the waters between Puteoli and Bauli… When all was ready, he put on the breastplate of Alexander (or so he claimed), and over it a purple silk chlamys, adorned with much gold and many precious stones from India; moreover he girt on a sword, took a shield, and donned a garland of oak leaves. Then he offered sacrifice to Neptune… and entered the bridge from the end at Bauli… and he dashed fiercely into Puteoli as if in pursuit of an enemy.*[17]

The purple chlamys echoes Ephippus' description of Alexander's attire, which is probably not coincidental in this context. The garland of oak leaves also has an indirect association with Alexander, because an exquisite gold oak wreath was one of the main finds from the tomb of Philip II at Aegae.

The darker side of Caligula's character included the opening of a brothel in the palace at which Roman matrons and freeborn youths were prostituted to raise cash for an exchequer bankrupted by his extravagances. He also perpetrated a range of casual murders, including the decapitation of his adopted brother, who had annoyed him by taking medicine to cure a persistent cough. Smelling the substance on his breath, Caligula accused him of taking an antidote to poison. The youth famously retorted, 'How can there be an antidote to Caesar?' Ptolemy of Mauretania, the last known descendant of Cleopatra, was another of the emperor's victims. It was no great surprise when Caligula was assassinated in the fourth year of his reign by two tribunes of the Praetorian Guard, whom he had long taunted by making them say lewd watchwords to one another all night long.

Nero intended to visit Alexandria in AD 64 and again in AD 66, although he remained in Greece on these occasions. Nevertheless, he perpetrated a royal piece of chicanery upon the Egyptian populace by calling in all the Ptolemaic coins in circulation and reissuing them in new types at the same denomination, but containing a lower weight of silver. A succession of such fiscal 'reforms' in the Roman Empire resulted in a gradual debasement of silver coinage. One of the new issues from the Alexandrian mint bore a personification of the city wearing the elephant–scalp headdress (fig. 4.8a). It

Figure 4.8a. Reverse of tetradrachm in billon dated AD 65 depicting Alexander the Great personifying the city of Alexandria and wearing the elephant-scalp headdress.

Figure 4.8b. Reverse of drachm in bronze dated AD 130 depicting Alexander the Great personifying the city of Alexandria and wearing a chiton, chlamys and elephant scalp and greeting Hadrian (r. AD 117-38) in the chariot. © A. M. Chugg

Figure 4.9 Bust of the Emperor Vespasian (r. AD 69-79) in marble (Flavian period), the Capitoline Museum, Rome. © Archivo Iconografico, S.A./CORBIS

could be a crude imitation of Ptolemy I Soter's tetradrachms, so perhaps a direct reference to Alexander was intended.[18]

Following Nero's suicide in AD 68 several generalissimos seized the purple in quick succession. Hence, AD 69 became known as the 'Year of Four Emperors'. In the eastern provinces the hierarchy favoured Vespasian, the governor of Syria (fig. 4.9), and in July the Egyptian legions became the first to declare for him at the urging of their prefect, Tiberius Alexander. Vespasian (r. AD 69-79) transferred his headquarters to Alexandria, since Egypt was strategically important because of its corn supplies to Rome (and to the imperial capital of Constantinople from the 4th century onwards). The new emperor is known to have visited the Serapeum and a visit to the Soma is also very likely given that he was based in the city for several months. His armies triumphed over his rival Vitellius at the battle of Cremona and he reigned securely for a decade. His son Titus, the future emperor (r. AD 79-81), who had accompanied his father to Egypt in AD 69, also revisited Alexandria in AD 71.[19]

In AD 115, in the reign of Trajan (r. AD 98-117), the Alexandrian Jews staged a major revolt against the Romans and the Alexandrian Greeks, but they were brutally subdued and a large proportion of them were massacred. From this time on the Jewish community in the city was never more than a pale shadow of its former self. It is believed that the main settlement area of Alexandria began to drift to western districts at about this time. This may be a critical factor in understanding the topography of the ancient metropolis. In any case, the city was in decline from its pre-eminence as the Ptolemaic capital, and the devastation of the Jewish suburbs in the eastern districts may well have contributed to this process.[20]

Two years later Hadrian (r. AD 117-38), the philhellene emperor, succeeded Trajan. In AD 122 there were further disturbances in Alexandria, but the emperor managed to quell them through diplomacy and exhortation, while based in the province of Narbonensis in southern Gaul. It was not until early August AD 130, escorted by his empress, Sabina, and his handsome young favourite, Antinous, that he began perhaps the most renowned and dramatic of all the Roman imperial visits to Egypt.[21]

Following the emperor's formal entry into Alexandria riding in a four-horse chariot (*quadriga*) (fig. 4.8b), he engaged in a round of sightseeing, which certainly took in the Soma, probably in the company of Antinous (fig. 4.10). The imperial party was enthusiastically feted by the Greek population, which saw Hadrian as a potential benefactor and an ally against their Jewish enemies. The emperor in turn lavished his patronage upon the city and its monuments, such as a life-size statue of a bull in black basalt, dedicated by Hadrian, that has been found in the ruins of the Serapeum. Hadrian soon managed to erode much of this goodwill by appointing cronies from other provinces to lucrative positions at the museum and by resisting pressure to allow the city to reconstitute its ancient council, which had been dissolved by Augustus. The atmosphere soured to the extent that Hadrian wrote to a friend at this juncture describing the Alexandrians as 'seditious, vain and spiteful'.[22]

A tangible link survives between Hadrian's visit and the Soma story manifest in several coin types (e.g. fig. 4.8b), which the emperor issued in Alexandria to commemorate the event. A description of one of these is given in the *Dictionary of Roman Coins*:[23]

> *The genius of Alexandria, or of Egypt in general, is figured in a brass medal of Hadrian* [struck in Egypt] *as a man, wearing on his own head the skin of an elephant, and holding in his right hand a bundle of corn ears. He takes with his left hand that of the emperor, and lifts it to his lips, as if to kiss it, in acknowledgement of Hadrian's benefits to the city and country. Round the coin is engraved ALEXANDREA and in the field LIE (Year XV [of the emperor]).*

The character in the elephant headdress has sometimes been identified as a young woman, through comparison with another group of coins

Figure 4.10 Statue of Antinous in marble, 'close friend' of the emperor Hadrian (2nd century AD), the National Archaeological Museum of Naples.
© Araldo de Luca/CORBIS

from the reign of Hadrian on which a personification of Africa as a reclining or kneeling woman wears an elephant scalp. These African coins were, however, minted in Rome and conform to general types used to commemorate visits to different provinces, whereas the Alexandrian coins were a special local issue. Also the figure in the Alexandrian coins is dressed in a *chiton* (tunic) and a *chlamys* (cloak), the same apparel described by Ephippus as the habitual garb of Alexander. These coins thus appear to represent an enduring association of the elephant-scalp motif

Figure 4.11a. Coin depicting the emperor Hadrian (r. AD 117-38), on the obverse side.
© A. M. Chugg

with Alexander dating from the earliest period of the Ptolemaic kingdom.[24]

Perhaps the clinching detail is the inclusion of a belt just beneath Alexander's breast in some examples. This is the 'Persian Girdle' or *zonam Persicam*, which Alexander wears in the 'Alexander Sarcophagus' reliefs from Sidon and in the 'Demetrio Alexander' statuette from 1st-century BC Egypt (now in the National Archaeological Museum at Athens). What could be better propaganda than for Hadrian to portray himself being greeted as an

Figure 4.11b. Reverse side of coin in fig. 4.11a, probably alluding to the foundation of Alexandria by Alexander on his return from the oasis at Siwa. © A. M. Chugg

equal by the personification of Alexandria in the guise of the city's deified founder?[25]

An elephant headdress is also worn by a naked male figure driving a chariot drawn by two winged serpents on various Alexandrian *drachmae* coins of the 2nd century AD (fig. 4.11b). The serpents wear the *skhent* crown of Upper and Lower Egypt in some examples, which suggests that the charioteer is a pharaoh of Egypt. He also casts seeds about him from a bag draped over his left arm. Arrian writes of Alexander's expedition to the Siwa oasis:[26]

> *Now Ptolemy son of Lagos says that two serpents preceded the army giving voice, and that Alexander told his leaders to follow them and trust the divinity; and the serpents led the way to the oracle and back again.*

Alexander most probably founded Alexandria on his way back from Siwa, famously marking the outline of its walls with barley seeds. Despite the iconography of these coins being reminiscent of Triptolemos, the Greek god of agriculture, it is known that the type was revived specifically in the year of the 500th anniversary of Alexandria. This tends to confirm that they were also considered to symbolise Alexander's foundation of the city, and the charioteer is likely to represent Alexander as pharaoh.[27]

If Otto Mørkholm is correct in suggesting that the representation of Alexander wearing the elephant headdress derives from a funerary statue at the Memphite tomb, then in these coins we may glimpse the transfer of the Memphite tomb to Alexandria, and the persistence of this symbolism deep into the Roman period. Possibly the funerary statue of Alexander wearing elephant spoils had accompanied his body in its move to the new capital and remained in the Soma in the time of Hadrian.[28]

In early October the imperial party embarked on a pleasure cruise up the Nile on a flotilla of barges. Even today, with most of the monuments in ruins and glimpses of modernity around every bend, this remains an atmospheric voyage. In the 2nd century AD most of the ancient architecture was relatively intact and the priests of the old gods still practised their mystical rituals as they had since the dawn of civilisation. For the Romans, Egypt was a land steeped in potent magic and the emperor and his entourage would have been engulfed by an almost tangible sense of sorcery and the occult. Hadrian had been suffering intermittently from a serious haemorrhagic illness, so he had planned the trip as a kind of pilgrimage to seek a cure from the magicians and diviners in this most supernatural of his realms.

The warlocks and diabolists assured the emperor that all the evils that beset him might be averted if a willing member of his retinue could be persuaded to sacrifice himself in Hadrian's stead, thus deflecting the bad luck, but no suitable volunteer could be found.

Another shadow oppressing the voyage was the spectre of famine hanging over the land in the wake of two successive failures of the Nile flood: a third drought would bring catastrophe. By timeless tradition the sacrifice of a youth or a virgin to the river gods was the only sure means of pacifying them and the proper occasion would be the festival to celebrate the Nile's flood on 22 October.

Antinous may have been further depressed by signs of a cooling in his relationship with the emperor. It seems likely, although the exact circumstances are shrouded in mystery, that the combination of these pressures led this impressionable youth to commit suicide by drowning himself in the river during the week following the Nile festival. Hadrian recognised in this act a gesture of supreme sacrifice and was profoundly moved. He plunged into an orgy of mourning, founding the city of Antinoopolis at the spot where the body was washed ashore, and establishing a cult for the worship of the deified Antinous throughout his empire. Hadrian seems to have modelled the new city on Alexandria at the time of its foundation and the worship of Antinous came to parallel that of Alexander himself in the succeeding centuries. Around AD 400 St John

Chrysostom denounced the Roman Senate for recognising Alexander and 'the favourite of Hadrian' as gods.[29]

Hadrian died seven years later and was buried at Rome in a mausoleum of similar design to that of Augustus. This monument still looms over the River Tiber, having been transformed in the medieval period into the papal fortress of Castel Sant'Angelo. The location of the tomb of Antinous, however, is another of antiquity's sepulchral mysteries. Some place it in his eponymous city beside the Nile, but the obelisk now standing on the Pincio in Rome bears Hadrian's epitaph for him and claims to mark his burial. Its original location is unknown, but in a crucial sentence its hieroglyphs translate as:

> O, Antinous! This deceased one, who rests in this tomb in the country estate of the Emperor of Rome.

This appears to be a reference to Hadrian's villa at Tibur just outside Rome. If Antinous was entombed there, then the Canopus section, modelled on the city of Canopus at the western mouth of the Nile, is a likely site.

The next emperor known to have visited the Soma was Septimius Severus (r. AD 193–211; fig. 4.12) in the course of his visit to Egypt in AD 199–200. He courted popularity in Alexandria by giving the city permission to reconstitute its town council and thereby administer itself. According to Dio Cassius, Augustus had dissolved the council 230 years earlier to punish the Alexandrians. Severus may also have removed a bar on Alexandrians serving in the Roman Senate, since Egyptians appear in the lists of its membership from early in the 3rd century AD.[30]

Severus was a disciplinarian and keen to root out potentially subversive influences. He seems to have been particularly intolerant of the Egyptian predilection for sorcery and the occult. A papyrus record of his edict against the magical divination of future events is preserved:[31]

Figure 4.12 Bust of the Emperor Septimius Severus (r. AD 193-211) in marble (late 2nd or early 3rd century AD), Gallery and Museum of the Ducal Palace, Mantua, Italy.

© Arte & Immagini srl/CORBIS

Therefore let no man through oracles, that is, by means of written documents supposedly granted under divine influence, nor by means of the parade of images or suchlike charlatanry, pretend to know things beyond human ken and profess [to know] *the obscurity of things to come, neither let any man put himself at the disposal of those who enquire about this or answer in any way whatsoever.*

The practical action taken by the emperor seems to have been to command the seizure of all the 'written documents' – the secret books of magic lore – that his soldiers and officials could lay their hands on.

Severus came from North Africa, but his empress, Julia Domna, was of Syrian origin. In light of their eastern roots, the Severan family no doubt identified themselves especially closely with Alexander and his legacy. Severus seems to have been shocked by the accessibility of the remains of his hero and he ordered the sealing up of the burial chamber. Dio Cassius (76.13) implies that the emperor took this opportunity also to seal the collection of secret books away in the tomb of Alexander:

[Severus] *inquired into everything, including things that were very carefully hidden; for he was the kind of person to leave nothing, either human or divine, uninvestigated. Accordingly, he took away from practically all the sanctuaries all the books that he could find containing any secret lore, and he sealed up the tomb of Alexander; this was in order that no one in future should either view his body or read what was mentioned in the aforesaid books.*

These facts are important, because of their implications for the preservation of the underground funerary chamber and its contents. Sealing in this context can hardly have meant a simple lock on the door. Rather we should look to the example of the sealing of the burial chamber of Mausolus at Halicarnassus, which was accomplished by inserting a huge block of masonry in the entrance passage (fig. 3.6). In this case there is a reasonable hope that the burial chamber and the sarcophagus might have survived the destruction of the building above it.

Septimius Severus had two sons by Julia Domna. The elder, named Antoninus, was a year older that his brother Geta. It is likely that they accompanied their father on his visit to Alexandria, when Antoninus was about 12 years old. It is easy to imagine how awe-inspiring the Soma would have been for a boy at such an impressionable age. As he grew up Antoninus came to identify himself closely with Alexander, but in ways that were symptoms of a terrifying megalomania. He also acquired a faintly deprecatory nickname – Caracalla, because of his habit of wearing a short military style of cloak. Although it was never used officially in his lifetime, he is known by this name historically thereafter (fig. 4.13).[32]

In AD 211 Severus died at York, leaving the Empire under the joint rule of his sons, who were then irreconcilably estranged. After a period of escalating tension Caracalla (r. AD 211-17) arranged to have Geta murdered in AD 212. His brother expired in their mother's arms, having been mortally wounded by Caracalla's henchmen. Yet this was just one of a long litany of murders and executions. It was a source of pride for Caracalla that an oracle had once referred to him as 'the Ausonian beast'.[33]

Caracalla's emulation of Alexander plumbed new depths after he became emperor. He wrote to the senate advising them that his hero had been reincarnated in his own person, and he raised a phalanx of 16,000 Macedonians, kitting them out as authentically as he could in old-fashioned armour and with long pikes like a set of lifesize toy soldiers. He is also said to have acquired certain cups and weapons, which he believed Alexander once owned. The Soma was a possible source for these artefacts, just as it had been for the cuirass sported by Caligula.[34]

In AD 215 he announced his intention to bless Alexandria with his presence, since he longed to see the city founded by his idol. He arrived in the summer amidst clouds of perfume, sweet music and showers of flowers

Figure 4.13 Bust of the Emperor Caracalla (r. AD 211-17) in marble (first quarter of the 3rd century AD), the Capitoline Museum, Rome. © Araldo de Luca/CORBIS

thrown by the enthusiastic crowd, who anticipated generous benefactions from an emperor so much obsessed with anything connected with Alexander. An account of his visit to the Soma was written by Herodian within a few decades of the event:[35]

> As soon as Antoninus entered the city with his whole army he went up to the temple, where he made a large number of sacrifices and laid quantities of incense on the altars. Then he went to the tomb of Alexander where he took off and laid upon the grave the purple cloak he was wearing and the rings of precious stones and his belts and anything else of value he was carrying.

Another ancient reference to the same visit has survived in an anonymous 4th-century manuscript:[36]

> After he had inspected the body of Alexander of Macedon, he [Caracalla] ordered that he himself should be called 'Great' and 'Alexander', for he was led on by the lies of his flatterers to the point where, adopting the ferocious brow and neck tilted towards the left shoulder that he had noted in Alexander's countenance, he persuaded himself that his features were truly very similar.

These accounts have the particular significance of being the last definite mentions of the existence of the tomb and the body in recorded history, though there are probable later references. Caracalla must have ordered the burial chamber to be unsealed for his visit, but it is likely that he had it resealed afterwards, because he would have been more jealously protective of its contents than his father.

The emperor set up his headquarters in the temple of Serapis, overlooking the city, where he plotted the most despicable of his crimes against the unsuspecting citizens of Alexandria. He had been receiving reports from his spies for several years regarding the behaviour of the

Alexandrians, who had been indulging in their characteristic lampooning of the reigning emperor. Caracalla represented a suitable target on account of his fratricide, rumours of incest with his mother and his emulation of Alexander, but the humour had been lost on Caracalla, who nurtured a foetid anger against the perpetrators of these remarks.

Accordingly, he assembled all the young men of the city in an open space under the pretence of recruiting a regiment for his army. While strolling among them smiling and chatting inconsequentially, his soldiers completed an encirclement of the parade ground. As the emperor withdrew with his guards he gave a prearranged signal and the trap was sprung. A ring of gnashing steel closed in upon the panic-stricken youths and methodically hacked them to pieces. This was but the prelude to a more generalised massacre as the troops were allowed to rampage on the streets to rape, pillage and slaughter the unfortunate inhabitants without restraint.

Caracalla remained in the city for several months, probably until early in AD 216, overseeing a plan to concentrate the main garrisons of Egypt in a fortress in the old palace quarter of the city known as the Bruchion. A great wall was constructed through the heart of the city to cordon off this district. Its imposing towers completed the humbling of the terrorised populace.[37]

Caracalla was now so steeped in the blood of friend and foe alike that he became increasingly fearful of assassination. He wrote to a friend in Rome asking him to consult the seers to discover any plots against him. The friend wrote back that he should beware of Macrinus, one of his military prefects. Ironically, Caracalla asked Macrinus to deal with the very batch of dispatches that included this reply. Naturally enough, the imaginary plot became an urgent reality. Macrinus recruited to his cause a centurion whose brother had recently been put to death by the emperor. When Caracalla was suffering from a bout of diarrhoea during a desert journey, he halted to relieve himself and his guards drew aside to give him some privacy. The vengeful centurion saw his chance. When the emperor's breeches were around his ankles, the assassin ran up to him as though responding to a summons and delivered a fatal stab wound with military precision. It was a fittingly ironic end for an emperor who revelled in opportunities to catch his victims off their guard.[38]

The last of the Severan dynasty was named Alexander (r. AD 222-35) in keeping with his family's traditional affiliation with the conqueror's memory. After his death in AD 235, the Roman Empire entered an era of serious political instability, sorely aggravated by the opportunistic incursions of various neighbouring nations. The empire was only saved from complete disintegration by a succession of powerful, authoritarian emperors, who imposed radical changes in the way it was governed and defended. At first Alexandria was relatively unaffected by these troubles, but in the second half of the century it became embroiled in a grievous series of wars and rebellions, from which it emerged terribly scarred and demoralised.

1   Lucan, *Pharsalia*, 10.14-20.
2   Julius Caesar, *The Civil War*, 3.106.
3   Dio Cassius, *Roman History*, 51.5.3; Josephus, *Contra Apion*, 2.58.
4   Plutarch, *Life of Antony*, 74.
5   Dio Cassius, *Roman History*, 51.8.6 and Zenobius, *Proverbia*, 5.24.
6   Plutarch, *Life of Caesar*, 49; Fraser, 1972, 305-35.
7   Arius was the probable author of the statement in Zenobius' *Proverbia* that Ptolemy Philopator had built the Soma, according to the Suidas. Suetonius, *Lives of the Caesars, Augustus*, 2.18.
8   Dio Cassius, *Roman History*, 51.16.5.
9   D. Shotter, 1991, 24-31.
10 A. Claridge, 1998, 175-184. For a detailed description of this monument, L. Richardson, 1992. 247-9.
11 Tacitus, *Annals*, 2.59-61; A. Ferrill, 1991, 51; Suetonius, *Lives of the Caesars, Caligula*, 4.10; Suetonius, *Caligula*, 4.9.
12 *Oxyrhynchus papyrus*, 25.2435 recto; Bowman, 1986, 44; Suetonius, *Caligula*, 4.3.
13 Suetonius, *Caligula*, 4.2, 11.
14 Suetonius, *Caligula*, 4.12.
15 Suetonius, *Caligula*, 4.52.
16 The Alexander Mosaic was modeled on a painting made within living memory of the Battle of Issus. The cuirass worn by Alexander is authentic. Stewart, 1993, 130-50. For the cuirass found in Philip's tomb, Dale M. Brown (ed.), 1994, 155.
17 Dio Cassius, *Roman History*, 59.17; Suetonius, *Caligula*, 4.19; Ferrill, 1991, 115.
18 Suetonius, *Nero*, 6.35; Dio Cassius, *Roman History*, 63.18.1; E. Christiansen, 1988, vol. 1, ch. 1, 104-6.
19 Suetonius, *Vespasian*, 8.6-7; Dio Cassius, *Roman History*, 65.8; *Oxyrhynchus papyrus*, 34.2725.
20 Eusebius, *Ecclesiastical History*, 4.2.1-5, Dio Cassius, *Roman History*, 68.32.1-3.
21 For details of the story of Hadrian and Antinous in Egypt, R. Lambert, 1984, 115-154.
22 J-Y. Empereur, 1998, 88.
23 S.W. Stevenson, C. Roach Smith and F.W. Madden, 1889, 35.
24 Bowman, 1986, 205.
25 Diodorus Siculus, 17.77.5; *Epitoma rerum gestarum Alexandri Magni* (Metz epitome), an anonymous 4th-century AD text, quoted by A. Stewart, 1993, 356, item T46.
26 Arrian, *Anabasis Alexandri*, 3.3.5.
27 For more detailed versions of these arguments, A.M. Chugg, 2001, 15.2.6-16 and 2003, 17.8.6-16.
28 O. Mørkholm, 1991, 63-4.
29 O. Montevecchi, 209, 1990, 183-195. John Chrysostom, Homily XXVI on the second epistle of St Paul the Apostle to the Corinthians.
30 *History*, 51.17.1-4.
31 J.R. Rea, 1977, 151-6; Bowman 1986, 190.
32 Dio Cassius, *Roman History*, 78.7-8.
33 Herodian, *History of the Empire*, 4.4 and Dio Cassius, *Roman History*, 78; Dio Cassius, *Roman History*, 78.23.4.

34 Dio Cassius, *Roman History*, 78.17.1-2.

35 The visit is recounted by Herodian, 4.86-9.8, and Dio Cassius, *Roman History*, 78.22-3, though only the former mentions the Soma visit. The visit is also mentioned by John of Antioch (7th century) in C. Müller, 1868, 4, 590, but this appears to be derived from Herodian.

36 *Epitome de Caesaribus Sexti Aureli Victoris*, 21.4 (quoted by Stewart, 1993, 348).

37 P. Flor. (papyrus from Florence, Museo Archeologico) 382 and BGU (Papyrus from the Aegyptische Urkunden aus den Königlichen (later Staatlichen) Museen zu Berlin, Griechische Urkunden) 1.266. The Roman garrison was moved from Nicopolis to the Bruchion at this time, J. Marlowe, 1971, 219. Details of the wall are provided by Dio Cassius, *Roman History*, 78.23.3.

38 Herodian, *History of the Empire*, 4.12-13.

5. Vanished from History

'You will know my lover, though you live far away:
And you will whisper where he's gone, that lily boy to look upon,
And whiter than the spray.'
'How should I know your lover, Lady of the Sea?'
'Alexander, Alexander, King of the World was he!'
'Weep not for him, dear lady, but come aboard my ship.
So many years ago he died, he's dead as dead can be.'
'O base and brutal sailor to lie this lie to me.
His mother was the foam-foot star-sparkling Aphrodite;
His father was Adonis, who lives away in Lebanon,
In stony Lebanon, where blooms his red anemone.
But where is Alexander, the soldier Alexander,
My golden love of olden days, the King of the World and me?'
She sank into the moonlight and the sea was only sea.

James Elroy Flecker, *Santorin, A Legend of the Aegean*

The legend of Alexander and the mermaid tells of a beautiful yet perilous marine enchantress who waylays ships to beg their crews for news of the conqueror. So long as they reply 'He lives and reigns', she departs satisfied. If they should mention his death, then she springs into a terrible rage and summons up a storm to drown them.

This fable probably owes its origin to the fantastical version of Alexander's career known as the *Alexander Romance*, implausibly attributed to Callisthenes, a great-nephew of Aristotle who travelled with Alexander as court historian. In particular, the *Romance* has a story of how Alexander dived to the bottom of the sea at Tyre in a glass jar held within a cage, where he saw all kinds of fish and an especially large specimen took the cage in its mouth and ferried the king to the shore. In later versions, an angel acted as Alexander's guide on his undersea adventure and the large fish grew into a gigantic sea-monster. The *Romance* seems to have been compiled in Greek by an uncritical conflation of earlier documents and legends some time in 3rd-century AD Egypt, probably Alexandria. It became a bestseller in Europe and the Middle East and has been reproduced in Latin, Armenian, Syriac, Coptic, Hebrew, Persian, Turkish, Arabic and Ethiopian versions.[1]

Herodian probably wrote his account of the visit of Caracalla (r. AD 211–17) to Alexandria in the late 240s AD. It is possible that he was a native of Alexandria, because a local grammarian, Aelius Herodian, a friend of the emperor Marcus Aurelius (r. AD 161–80), may have been his father. His *History* closed in AD 238 without any mention of the Soma's destruction, so providing negative evidence that the monument remained intact until about the middle of the 3rd century AD. Interestingly, the Syriac version of the *Romance* mentions the contemporaneity of Alexander's tomb: 'and they call that place the *Tomb of Alexander* unto this day.' The *Romance* may be later than Herodian, in which case it is the last piece of documentary evidence which treats the existence of the Soma mausoleum as self-evident.[2]

Although the Soma probably survived until at least the second half of the 3rd century AD, it is equally likely that it had been destroyed by the end of the 4th century. The best evidence for this comes from a section of a sermon by John Chrysostom (lived *c.* AD 340–407), a cleric from Antioch, and later Bishop of Constantinople. This homily may be dated to the last quarter of the 4th century or very early in the 5th century AD. His words shed fascinating light on the battle for hearts and minds, raging at the time between the Church and the disparate pagan forces, spearheaded by the Senate in Rome:[3]

For thus it was that idolatries gained ground at first; men being held in admiration beyond their desert. Thus the Roman senate decreed Alexander to be the thirteenth God,[4] for it possessed the privilege of electing and enrolling Gods. For instance, when all about Christ had been reported, the ruler of the nation sent to inquire, whether they would be pleased to elect Him also a God. They however refused their consent, being angry and indignant that previous to their vote and decree, the Power of the Crucified flashing abroad had won over the whole world to its own worship. But thus it was ordered even against their will that the Divinity of Christ was not proclaimed by man's decree, nor was He counted one of the many that were by them elected. For they counted even boxers to be Gods, and the favorite of Hadrian; after whom the city Antinous is named. For since death testifies against their immortal nature, the devil invented another way, that of the soul's immortality; and mingling therewith that excessive flattery, he seduced many into impiety. And observe what wicked artifice. When we advance that doctrine for a good purpose, he overthrows our words; but when he himself is desirous of framing an argument for mischief, he is very zealous in setting it up. And if any one ask, 'How is Alexander a God? Is he not dead? and miserably too?', 'Yes, but the soul is immortal,' he replies. Now thou arguest and philosophizest for immortality, to detach men from the God Who is over all: but when we declare that this is God's greatest gift, thou persuadest thy dupes that men are low and grovelling, and in no better case than the brutes. And if we say, 'the Crucified lives,' laughter follows immediately: although the whole world proclaims it, both in old time and now; in old time by miracles, now by converts; for truly these successes are not those of a dead man: but if one say, 'Alexander lives,' thou believest, although thou hast no miracle to allege. 'Yes,' one replies; 'I have; for when he lived he wrought many and great achievements; for he subdued both nations and cities, and in many wars and battles he conquered, and erected trophies.' If then I shall show [something] which he when alive never dreamed of, neither he, nor any other man that ever lived, what other proof of the resurrection wilt thou require? For that whilst alive one should win battles and victories, being a king and having armies at his disposal, is nothing marvellous, no, nor startling or novel; but that after a Cross and Tomb one should perform such great things throughout every land and sea, this it is which is most especially replete with such amazement, and proclaims His divine and unutterable Power. And Alexander indeed after his decease never restored again his kingdom, which had been rent in pieces and quite abolished: indeed how was it likely he, dead, should do so? but Christ then most of all set up His after He was dead. And why speak I of Christ? seeing that He granted to His disciples also, after their deaths, to shine? For, tell me, where is the tomb of Alexander? show it me and tell me the day on which he died. But of the servants of Christ the very tombs are glorious, seeing they have taken possession of the most loyal city; and their days are well known, making festivals for the world. And his tomb even his own people know not, but This Man's the very barbarians know. And the tombs of the servants of the Crucified are more splendid than the palaces of kings; not for the size and beauty of the buildings, (yet even in this they surpass them,) but, what is far more, in the zeal of those who frequent them. For he that wears the purple himself goes to embrace those tombs, and, laying aside his pride, stands begging the saints to be his advocates with God, and he that hath the diadem implores the tent-maker and the fisherman, though dead, to be his patrons.

Careful scrutiny of this quotation indicates that the bishop was suggesting that Alexander's tomb did not exist in his time. By contrast, he stated that Christ's tomb was then known and was famous throughout the world. This is validated by our knowledge that St Helena, the mother of Constantine the Great (r. AD 306–37), undertook a pilgrimage to Jerusalem around AD 326, where she 'rediscovered' various biblical sites including the tomb of Jesus.[5] Alternatively, John Chrysostom might have been referring to the tomb of St Paul in Rome, since a letter from St Paul was the main theme of his sermon.

It is possible to interpret Chrysostom's words as an expression of ignorance about the Soma, which would argue in favour of the building's destruction long before. It is also possible to take the view that this educated and cosmopolitan man chose the example of the Soma because he had some knowledge of its destruction and knew it would be impossible for his audience to respond to his request to show it to him. In this case he would have been more likely to be mindful of the event if the destruction had been quite recent. On balance, therefore, his words are ambiguous regarding how recently the Soma had ceased to exist. Its disappearance is, however, corroborated by Theodoret, who listed Alexander among famous men whose tombs were unknown in the mid-5th century AD.[6]

Having established that the end of Alexander's monument occurred between the mid-3rd century and the last quarter of the 4th, it is feasible to sieve through the history of Alexandria in that period in an attempt to find a reason for its disappearance. Coincidentally, in this period the city suffered several of the most tumultuous upheavals in its history.

Alexandria's troubles in the 3rd century began in AD 260 with an argument between a servant and a legionary over a pair of shoes. This trivial dispute escalated into a classic Alexandrian mob riot. Marcus Julius Aemilianus, the Roman prefect of Egypt, had recourse to order his garrison troops to quell the disorder. The empire had just suffered the ignominious defeat and capture of the emperor Valerian (r. AD 253-59/60) by the Persians in Syria. His son, Gallienus (r. AD 253-68), assumed supreme power, and seems to have been particularly unpopular with the army contingents in Egypt, so they seized the opportunity to back Aemilianus as a rival claimant to the throne.[7]

The rebellion of Aemilianus endured for two years, until Gallienus sent his leading general, Theodotus, into Egypt to destroy the usurper. Aemilianus seems to have been besieged for two more years in the Bruchion fortress, but was eventually defeated, captured and strangled. Consequently, much of Alexandria was a virtual battlefield in the years AD 262-4. Eusebius has preserved a (rather hyperbolical) description of the consequences of this revolt for the city of Alexandria:[8]

It would be easier for one to go, not only beyond the limits of the province, but even from the East to the West, than from Alexandria to Alexandria itself. For the very heart of the city is more intricate and impassable than that great and trackless desert which Israel traversed for two generations. And our smooth and waveless harbours have become like the sea, divided and walled up, through which Israel drove and in whose highway the Egyptians were overwhelmed. For often from the slaughters there committed they appear like the Red Sea.

He goes on to describe an outbreak of pestilence, possibly plague, which killed a third of the population of Alexandria in the grim aftermath of the insurrection.

In Syria the Roman cause was being preserved from obliteration by the wealthy merchant city of Palmyra. Its king, Odenath, was nominally an ally of Rome and an effective bulwark against the expansionist Persians. He organised and led a highly successful counter-offensive against the Persian monarch Shapur I (r. AD 241-72), driving him back across the Euphrates. Impressed by this achievement Gallienus manoeuvered to keep Odenath in the Roman fold by appointing him commander of the Orient. This ploy seems to have worked while Odenath lived, but in the late 260s he perished and was succeeded by Zenobia (r. AD 267/8-72) (fig. 5.1), his ambitious and formidable queen. She is said to have claimed descent from Cleopatra, which may help to explain her actions, breaking the alliance with Rome in dramatic fashion by invading and capturing Egypt in AD 269-270. The Roman garrison barely managed to hold out in the Bruchion fortress, behind Caracalla's immense ramparts.[9]

Fortunately for Rome, Aurelian (r. AD 270-75) ascended the throne at this time, and through his efforts the empire, assailed on all fronts, was retrieved from the brink of collapse. He had been a member of an elite corps of senior officers, the *Protectores*, who had begun to develop new military strategies based on mobility and the ability to launch rapid and

Figure 5.1 Relief depicting Queen Zenobia (r. AD 267/8-72) in marble, accompanied by an eagle, female dog and female servant (second half of the 3rd century AD), National Museum, Damascus. © Giraudon/Bridgeman Art Library

effective offensives across great distances. In AD 272 Aurelian deployed these tactics in a war against the troublesome Palmyrenes. Leading his armies on forced marches across vast tracts of desert, he routed Zenobia's forces in two great battles. Palmyra was besieged, but capitulated on honourable terms proffered by the emperor. One version of events states that Zenobia was compelled to march through the streets of Rome as the centrepiece of Aurelian's triumph, although this has been disputed.[10]

Firmus, a wealthy Alexandrian merchant and supporter of Zenobia, is said to have instigated a fresh rebellion after her defeat by declaring himself emperor.[11] Unsurprisingly, he was speedily routed, taken captive, tortured and put to death. Aurelian may have led the attack on him in person, since a papyrus from the town of Oxyrhynchus in Upper Egypt records the decision of its council to present a golden statue of the goddess Victory to the emperor to commemorate his successes. Writing over a century later, probably in the late 380s AD, Ammianus Marcellinus noted the devastation of Alexandria, particularly in the Bruchion district as a result of these wars:[12]

> But Alexandria herself, not gradually (like other cities), but at her very origin, attained her wide extent; and for a long time she was grievously troubled by internal dissension, until at last, many years later under the rule of Aurelian, the quarrels of the citizens turned into deadly strife; then her walls were destroyed and she lost the greater part of the district called Bruchion, which had long been the abode of distinguished men.

For a quarter of a century after the wars Alexandria seems to have basked in relative tranquillity, but in AD 297, during the reign of the great reforming emperor, Diocletian (r. AD 284-305; fig. 5.2), the empire came under a renewed threat in the East from the Persian king Narses (r. AD 293-302). A simmering mood of nationalism expressed itself in Egypt, provoked by an unpopular tax reform, while the imperial armies were preoccupied by the Persian emergency. The province revolted in the name of a new Egyptian emperor, Lucius Domitius Domitianus, although he remained little more than a figurehead since the real power was wielded by Achilleus, the self-styled 'Corrector of Egypt'.[13]

In Syria, despite an initial victory over the Romans, the Persians had been fought to a standstill. While hostilities were interrupted by the summer heatwave, Diocletian led a large detachment by forced marches to counter the rebellion in Egypt. They joined up with the remnants of the former Roman garrisons and commenced a systematic campaign to reduce the rebel-held towns. By early winter Diocletian's army was arrayed before the walls of Alexandria itself. Achilleus maintained a stubborn and desperate resistance, perhaps hoping that the Persians might relieve the siege, although Galerius, Diocletian's deputy, was successfully holding the Roman position in Syria. Diocletian's policy was to cut the aqueducts supplying fresh water to the city and bide his time.

After eight months of dreadful hardship the city capitulated in the spring of AD 298. The furious emperor commanded that an example should be made of the city and all those who had supported the rebellion should be put to the sword. Only when the blood flowed above his horse's knees, he vowed, should the killing stop. But when his mount suddenly stumbled so that its knees actually touched the earth, the superstitious Diocletian saw it as an omen and relented. With their characteristic black humour, the Alexandrians erected a bronze statue of the emperor's steed to commemorate their deliverance.

Diocletian raised a great column near the Serapeum, surmounted by a statue of the victorious emperor (fig. 5.3). This is virtually the only major monument from ancient Alexandria that is preserved, although the actual statue has long since disappeared and the pillar is erroneously named after Julius Caesar's rival, Pompey.[14]

Scholarly opinion has tended to endorse the idea that the Soma was smashed or razed in the course of one of the three calamitous periods of warfare during the second half of the 3rd century, most likely by Aurelian in his campaigns against Zenobia and Firmus. The reasoning behind this is that Strabo located the Soma in what he called the 'Royal Quarter', believed to correspond with the district known to the Romans as the Bruchion, although this was probably smaller than the Royal Quarter. Ammianus observed that the Bruchion was a ruin in his day, since it had been destroyed in the time of Aurelian, and Epiphanius also noted that the Bruchion was a wilderness at about the same date. There are several problems with this theory.[15]

The boundary of the Bruchion in Late Roman times was defined by the wall built by Caracalla. Although the exact location of this wall is unknown, the line of the Tulunid fortifications erected by the Sultan Ahmed Ibn Tulun (r. *c.* AD 868-84), is marked as 'Murs d'enceinte de la ville des Arabes' on the map of Alexandria drawn in 1866 by Mahmoud Bey (fig. 3.1). A north-eastern stretch of these walls ran from the 'Tower of the Romans' near the coast towards the eastern gate of the city. A long section ran roughly along the course of a major east-west street in the Graeco-Roman period, designated as L2. The Tower of the Romans, preserved until the early 20th century (fig. 5.4), seems to have been built in the Hellenistic style and probably dates from no later than the early Roman period. Its survival may be the result of successive incorporations into the walls of Caracalla and the Tulunids.[16]

This section of the Tulunid walls is indented from the coastline, excluding the Bruchion district from the old Islamic city of Alexandria. On the basis of these clues it seems plausible that the Tulunid walls followed the line of Caracalla's in their north-eastern sector. If so, then the central crossroads of Ptolemaic Alexandria lay at least several hundred metres outside the Bruchion wall. Since this crossroads is the most likely location of the Soma, the Bruchion's destruction in the 3rd century may not be directly relevant to the fate of Alexander's tomb.[17]

The sarcophagus of Julius Philosyrius (fig. 3.9) provides a further hint

Figure 5.2 Portrait head of the emperor Diocletian (r. AD 284-305) in marble (period of the Tetrarchy), Archaeological Museum, Istanbul.

© *The Art Archive/Archaeological Museum Istanbul/Dagli Orti*

Figure 5.3 Aquatint of 'Pompey's Pillar' erected by Diocletian (r. 284-305) to commemorate his sack of Alexandria in AD 298. A 4m-high statue of the emperor once adorned its summit; the cylindrical shaft is 30m high, making it the largest known example of this kind of Roman monument. Engraved in 1802 from a drawing of the last quarter of the 18th century, by L. Mayer, Views in Egypt: from the original drawings, in the possession of Sir Robert Ainslie, *London, 1805.*

that the Soma may still have existed after Diocletian erected Pompey's Pillar, and thus survived all three episodes of warfare.

Ammianus relates two other intriguing stories about Alexandria, which together suggest that the Soma was a victim of a natural disaster around AD 365. The first of these accounts concerns the downfall of Bishop Georgius, who was appointed Patriarch of Alexandria late in the reign of Constantius II (r. AD 337-61). Georgius made himself disastrously unpopular with the Alexandrians by acting as an informer against them to the emperor:[18]

> *And, among other matters, it was said that he maliciously informed Constantius also of this, namely, that all the edifices standing on the soil of the said city [Alexandria] had been built by its founder, Alexander, at great public cost, and ought justly to be a source of profit to the treasury. To these evil deeds he added still another, which soon after drove him headlong to destruction. As he was returning from the emperor's court and passed by the splendid temple of the Genius [speciosum Genii templum], attended as usual by a large crowd, he turned his eyes straight at the temple, and said: 'How long shall this tomb [sepulcrum] stand?' On hearing this, many were struck as if by a thunderbolt, and fearing that he might try to overthrow that building also, they devised secret plots to destroy him in whatever way they could.*

Following the death of Constantius and the accession of the pagan emperor Julian (r. AD 361-3), the Alexandrian mob seized Georgius and tore him limb from limb.[19]

Ammianus' description of a 'splendid temple of the Genius', which Georgius calls a tomb, is tantalising because it sounds like a description of the Soma mausoleum. In Latin the word *genius* normally refers to a tutelary (guardian) deity or the sacred and spiritual essence of a place, person or thing. It is very rare for Latin authors to use it to refer to intellectual genius, its most common form in English. It is reasonable that Ammianus should refer to the deified Alexander as the *genius* or guardian spirit of a city which

Figure 5.4 The Tower of the Romans and the Caesareum Obelisks. The fallen obelisk is now Cleopatra's Needle on the Thames Embankment, London; the standing example was removed to Central Park, New York. The Description de l'Égypte *(Panckoucke edition), Paris, 1821-29, Antiquités Volume V, Plate 32.* © A. M. Chugg

he founded, especially since he mentioned him two sentences earlier. This idea is strengthened by Alexander's possible role as *genius* in some of the Alexandrian coin issues of Hadrian (fig. 4.8b). Some experts have challenged this because there was a snake spirit called the Agathos Daimon (fig. 5.5), which also fulfilled this role in some cases.[20]

It is doubtful whether Ammianus was as well informed on the cultural

155

Fig. 5.5 Ancient sculpted relief of the Agathos Daimon serpent god found in Alexandria, now in the Graeco-Roman Museum. © Archives CEAlex/CNRS

nuances of Alexandrian tradition as modern scholars. He came from Antioch and, although he probably visited Alexandria in the late 360s AD, he makes some bad mistakes concerning the city's history. For instance, he asserts that Cleopatra built the Pharos lighthouse, when it was certainly constructed over two centuries earlier. Ammianus probably wrote his history in Rome, where the *genius* of the emperor Augustus is known to have been worshipped.[21]

The idea that the tutelary deity of Alexandria is always the Agathos Daimon is erroneous since Sozomenus, also writing in the Late Roman period, attributes this role to Serapis. Christopher Haas, on the other hand, identifies Ammianus' *genius* as the Tyche of Alexandria, a female personification of the city's *fortune* derived from Isis. At least four deities have accordingly been recognised as the *genius* of Alexandria, yet only one of these was entombed in a 'splendid temple' in the city. On balance, the most credible interpretation of Georgius' remarks is that he was referring to the Soma mausoleum. If so, the building survived until at least AD 361.[22]

The other significant story told by Ammianus is a gripping account of a powerful earthquake followed by a devastating tidal wave, which struck the eastern Mediterranean in AD 365. The quake probably occurred on one of the major geological fault lines that lie beneath the sea to the south of Crete, and Alexandria seems to have been particularly badly hit:[23]

On the 21st of July in the first consulship of Valentinian with his brother, horrible phenomena suddenly spread through the entire extent of the world, such as are related to us neither in fable nor in truthful history. For a little after daybreak, preceded by heavy and repeated thunder and lightning, the whole of the firm and solid earth was shaken and trembled, the sea with its rolling waves was driven back and withdrew from the land, so that in the abyss of the deep thus revealed men saw many kinds of sea-creatures stuck fast in the slime; and vast mountains and deep valleys, which Nature, the creator, had hidden in the unplumbed depths, then, as one might well believe, first saw the beams of the sun. Hence, many ships were stranded as if on dry land, and since many men roamed about without fear in the little that remained of the waters, to gather fish and similar things with their hands, the roaring sea, resenting, as it were, this forced retreat, rose in its turn; and over the boiling shoals it dashed mightily upon islands and broad stretches of the mainland, and levelled innumerable buildings [aedificia] in the cities and wherever else they are to be found; so that amid the mad discord of the elements the altered face of the earth revealed marvellous sights. For the great mass of waters, returning when it was least expected, killed many thousands of men by drowning; and by the swift recoil of the eddying tides a number of ships, after the swelling of the wet element subsided, were found to have been destroyed, and the lifeless bodies of shipwrecked persons lay floating on their backs or on their faces. Other great ships, driven by the mad blasts, landed on the tops of buildings – as happened at Alexandria – and some were driven almost two miles inland, like a Laconian ship which I myself in passing that way saw near the town of Motho, yawning apart through long decay.

A description of the effects of this disaster at Alexandria is given by Sozomenus, although (as a Christian writer) he attributes it to the wrath of God and incorrectly dates the episode to the reign of Julian in AD 363:[24]

It is, however, very obvious that, throughout the reign of this emperor [Julian], God gave manifest tokens of His displeasure, and permitted many calamities to befall several of the provinces of the Roman Empire. He visited the earth with such fearful earthquakes, that the buildings were shaken, and no more safety could be found within the houses than in the open air. From what I have heard, I conjecture that it was during the reign of this emperor, or, at least, when he occupied the second place in the government, that a great calamity occurred near Alexandria in Egypt, when the sea receded and again passed beyond its boundaries from the re-flux waves, and deluged a great deal of the land, so that on the retreat of the waters, the sea-skiffs were found lodged on the roofs of the houses. The anniversary of this inundation, which they call the birthday of an earthquake, is still commemorated at Alexandria by a yearly festival; a general illumination is made throughout the city; they offer thankful prayers to God, and celebrate the day very brilliantly and piously.

These compelling accounts may be related to the geography of ancient Alexandria by examining Mahmoud Bey's 19th-century map (fig. 3.1). The central crossroads seems to have lain in a shallow declivity in the landscape, which stretched from the Mediterranean coast near the Lochias peninsula across the city to Lake Mareotis. Buildings in this valley would have been particularly exposed to the effects of a tidal wave approaching from the north. If, as Ammianus suggests, innumerable buildings were levelled by the wave, then the devastation in this area of the city may have been such that it was difficult to recognise the precise location of Alexander's tomb. Georgius' question, 'How long shall this tomb stand?' also acquires extra resonance if the building was destroyed soon after by 'divine wrath'. In the devastation wrought by this event can be recognised perhaps the most convincing explanation of why the Soma mausoleum subsequently vanished so completely from the historical record.

Until very recently the Ammianus reference was believed to be the latest text to allude to the continued existence of Alexander's remains in ancient Alexandria. But now, thanks to the diligent research of Judith McKenzie, a previously unrecognised comment by a late 4th-century writer pertaining to the fate of Alexander's corpse has come to light. This occurs in an oration addressed to the emperor Theodosius I (r. AD 378-95) by the pagan scholar Libanius, a resident of the great metropolis of Antioch in Syria. This work seems to have been composed whilst Tatianus was praetorian prefect in the East, dating it to between AD 388 and 392. It is difficult for it to be later than early AD 391, because Theodosius conceived a fierce antipathy towards the pagans from that point onwards. The speech constitutes a fierce attack upon the behaviour and performance of the city councillors in Syria and elsewhere. In the relevant section Libanius speculates whether even tombs are safe from their desecrations:[25]

Who could be the friend of such as these? When they behave like this for money's sake, would they keep their hands off temple offerings or tombs? If they were travelling with some companion who had a gold piece, would they not kill him and rob him of it, if they had the chance. And this evil, King, is universal, whether you mention Paltus or Alexandria where the corpse of Alexander is displayed, whether Balaneae or our own city [Antioch]. *They may differ in size, but the same ailment afflicts them all.*

In this context, the mention that the corpse of Alexander was displayed in Alexandria appears to be a deliberate illustration of the threat posed presumably by city councillors to the sanctity and integrity of tombs. It suggests that the body had been extracted from its tomb to be publicly exhibited by the orders of such councillors.

It is necessary to express some caution regarding the identity of this Alexander, since Libanius was mainly discussing the situation in his home provinces of Syria. The other three towns he mentions are all in Syria and there was an Alexandria in Syria located near the site of Alexander's battle at Issus. There were also a number of important individuals named Alexander in the East at that time. In particular, another Alexander had been governor of Syria in the early 360s under Julian the Apostate, and letters to him from Libanius survive. Nevertheless, Libanius is seeking to demonstrate the universality of the problem in this passage and he seems to be referring to Alexandria in Egypt as a parallel example to his own city of Antioch – the emperor could only have read it that way. For this reason it may be concluded, on the balance of probabilities, that this is a reference to the corpse of Alexander the Great on public display in the Egyptian city of Alexandria in or just before AD 390.

It may be added that the idea that the Soma mausoleum was destroyed by the catastrophe of AD 365 is perfectly consistent with this new fragment of evidence. Such a calamity would have provided a motive, an opportunity and an excuse to excavate the subterranean burial chamber and rescue the famous remains. Libanius' remark also sets the scene for a ready explanation of the subsequent disappearance of the corpse. Shortly after he composed his speech, in AD 391 the roof fell in on the pagans and literally so in the case of many of their temples, for that year marked the end of official tolerance of paganism in the Roman Empire. Something drastic would have been required to save such a potent pagan relic as Alexander's corpse from oblivion.

There are some who believe that the Soma may have survived the disaster of AD 365, and they point to the rioting and religious violence at the end of the 4th century to explain its disappearance. At this time the remaining vestiges of the pagan past were systematically suppressed and destroyed as the new Christian orthodoxy became ever more intolerant of rival religions. This trend was pronounced under the Emperor Theodosius (r. AD 378-95). During his reign, in AD 385, Theophilus became patriarch in Alexandria and pursued a staunch anti-pagan policy, backed up by a militia of zealots known as the *parabolani*. In early AD 391 the emperor abandoned his policy of religious tolerance and respect for paganism by enacting a series of increasingly radical laws banning sacrifice, closing pagan shrines and temples and outlawing virtually every expression of pagan beliefs.[26]

In Alexandria, Theodosius supported Theophilus against the imperial prefect, who had sought to maintain the peace between the Christian and pagan factions in the city. Theodosius ordered that the Serapeum, the principal shrine of the pagans, should be attacked and then demolished, together with all other remaining pagan temples. Theophilus and his henchmen duly tore the magnificent temple apart, exposing the mechanisms of its wonders, such as a life-size statue made to float on air by means of magnets, and leaving it a pile of rubble. It can scarcely be doubted that any other surviving pagan shrines shared its fate at this time (or were perhaps converted into churches, as happened to the Caesareum), but the fact that no specific mention is made of the Soma tends to support the contemporary view of John Chrysostom, that by this date it had already ceased to exist.

Having worked through the evidence relating to the disappearance of Alexander's tomb, it is possible to draw some tentative conclusions concerning its fate. Notwithstanding the lack of any direct evidence for the event, it is probable that the Soma was destroyed some time between AD 262 and 365. Whereas the various episodes of warfare in the late 3rd century remain possibilities, the earthquake and tidal wave at the end of this period are the best candidates for its demolition. This does not necessarily mean that the burial chamber was destroyed at the same time. Indeed, if the Soma was as large a building as the sources imply, and if it collapsed over a burial chamber that was already sealed up, then it will have made the excavation of Alexander's sarcophagus very difficult. Nevertheless, there is now evidence that the sarcophagus and corpse had been exhumed by the late 380s.

Fig. 5.6 Pompey's Pillar with Kom el-Dikka in the background, from a painting of the 1840s by David Roberts (published 1854).

1   Stoneman, 1991, 2.38; G. Benwell and A. Waugh, 1961, 51-7. Although the earliest surviving version dates to the 3rd century AD, parts of the *Romance* go back to the 3rd century BC. While some episodes in it are fantastical, it includes topographical details which often accord with details in other sources.
2   C. R. Whittaker, 1969, xxv.
3   John Chrysostom, *Homily XXVI on the second epistle of St Paul the Apostle to the Corinthians*; E. D. Clarke, 1805, 12-13; John Chrysostom, *Opera*, VI, 610, (edit. Savil. Eton., 1612).
4   Clement of Alexandria, *Exhortation to the Greeks*, 10; Lucian, *Dialogues of the Dead*, 13.
5   Socrates Scholasticus, *Ecclesiastical History*, 1.17.
6   Theodoret, *Graecarum Affectionum Curatio*, 8.61; A. Erskine, 2002, 179.
7   J. Marlowe, 1971, 220.
8   Eusebius, *Ecclesiastical History*, 7.21.
9   S. Williams, 1985, 29; Marlowe, 1971, 220-1.
10 Williams, 1985, 30.
11 Bowman, 1986, 39-40.
12 E. Gibbon, 1782 (revised 1845), Ch. 11; Bowman, 1986, 44; Oxyrhynchus Papyrus, 1413 (perhaps AD 271/2); Ammianus Marcellinus, *Res Gestae*, 22.16.15.
13 Williams, 1985, 78-83.
14 Empereur, 1998, 100-109.
15 Strabo, *Geography*, 17.1.8; Epiphanius, *On Weights and Measures*, col. 250C.
16 According to Mahmoud Bey's labelling convention for the longitudinal streets.
17 Probably at the intersection of L1 with R1, but in any case somewhere on L1.
18 Ammianus Marcellinus, *Res Gestae*, 22.11.7.
19 Socrates Scholasticus, *Ecclesiastical History*, 3.2.
20 D. G. Hogarth, 1894-5, 23, note 3; L. Ross Taylor, 1927, 168. Fraser, 1972, vol. 2, 356-7, note 164.
21 J. C. Rolfe, 1937, xiii; W. W. Tarn, 1928, 216.
22 Sozomenus, *Ecclesiastical History*, 5.7; C. Haas, 1997, 287.
23 Ammianus Marcellinus, *Res Gestae*, 26.10.15-19.
24 Sozomenus, *Ecclesiastical History*, 6.2.
25 Libanius, *Oration*, XLIX, 11-12.
26 Marlowe, 1971, 280-1; S. Williams and G. Friell, 1994, 119-33.

6.   The Mysteries of the Mosques

When suddenly there is heard at midnight
A company passing invisible
With wondrous music, with voices,
Your fortune giving way now, your works
All turned to illusions, do not mourn vainly.
As one long since prepared, courageously,
Say farewell to her, to Alexandria who is leaving.
Above all do not be fooled, never say it was
All a dream, and that your hearing was deceived;
Do not stoop to such vain hopes as these.
As one long since prepared, courageously,
As becomes one worthy as you were of such a city,
Firmly draw near the window,
And listen with feeling, but not
With the complaints and entreaties of cowards,
Listen, your last enjoyment, to the sounds,
The exquisite instruments of the mystic troupe,
And say farewell, farewell to Alexandria you are losing.

The God Forsakes Antony, Constantine Cavafy, 1911

The character of Alexandria was greatly altered under the Islamic Caliphate. The classical city of spacious marble colonnades and monumental classical architecture in a rectilinear street plan was already much decayed in the Late Roman period. But the Christianised Romans had been energetic builders of illustrious churches with huge, echoing interior spaces, decorated with splendid mosaics and marble revetments, capped by domes and vaulted ceilings and decorated with glinting cupolas. With the arrival of the Arabs in AD 642 this architecture steadily crumbled to rubble to be replaced by mosques and bazaars typical of Middle Eastern trading cities, presided over by the continual song of the *muezzins* in the pinnacles of a hundred minarets.

Perhaps surprisingly, the Arab rulers seem to have been more tolerant of Alexander's memory than their Christian predecessors. This may be because Alexander appears as a kind of prophet in the Islamic holy book, the *Koran* (or *Quran*), in the guise of Dulkarnein (Dhulkarnein, Dzoul Karnein or Dhul-Qarnain). This title translates as something like 'Two-Horned Lord' and clearly derives from Alexander's appearance on the widely circulated coins of his generals Ptolemy, Seleucus and Lysimachus, where he variously wears the ram's horns of Ammon, a helmet with bull's horns and the tusks of an elephant.[1]

Some time in the 9th century, but prior to his death in AD 871, the Arab historian Ibn Abdel Hakim compiled an account of the mosques then existing in Alexandria. Among them he recorded, 'The Mosque of Dulkarnein, situated near the Gate of the City and its exit.' In the next century (AD 943-4) the commentator Al-Massoudi (or Maçoudi) mentioned the existence of a modest building in Alexandria called the 'Tomb of the Prophet and King Eskender'. Since both accounts were written within a century of one another, they may well be describing the same shrine. Hakim's account is especially striking, because he probably wrote near the time that the Tulunid walls were constructed. According to Mahmoud Bey's map (fig. 3.1), the main Graeco-Roman crossroads of Alexandria – the most likely location of the Soma – lay just within the main eastern gate in these fortifications.[2]

The shrine seems to be too small to be the Soma itself, but the relatively early date, and the possible consistency with the location suggested by the ancient Greek accounts, makes it feasible that it had been constructed at the remembered site of Alexander's tomb. It also tends to reinforce the theory that the Soma was situated near the main crossroads.

Following the observations of Hakim and Massoudi there is a gap of five centuries before anything more is heard of Alexander's tomb. This was a period of gentle decline for Alexandria, due to the establishment of the new Arab capital of Egypt at Cairo and the diminished Mediterranean trade on account of the political and religious divide between its northern and southern shores. The trading climate only began to improve in the wake of the Veneto-Ottoman Treaty of 1517, when the Ottoman sultan took over Egypt from the Mamelukes.

Early in the 16th century another Arab writer, Leo Africanus (1494/5–1552), noted the existence of Alexander's tomb in Alexandria. The following extract comes from an Italian translation made in 1550 of the lost Arabic manuscript of 1526 for his *Description of Africa*:[3]

> *It should not be omitted, that in the middle of the city amongst the ruins may be seen a little house in the form of a chapel, in which is a tomb much honoured by the Mahometans; since it is asserted that within it is kept the corpse of Alexander the Great, grand prophet and King, as may be read in the Koran. And many strangers come from distant lands to see and venerate this tomb, leaving at this spot great and frequent alms.*

Several decades after Leo's visit the Spanish traveller Marmol visited Alexandria in AD 1546. His account of the tomb of Alexander also locates it in a house in the form of a temple in the centre of the city amongst ruins, almost paraphrasing the words of Leo Africanus, and adding only that Alexander was called 'Escander'. Contrary to several later authors, Marmol did not write that this chapel lay near the Church of St Mark, but mentioned the chapel immediately after describing the church. George Sandys, who visited the city in AD 1611, and Michael Radzivill Sierotka, writing in AD 1582-4, have provided a similar account. The parallels are striking enough to suggest a connection between the various descriptions. Perhaps the later visitors were using a version of Leo Africanus as their guidebook.[4]

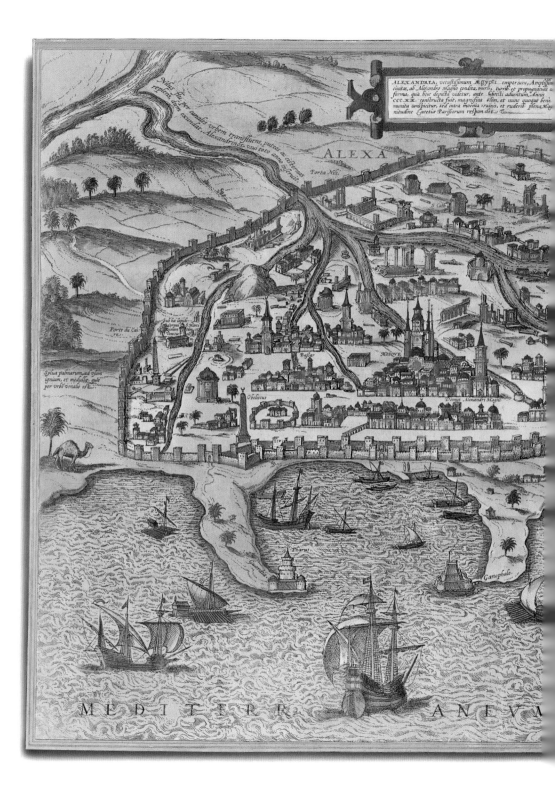

ALEXANDRIA, vetustissimum Ægypti ... emporium, Amplissa
ciuitas, ab Alexandro Magno condita, muris, turrib et propugnaculis o
forma, qua hic depicta cauetur, ante Christi aduentum, Annis
CCC.XX. constructa fuit, magnifica olim, et nunc quoque bene
munita conspicitur, sed intra moenia ruinis, et ruderib plena, Ma
nitudine Lutetia Parisiorum respondet.

ALEXA

Torta Nili.

Ndus hic per canales urbem transfluens, puteos ac cisternas
replens adim exundat. Alexandrini, uni toto anno usus fruit.

Sub hoc lapide
corpus D. Marci
fuisse
Porte du Cai
res.

Siluia palmarum ad usum
ignium, et medullae quæ
per urbē venalis est.

Bassar

Mosque

Domus Alexandri Magni

Obeliscus

Pharus

Granelle

Ganophalo

MEDITERR ANEVM

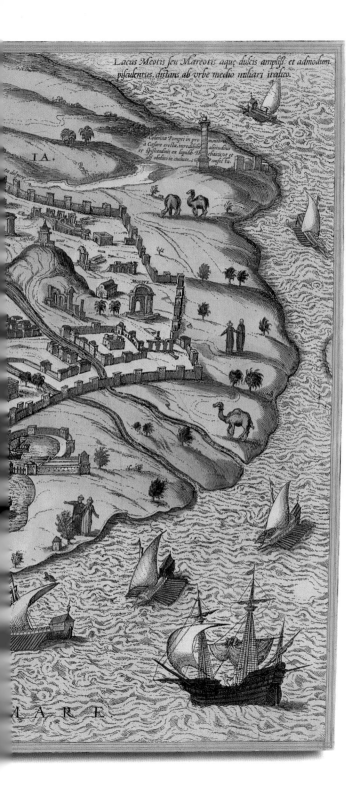

Within the illustration, the following engraved captions appear:

Lacus Meotis seu Mareotis aquæ dulcis amplifs. et admodum piscuëntus, distans ab vrbe medio miliari italico.

Colurina Pompei in pro montorio a Cæsare erecta, incredibilis altitudinis et pulchritudinis ex lapide Arabachiq; et cōfecta.

IA.

Mosgvi

MARE

*Figure 6.1 Map of Alexandria
by G. Braun and F. Hogenberg
(Civitates Orbis Terrarum),
Cologne, 1573, based on
information supplied by the
Cologne merchant Constantin
van Lyskirchen (from the late
16th or early 17th century).*
© A. M. Chugg

The most significant detail in Leo's description, when compared with that of Ibn Abdel Hakim, is the location of the tomb in the centre of Alexandria. This is difficult to reconcile with a location near an important exit gate, so it seems unlikely that the tomb cited by Leo (and his 16th- and 17th-century plagiarists) is in the same place as Hakim's Mosque of Dulkarnein. Leo's mention of the importance of the tomb as a source of 'alms' from foreigners indicates that the Alexandrians had a strong financial interest in maintaining a 'tomb of Alexander'. The cynical view might be that a suitable shrine would have been established for the sake of the local tourism industry, whether or not the natives had any genuine knowledge of the tomb's location.

In AD 1570 Ortelius published his *Theatrum Orbis Terrarum (Theatre of the World)*, the first modern atlas. Two years later, apparently as a companion volume to Ortelius' work, Georg Braun and Frans Hogenberg of Cologne published their *Civitates Orbis Terrarum (Cities of the World)*, comprising plans of most of the prominent cities then known. Among them was a lovely map of ancient and contemporary Alexandria (fig. 6.1).

The earliest medieval plan of Alexandria is Ugo Comminelli's panorama in the *Codex Urbinate* of 1472, but Braun and Hogenberg's plan is the most seductive of the antique images of the metropolis, providing a vivid – if slightly impressionistic – insight into the layout and atmosphere of the late medieval city. The map seems to have been based on reasonably good first-hand information supplied to the cartographers by the Cologne merchant Constantin van Lyskirchen. Its accuracy is limited by various distortions of scale and perspective, but it faithfully represents certain deviations of the Tulunid walls and other authentic details. Pompey's Pillar is depicted in the top left beyond the walls and the fort of Qait Bey is shown on the right-hand of the two promontories of the Great Harbour. This fort was built in AD 1477-80 on the foundations of the ruined Pharos lighthouse by the Mameluke sultan whose name it bears. The Pharos itself had been progressively damaged by a succession of earthquakes from AD 796 onwards, the most destructive of which seems to have occurred on 8 August AD 1303, razing it almost entirely.[5]

Close inspection of the exact centre of Braun and Hogenberg's panorama (fig. 6.2) reveals the dramatic legend '*Domus Alexandri Magni*' ('House of Alexander the Great'). This wording recalls the accounts of Marmol and Leo Africanus, both of whom describe Alexander's tomb as lying within a house (*casa* in the Italian and Spanish manuscripts). The label appears to refer to a modest building with a domed roof, next to the tower of a mosque at the right-hand corner of the central cluster of buildings a little to the north of the Canopic Way. Given that this map was engraved just a few decades after Leo and Marmol's visits, it is likely that this building is a representation of the same tomb of Alexander as referred to by them.

In the mid- to late 18th century a number of European travellers

*Figure 6.2 The House of Alexander the Great (*Domus Alexandri Magni*) detailed by G. Braun and F. Hogenberg.* © *A. M. Chugg*

reported the existence of a tomb inside a small shrine within the courtyard of the Attarine Mosque in Alexandria. In 1737 Richard Pococke could glean 'no account of it', whereas Johannes Van Egmont with Johannes Heyman failed to gain entry, since infidels were forbidden admission by the religious authorities at that time. Nevertheless, the intrepid Eyles Irwin managed to enter secretly in 1777, Charles Sigisbert Sonnini visited the shrine a little before 1780 by means of bribery, and William George Browne saw it in 1792. All provided accounts in their travelogues, yet none of them seems to have explicitly linked the shrine with Alexander.[6]

Alexandria emerged from its medieval torpor and decay, becoming fully accessible to the inquisitive gaze of the modern world in 1798 with the arrival of Napoleon Bonaparte in Egypt. He was escorted by a powerful army and accompanied by a team of scholars and scientists, whom he commissioned to compile a magnificent survey of the country called the *Description de l'Égypte*. It incorporates 1,000 plates of the finest engravings; 29 of these provide a beautifully accurate record of Alexandria at the close of the 18th century.

Napoleon's expedition came to grief when the English fleet under Nelson destroyed his ships in the Battle of the Nile at Aboukir Bay. The French expeditionary force remained in Egypt for three years until they were routed by the English under General Abercrombie in a land battle at Alexandria in 1801. In 1799 they discovered the famous Rosetta Stone with simultaneous texts in hieroglyphic script, Demotic and Greek of a proclamation marking the first anniversary of the coronation of Ptolemy V (r. 205-181 BC). This priceless artefact was ceded to the British upon the surrender of Alexandria in September 1801.[7]

During their stay, the French scholars Dominique Vivant Denon and Déodat Gratet de Dolomieu also discovered the small building in the courtyard of the Attarine Mosque in Alexandria, and circumstances suggest that they were told by the Egyptians that it was venerated as the tomb of Alexander. It contained a substantial and magnificent (but empty) green granite (or 'breccia') sarcophagus weighing 7 tonnes and covered all over with ancient hieroglyphs (fig. 6.3). This was also secured by the British and shipped to the British Museum in 1802 by Edward Daniel Clarke, who published his account of this object in a book entitled *The Tomb of Alexander* in 1805. Concerning the discovery of the sarcophagus in 1801, he explains how its whereabouts and its identity were made known to him:[8]

We had scarcely reached the house in which we were to reside, when a party of the merchants of the place, who had heard the nature of our errand, came to congratulate us on the capture of Alexandria, and to express their anxiety to serve the English. As soon as the room was clear of other visitants, speaking with great circumspection and in a low voice, they asked if our business in Alexandria related to the antiquities collected by the French? Upon being answered in the affirmative, and, in proof of it, the copy of the Rosetta Stone being produced, the principal of them said, 'Does your Commander in Chief know that they have the Tomb of Alexander?' We desired them to describe it; upon which they said it was a beautiful green stone, taken from the mosque of St Athanasius; which, among the inhabitants, had always borne that appellation. Our letter and instructions from Caïro evidently referred to the same monument. 'It is the object,' they continued, 'of our present visit; and we will shew you where they have concealed it.' They then related the measures used by the French; the extraordinary care they had observed to prevent any intelligence of it; the indignation shewn by the Mahometans at its removal; the veneration in which they held it; and the tradition familiar to all of them respecting its origin. I conversed afterwards with several of the Mahometans, both Arabs and Turks, on the same subject; not only those who were natives and inhabitants of the city, but also dervises and pilgrims; persons from Constantinople, Smyrna, and Aleppo, who had visited, or who resided in Alexandria; and they all agreed in one uniform tradition, namely, ITS BEING THE TOMB OF ISCANDER (Alexander), THE FOUNDER OF THE CITY OF ALEXANDRIA. We were then told

Figure 6.3 Sarcophagus of Nectanebo II (r. 360-43 BC) in green granite, possibly used as a container for Alexander's coffin in Memphis and Alexandria, presently in the British Museum, E.D. Clarke, The Tomb of Alexander, a dissertation on the sarcophagus from Alexandria and now in the British Museum, *Cambridge, 1805, Plate I.* © A. M. Chugg

T. Medland sculp.

177

it was in the hold of an hospital ship, in the inner harbour; and being provided with a boat, we there found it, half filled with filth, and covered with the rags of the sick people on board.

In the early 19th century many were convinced by Clarke's arguments that the sarcophagus in the British Museum was indeed that of Alexander the Great, although his book does not provide any hard evidence for this conclusion, apart from the statements of local merchants. The next twist in the tale came in 1822, when Jean-François Champollion learnt how to decipher Egyptian hieroglyphs which had remained unintelligible for 12 centuries by studying the inscriptions on the Rosetta Stone. When the hieroglyphs on the sarcophagus were translated, an Egyptian funerary text was revealed liberally interspersed with the cartouche of Nectanebo II (r. 360-343 BC), the last native Egyptian pharaoh, who had been overthrown by the Persians in 343 BC. This direct association between the sarcophagus and Nectanebo II has led many scholars to reject its purported use by Alexander. However, surprisingly, there seem to be some striking pieces of circumstantial evidence, which tend to support its association with the king, of which Clarke was unaware.

Clarke's book contains an engraving of the courtyard of the Attarine Mosque (fig. 6.4 and also shown in 6.5) prepared from a drawing by Vivant Denon. This depicts the small building, which housed the sarcophagus, being venerated by several Islamic worshippers. This corresponds with the 'House of Alexander the Great' situated beside the minaret of a mosque at the exact centre of Braun and Hogenberg's map. Interestingly, the location of the mosque in this map closely matches the actual position of the Attarine Mosque within the Arab city. It would seem that the shrine in the Attarine Mosque and the 'little house in the form of a chapel' described by Leo Africanus are probably the same place. Previously, this has been doubted, because the significance of the '*Domus Alexandri Magni*' legend in the map does not seem to have been recognised. It is now possible for the first time to argue with confidence that the association of the sarcophagus with Alexander dates back at least as far as the medieval period.[9]

In the Late Roman period it is believed that the Church of St Athanasius stood on the site of the Attarine Mosque (Attarine being a derivative of Athanasius). Intriguingly, Athanasius was Patriarch of Alexandria in AD 365,

Figure 6.4 Courtyard of the Attarine Mosque c. 1798, detailing the chapel which contained the Nectanebo sarcophagus, E.D. Clarke, 1805, Plate II.
© A. M. Chugg

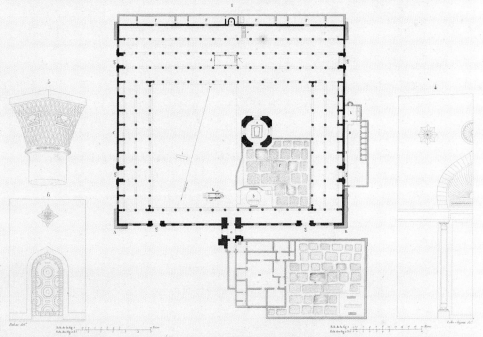

PLAN, ÉLÉVATION, COUPE ET DÉTAILS D'UNE ANCIENNE BASILIQUE, VULGAIREMENT
NOMMÉE MOSQUÉE DE St ATHANASE.

when the tidal wave struck. The Late Roman church that originally stood on the site of the Attarine Mosque was probably constructed just decades after the likely date for the destruction of the Soma mausoleum. If Athanasius had arranged for the rescue of Alexander's remains from beneath the rubble of the Soma, then this could explain how the sarcophagus ended up in a church bearing his dedication. Some doubt arises from the fact that Athanasius had been a protégé of the preceding patriarch, Alexander. Could the tomb of the patriarch Alexander have become confused with the tomb of the city's founder? This would be entirely feasible, except for the fact that it would be highly aberrant to find an Alexandrian patriarch entombed in the pagan sarcophagus of a pharaoh, whereas there are strong circumstantial links between Nectanebo's sarcophagus and Alexander the Great.[10]

The Attarine tomb and mosque, including the 'House of Alexander the Great', was destroyed in 1830, but the mosque was entirely rebuilt on an adjoining site in the second half of the 19th century. An interesting attempt was made to resuscitate the Attarine tomb theory in 1948 by Alan J. B. Wace. He pointed out that the sarcophagus may well have been vacant and available at the time of Alexander's death, because Diodorus says that Nectanebo fled to Ethiopia to escape the Persian invasion of 343 BC and he may well have died there. Wace suggested that the use of the sarcophagus by Alexander instead was the inspiration for a story in the *Alexander Romance* about Nectanebo being Alexander's father. Wace further explained the presence of the sarcophagus at Alexandria by postulating the (otherwise unattested) existence of a royal cemetery on the site before Alexander founded the city.[11]

This royal cemetery hypothesis is dubious but need not count against the general theory, because it is virtually certain that Alexander's original entombment took place at Memphis. Also, the circumstantial evidence suggests that the sarcophagus was left at Memphis, possibly at the Serapeum, when Nectanebo went into exile.

Fraser has conceded that 'the presence of this mighty sarcophagus in

Figure 6.5 Plans of the Attarine Mosque, drawn in 1798-1801, from the Description de l'Égypte *(Panckoucke edition), Paris, 1821-29, Antiquités Volume V, Plate 38.*
© A. M. Chugg

Alexandria is surprising.' In fact, it is well established that the Ptolemies transported large numbers of sphinxes, obelisks and similar architectural embellishments to Alexandria. Most of these were robbed from the Egyptian city of Heliopolis, which had fallen into ruin before the Ptolemaic era. Logically, the only obvious use for a pharaoh's sarcophagus would have been the entombment of a king. Indeed, it is likely that its exploitation for any lesser purpose would have been considered sacrilegious by the native Egyptians. Thus, it is difficult to imagine that anyone would have expended the considerable human and financial resources required to move the sarcophagus from Memphis to Alexandria, unless it was their intention to use it for a pharaonic sepulchre. The only scenario that seems to make sense of the conundrum is to suppose that the tradition concerning this relic is essentially true. If Ptolemy I Soter had used it for Alexander's corpse in the Memphite tomb in 321 BC, then it would probably have been transported to Alexandria with Alexander's body by Ptolemy II Philadelphus, thus neatly solving the mystery of how it came to lie in a city founded at least 12 years after it was sculpted.[12]

Regarding the sarcophagus, Fraser concludes, 'I do not think it can seriously be maintained that [Ptolemy I] Soter or [Ptolemy II] Philadelphus would have buried the Founder in this manner.' Initially, I tended to agree with him, since it seemed extraordinary that Ptolemy should have placed Alexander's remains within a vessel emblazoned with Nectanebo's cartouches. However, a detailed analysis of the political context of the Memphite entombment strongly suggests that this view is not sustainable. At that time Ptolemy was avidly seeking to ingratiate himself with the native Egyptians in order to help cement his power base. For example, on the 'Satrap Stele' of 311 BC he firmly links himself with an Egyptian leader called Khabbash, who seems to have led an insurrection against the Persians in about 338 BC. Ptolemy II Philadelphus is actually attested to have used an obelisk quarried by Nectanebo for a shrine to his sister-wife, Arsinoë. In these circumstances the association of Alexander's tomb with the last native pharaoh may well have seemed an astute gambit, especially since it also circumvented the need for a considerable financial outlay and a delay of several years for a fresh sarcophagus to be fashioned.[13]

That the sarcophagus was made for Nectanebo II is consistent with it being available to Ptolemy in a vacant state when he entombed Alexander at Memphis. This explains how the sarcophagus reached Alexandria and most significantly why a group of Greek statues, independently linked to Alexander's tomb by Dorothy Thompson, guarded the entrance to the temple of Nectanebo at the Serapeum at Saqqara. It is unlikely that the sarcophagus should turn out to connect two independently recognised sites for Alexander's tomb by chance. Supposing it to be a forgery, the perpetrators would have been incredibly sophisticated in their choice of this particular sarcophagus. They probably needed to be able to read the pharaoh's name in its cartouches, yet hieroglyphics died out at the end of the 4th century AD, very shortly after Alexander's Alexandrian tomb was destroyed. This would tend to date the forgery to within a few generations of the existence of the original, but at such an early date Alexandrian records and recollections should still have been sufficient to expose such a deception.

If this sarcophagus was genuinely used for Alexander's corpse, then an immediate implication is that the funeral chamber beneath the destroyed mausoleum of the Soma was pillaged in Late Antiquity, probably towards the end of the 4th century AD.

A further implication is that the semicircle of statues at the Serapeum guarded the entrance to the first tomb of Alexander, which was therefore located within the temple of Nectanebo. Returning to Mariette's detailed plan (fig. 6.6), it is apparent that besides the temple proper the entrance guarded by the statues also leads via a side-passage to a small adjoining chamber (A). The Nectanebo sarcophagus actually fits within this chamber in the section to the east of its entrance, leaving space for a votive sculpture in its western end. There are also some hints in the plan of the temple that the side chamber may have been appended after its original construction:

i. The hypothetical outline of an original symmetrical plan for the temple may be superimposed on the plan defined by Mariette (fig. 6.6).

ii. The southern exterior face of the hypothetical original temple is in line with the fine quality stone (light grey) façade wall containing entrance B.

iii. The southern exterior face of the hypothetical original temple coincides with an interior face of the possible tomb chamber.

iv. One wall of the passage to the tomb chamber coincides with the interior face of the southern wall of the hypothetical original temple.

It is also potentially significant that Mariette shows a side-entrance to the temple at the corner of the southern wall (B in fig. 6.6), for this too was guarded by sculptures representing four lions in the Greek style (2 in fig. 6.6). Similar lions were a symbol of the Macedonian monarchy and are a prominent feature of the tombs of the Macedonian magnates of the Hellenistic world, such as the Lion Tombs of Knidos, Amphipolis and Gerdek Kaya and the Lion of Hamadan. Significantly, a pair of golden lions had guarded the entrance to Alexander's catafalque. Clearly the chamber appended to the Nectanebo temple at the Serapeum is an excellent candidate for Alexander's first tomb.[14]

Further, the use of Nectanebo II's sarcophagus for Alexander's tomb is consistent with the newly identified comment by Libanius referring to Alexander's corpse having been exhibited in Alexandria in about AD 390. The authenticity of the sarcophagus requires that it should have been exhumed from beneath the presumed ruins of the Soma at some point and unambiguously attributed to Alexander. This step is necessary in order that

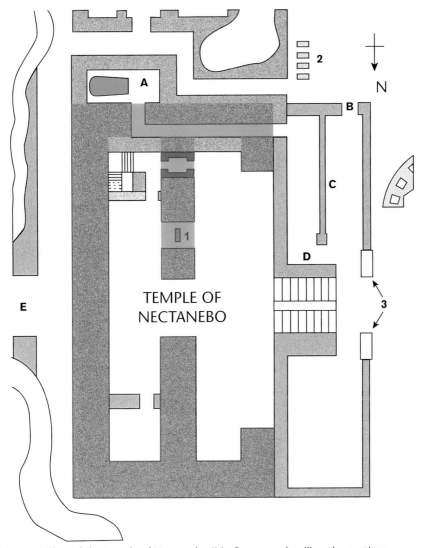

Figure 6.6 Plan of the temple of Nectanebo II in Saqqara, detailing the southern antechamber which may have been used to entomb Alexander before the subsequent removal of his remains to Alexandria (adapted from Figure 2.9). © A. M. Chugg

Figure 6.7. The Nabi Daniel Mosque depicted in an engraving of c. 1840 by A. Rouargue of Paris, viewed from Kom el-Dikka with the late Arab city still confined to the isthmus in the centre background. Qait Bey fortress and the Pharillon are depicted at each end of the harbour mouth with one of Cleopatra's Needles standing between these locations (from a drawing of the 1830s by W.H. Bartlett of London). © A. M. Chugg

the sarcophagus should have found its way into the courtyard of the Attarine Mosque, whilst retaining its association with Alexander. The Libanius reference suggests that the sarcophagus was recovered prior to the final outlawing of paganism in AD 391, and sets up the rioting and turmoil that broke out in Alexandria in that year as the most likely occasion for the final disappearance of Alexander's corpse, especially since John Chrysostom and Theodoret both claimed that Alexander's tomb had been lost by the early 5th century.

By virtue of Alexander's deification, his remains were sacred pagan relics. Butler provides a fascinating illustration of the kind of fate typically suffered by pagan religious artefacts in 4th-century Alexandria. He quotes the *Coptic Synaxary* and Eutychius to show that the Christian Patriarch of Alexandria under the Emperor Constantine – coincidentally also named Alexander – wished to abolish a pagan feast day and destroy an associated statue of Saturn, to which the Alexandrians offered sacrifices. Resistance from the populace persuaded him to retain the festival as a Christian celebration and to fashion a cross from the bronze of the statue. We also hear that the Caesareum temple became the Christian cathedral of the city in the mid-4th century. Popular sentiment often favoured the adaptation and absorption of the pagan legacy in the service of Christianity, in preference to the wanton destruction occasionally perpetrated by the fanatics.[15]

Another traditional site of the Soma in Alexandria has gripped the imaginations of successive generations of tomb-hunters even more tenaciously than the story of the sarcophagus, but perhaps with less justification. It is the Nabi Daniel Mosque in the modern Nabi Daniel Street (fig. 6.7), often marked, rather speculatively, on plans of the ancient city as the 'Street of the Soma'. Nabi is the Arabic word for a prophet, but the Arab legend of the prophet Daniel, though probably having its origins in the Old Testament story, differs considerably from the biblical account. The source has been traced back to at least the 9th century AD via two Islamic astronomers: Mohammed Ibn Kathir el Farghani and Abou Ma'shar. Their story is interesting, because it contains some elements which seem to have been inspired by Alexander's career. In particular, their Daniel was promised victory over all Asia, acquired support from the Egyptians, founded Alexandria and was buried in a golden sarcophagus in the city. This was later stolen by the Jews to mint coins, and replaced with a stone casket.

Notwithstanding this traditional source for the dedication of the mosque, some Islamic scholars have suggested that its name derives from Sheikh Mohammed Daniel of Mosul, who lived in Alexandria in the 15th century AD. He is said to have made the mosque, supposed previously to have been known as the 'Mosque of Alexander', into a centre of religious teaching and was buried within it when he died. The confusion between him and the eponymous prophet possibly resulted in the modern name of the building.[16]

The present mosque seems to have been built or rebuilt mainly under Mohammed Ali in 1823. Interestingly, there are two empty tombs in a subterranean vault under the mosque, which local tradition attributes to the prophet Daniel and a legendary religious storyteller called Sidi Lokman. This basement appears to be of earlier date than the overlying building. A Russian monk, Vassili Grigorovich Barskij, visited Alexandria in 1727 and 1730 and identified a small shrine in his plan of the city, a possible precursor of the mosque, but other map evidence belies the existence of a substantial building on the site in the 18th century.

Ambroise Schilizzi, a dragoman at the Russian Consulate in Alexandria in the middle of the 19th century, claimed to have gone into the vault beneath the mosque in 1850 while escorting some European travellers. The story goes that he descended into a narrow and dark subterranean passage and came to a worm-eaten wooden door. Looking through the cracks of the planks he glimpsed a body bent up in a throne or somehow raised up in a crystal or glass cage or sarcophagus. On the head of the corpse was a golden diadem and scattered around lay papyrus scrolls and books. Schilizzi sought to investigate further, but was dragged away by one of the keepers of the mosque.[17]

This tantalising tale conflates details from Strabo (the crystal sarcophagus), Suetonius (the diadem left by Augustus) and Dio Cassius (the secret books gathered by Septimius Severus). Papyrus would almost certainly have perished over such a long period, given Alexandria's dank climate and the fact that capillary action tends to draw dampness upwards through the soil from the water table. No ancient papyri have ever been found in Alexandria. Schilizzi emerges as having been well read among the ancient sources, but his account is quite certainly a shameless hoax.[18]

The Nabi Daniel tradition seems first to have been given written form by Mahmoud Bey. In his book published in Copenhagen in 1872, while conceding that this location for Alexander's tomb derives from a purely oral tradition, he nevertheless seeks to build on the theory with several further lines of argument:[19]

i.   The site reconciles the statements of Strabo that the Soma was part of the Royal Quarter, and of Achilles Tatius, that the 'place of Alexander' lay at a central crossroads on the Canopic Way. However, according to Mahmoud Bey's own map the site is far from the principal crossroads, is offset from the Canopic Way and seems a little too distant from the main palace district readily to be assigned to the Royal Quarter.

ii. The adjacent hill, Kom el-Dikka (fig. 6.8), means the mosque is on rising ground, which can help to preserve a corpse from the effects of dampness. (But the hill is now known to be a medieval spoil-heap above Roman ruins.)

iii. Bones dating back to pagan times were found buried in the vicinity of the mosque and a small subterranean tomb chamber with a damaged marble statue was discovered at the foot of the mound on which the mosque is constructed. Nonetheless, more recent archaeological investigations have shown that none of the nearby inhumations is older than the Christian period.[20]

iv. The Prophet Daniel died long before Alexandria was founded and he spent nearly all his life in captivity in Babylon, so he could not be buried in the city.

Figure 6.8. Map of Alexandria as it appeared in the Baedeker Guide, Leipzig, 1913.

© A. M. Chugg

1. Site of Pharos lighthouse
2. Site of Caesareum (Cleopatra's Needles)
3. Site of Lochias peninsula
4. Shallalat Gardens
5. Chatby necropolis
6. Alabaster Tomb
7. Ancient wall fragment
8. Site of Rosetta Gate
9. Kom el-Dikka
10. Nabi Daniel Mosque
11. Pompey's Pillar
12. Catacombs of Kom el-Shuqafa
13. Attarine Mosque
14. Island of Pharos

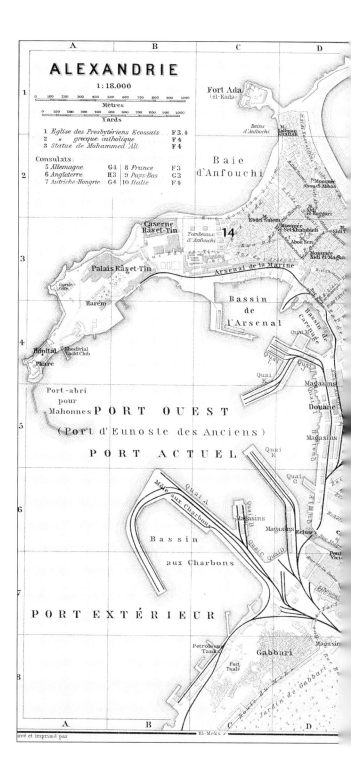

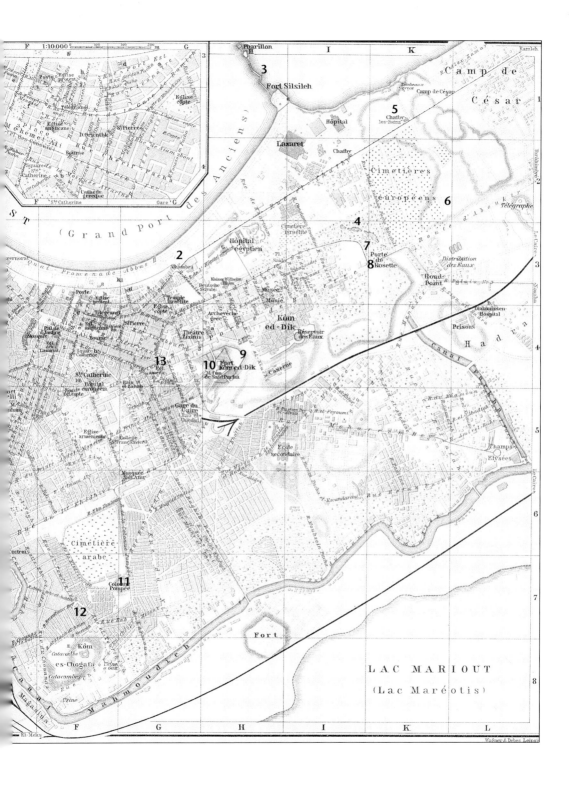

v. The mound on which the mosque is built is called Kom el-Demas, which means the 'hill of the bodies' in Arabic, so there is a continuity in the name of the spot, since it was called the Soma ('body' in Greek). But the name could also refer to the two tombs in the crypt of the mosque.

Although Mahmoud Bey does not mention the fact, there is also a fantastical story in the *Alexandrian Synaxary* of the erection of a church dedicated to Elias and John on a site called Dimas-Demas, which Breccia states is identical to Kom el-Demas. During the clearance of the site a treasure of golden ornaments dating to the time of Alexander was discovered, but there is no definite connection with the Soma in any of this.[21]

Alexandre-Max de Zogheb also tells of a visit by Mahmoud Bey to the vaults beneath the Nabi Daniel Mosque. He entered a large chamber with an arched roof on the ground level of the ancient town. From this paved crypt inclined corridors ran out in four directions, too lengthy and dilapidated for him to survey properly. He was subsequently forbidden to return and the entrances were walled up.[22]

Zogheb also quotes a letter from Yacub Artin Pacha written early in the 20th century attesting to the traditional association of the mosque with the site of Alexander's tomb:[23]

For as long as I can recall, I remember the mosque of Nabi Daniel, and its memory is indissolubly linked in my mind with the name of Alexander the Great; as I have always been told that it contained the tomb of the Macedonian and I also believe that in 1850 this was the general belief in Alexandria.

In 1879 a mason working in the basement of the Nabi Daniel Mosque also broke through to the vaulted chamber. The Sheikh of the mosque accompanied him in a brief exploration of an inclined passage. After observing granite monuments with an angular summit, the Sheikh then insisted that they return. The entrance was subsequently walled up and the mason was asked not to reveal the incident.[24]

Inspired by Mahmoud Bey's evocative legend, a long succession of archaeologists has excavated in the vicinity of the Nabi Daniel Mosque and across the nearby hill of Kom el-Dikka, starting with Hogarth at the end of the 19th century. Heinrich Schliemann, the famous discoverer of Troy, even failed to acquire a permit to dig at the site in 1888. Evaristo Breccia, who actually excavated in the vault beneath the mosque, found nothing that could be considered ancient down to the foundations of the building. Achille Adriani found sections of a Roman street 9m beneath Kom el-Dikka and beneath these, at the level of the water table, lay some Ptolemaic wall foundations. More recently, a team of Polish excavators has clarified the probable nature of the 'passages' discovered beneath the mosque in the 19th century, confirming that the building lies above ancient cisterns on two levels, which were fed by artificial water channels.

The excavations have been sufficiently extensive, one may reasonably conclude, to virtually rule out the possibility of the Soma having been located beneath the Nabi Daniel Mosque or the nearby hill. Also doubtful is whether the legendary association between this building and the Soma predates the middle of the 19th century. Sadly, the most romantic of the sites for Alexander's tomb is perhaps now among those parts of ancient Alexandria that can probably be excluded from further investigation.

Nonetheless, such mythology is self-perpetuating, quite independent of the restraints of truth and evidence. Many popular guides to Egypt and Alexandria still confidently assert that the Nabi Daniel Mosque overlies the site of the Soma. Even academic archaeologists are not immune to its allure: applications for permits to dig for Alexander's tomb around this mosque were still being received during the 1990s.[25]

Although the evidence for the tomb of Alexander at the Nabi Daniel Mosque disintegrated when subjected to archaeological investigation, it has emerged that Mariette's excavations at the Serapeum in Saqqara provide a remarkable vindication of the once discredited tomb in the Attarine Mosque. The superficially damning evidence that the Attarine sarcophagus was made for Nectanebo II appears on closer analysis actually to support its use for Alexander's corpse. Furthermore, it points directly at a candidate for the first tomb of Alexander at Saqqara, which might reasonably be subjected to fresh archaeological investigation.

Fig. 6.9 Cleopatra's Needles, from a painting of the 1840s by David Roberts (published 1854).

1   *Koran, Surah* 18; O. Mørkholm, 1991, 63-5, 72 and 81.

2   Fraser, 1972, vol. 2, 36-9 (section 1 of note 86); B. de Meynard and P. de Courteille, 1861-1917, II, 259; the dates for Sultan Ibn Tulun are AD 868-84 (Empereur, 1998, 86), so the Tulunid walls most probably post-date Hakim.

3   Leo Africanus made several visits to Egypt, probably between 1515-20; his account of Alexandria was drafted in 1526; Fraser, 1972, vol. 2, 37 (section 1 of note 86); Pory, 1896, 864-5.

4   N. Perrot, 1667, III, 276; Fraser, 1972, vol. 2, 36-9 (section 1 of note 86); G. Sandys, 1617, 112; M. Radzivill Sierotka, 1601 [1925], 120.

5   Constantin van Lyskirchen supplied views of many towns in Asia and Africa to Braun and Hogenberg, including Alexandria. They may have used other sources as well; Oscar Norwich, 1997, 380. Empereur, 1998, 86-7; M. A. Taher in C. Décobert and J.-Y. Empereur (eds.), 1998, 51-6.

6   R. Pococke, 1743, I, 4; J. A. van Egmont and J. Heyman, 1759, II, 133; E. Irwin, 1780, I, 367; C. S. Sonnini, 1800, I, 67; W. G. Browne, 1799, 6.

7   B. Lavery, 1998, 298-300.

8   Vivant Denon in the company of Dolomieu arrived with Napoleon's expedition on 4 July 1798 (D. Vivant Denon, 1802, 19-30). This account also omits mention of Alexander's name, but it appears from subsequent events and the great secrecy with which they acted that the French were at some point told about the connection between the sarcophagus and Alexander. E. D. Clarke, *The Tomb of Alexander*, 1805, 39-40.

9   There are also a number of views and plans of the Attarine Mosque and the sarcophagus in the *Description de l'Égypte, Antiquités* 5, plates 35, 38-41.

10 Fraser, 1972, vol. 2, 39-40 (section 2 of note 86). The Attarine mosque building seen by Napoleon's scholars was probably an 11th-century construction, since its foundation inscriptions give the date AD 1084, B. Tkaczow, 1993, 78-9, item 25. It remains possible that the courtyard chapel was older. A Greek inscription in Roman letters preserving the word 'Constantinon' on the pavement beside the tomb is preserved from the earlier church, C.S, Sonnini, I, 1800, 67. Marlowe, 1971, 264-78. Athanasius returned to Alexandria after the death of Julian the Apostate in AD 363 and remained there until his death in AD 373; Haas, 1997, 353-4.

11 B. Tkaczow, 1993, 78-9, item 25; A. J. B. Wace, 1948, 1-11; Diodorus Siculus, 16.51; Stoneman, 1991, 35-44.

12 Fraser, 1972, vol. 2, 40 (section 2 of note 86); Empereur, 1998, 117-8.

13 Bowman, 1986, 22; Pliny, *Natural History*, 36.14.67.

14 J. Fedak, 1990, 76-78 and 100; Diodorus 18.27.1.

15 A. Butler, [1902] 1978, 374 (note); *The Coptic Synaxary*, for 12 Ba'ûnah; Eutychius in J.-P. Migne, *Patrologia Graeca* 111, col. 1005.

16 Fraser, 1972, vol. 2, 38 (section 1 of note 86).

17 Breccia, 1922, 99; A.-M. de Zogheb, 1909, 170-1.

18 E. G. Turner, 1980, 43.

19 Mahmoud Bey, 1872, 49-52.

20 Empereur, 1998, 149.

21 Breccia, 1922, 99.
22 A.-M. de Zogheb, 1909, 171-2.
23 Fraser, 1972, vol. 2, 39 (section 1 of note 86).
24 Zogheb, 1909, 173.
25 D. G. Hogarth and E. F. Benson, 1895, 1-33; L. Deuel, 1977; Fraser, 1972, vol. 2, 41 (note 88); Fraser, 1972, vol. 2, 41 (note 90); Fraser, 1972, vol. 2, 41 (note 88); M. Rodziewicz, 1984.

7.   The Astronomer's Chart

As when it happeneth that some lovely town
Unto a barbarous besieger falls,
Who there by sword and flame himself instals,
And, cruel, it in tears and blood doth drown;
Her beauty spoiled, her citizens made thralls,
His spite yet so cannot her all throw down,
But that some statue, arch, fane of renown
Yet lurks unmaimed within her weeping walls:
So, after all the spoil, disgrace, and wrack,
That time, the world and death could bring combined,
Amidst that mass of ruins they did make,
Safe and all scarless yet remains my mind:
From this so high transcending rapture springs,
That I, all else defaced, not envy kings.

William Drummond of Hawthornden, *Sonnet XXIV,* 1623

This chapter provides an overview of what is known of the layout (topography) of ancient Alexandria and its evolution through the centuries, especially regarding points of importance to the form and location of Alexander's tomb. Although it may not be immediately obvious that such a detailed introduction is required, it will emerge that some familiarity with the organisation of the Graeco-Roman city is essential both to recognise the flaws in false theories and in order to appreciate the attractions of new hypotheses presented in the next chapter.

The population of ancient Alexandria has been estimated at around half a million in the 1st century BC. A larger number than this would have been

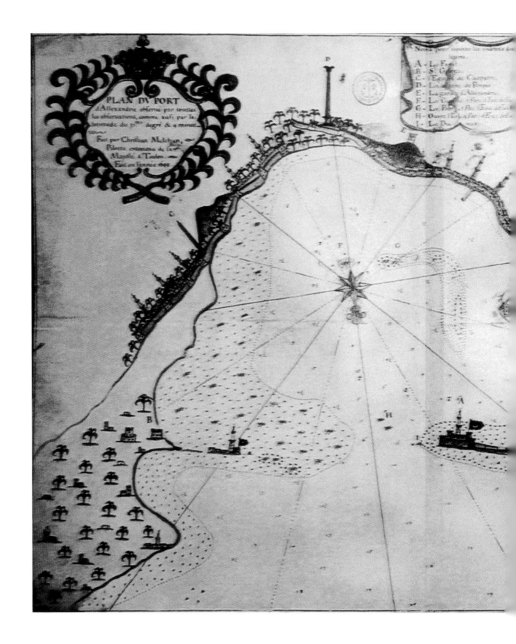

Figure 7.1 Chart of Alexandria by C. Melchien (AD 1699), from G. Jondet, L'Atlas Historique de la Ville et des ports d'Alexandrie, *Tome II, Cairo, 1921, Plate IX.*

201

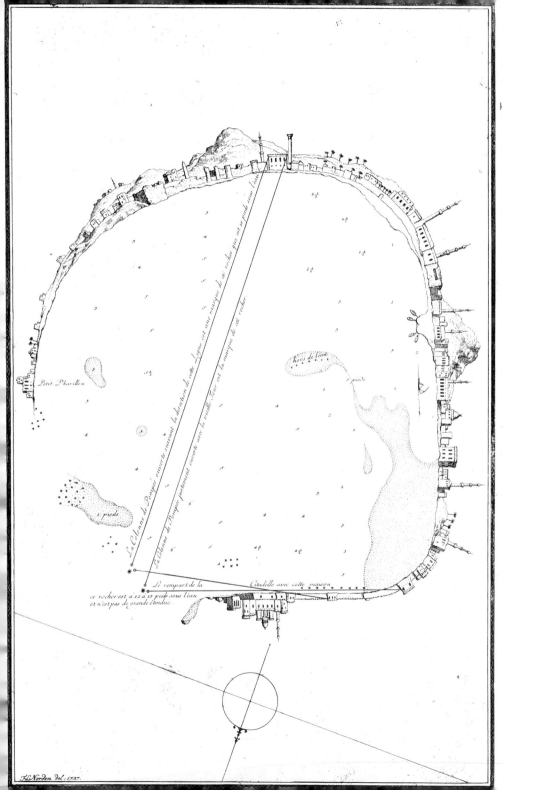

Petit Pharillon

hors de l'eau

La Colonne de Pompée ouverte suivant la direction de cette Ligne est une marque de ce rocher qui est 12 pieds sous l'eau

La Colonne de Pompée justement ouverte avec la vieille Tour est la marque de ces rocher

2 pieds

Le rempart de la   Citadelle avec cette maison

ce rocher est à 12 à 13 pieds sous l'eau
et n'est pas de grande étendüe

F.L.Norden del: 1737.

difficult to accommodate within the known extent of the Ptolemaic city, because the evidence implies that Alexandria lacked high-density accommodation such as imperial Rome's multi-storey tenement blocks, the so-called '*insulae*'. Ancient papyri suggest a slow decline in the Roman period, exacerbated at times by poor economic conditions, wars, plagues and natural disasters. By the 4th century AD the population had probably diminished to around 180,000. This number probably increased in the period *c.* AD 450-600, when Alexandria experienced an economic boom as the main provider of wheat to the imperial capital of Constantinople. The early 7th century heralded a period of decline ushered in by the Persian invasion of 619, and after their expulsion from the Byzantine Empire by the Emperor Heraclius (r. AD 610-41), Alexandria suffered another hammer blow when Palestine, Syria and parts of Egypt were conquered by the Arabs in AD 636-40. Alexandria herself was surrendered by treaty in AD 642 after a long siege.[1]

The '40,000 tributary Jews' mentioned by the Arab general 'Amr may be interpreted as a surprisingly low approximation of Alexandria's population at this time. In the 9th century the Arab historian Ibn Abdel Hakim estimated the population at the time of the Arab conquest at 200,000, but a value between the two limits is more realistic. The relative areas of the Ptolemaic and Arab cities defined by the circuits of their defensive walls suggest a 9th-century population below 100,000.

Alexandria languished ever more deeply in the shadow of Cairo and was extensively quarried to recycle luxurious architectural materials to such a degree that by the time the map of Braun and Hogenberg was completed in the mid-16th century there were large open areas within the Tulunid walls. By then the Heptastadion causeway had silted up, producing a broad, flat isthmus between the harbours. As the old Arab city began to suffer irreparably from the ravages of time and stone robbers, the Ottomans (who took over the rule of Egypt from the Mamelukes in 1517) found it convenient to build the town afresh on the virgin soil of the isthmus. This

Figure 7.2 Plan of the Great Harbour of Alexandria in 1737 by F. L. Norden. © A. M. Chugg

Figure 7.3 (overleaf). Map of Alexandria c. 1800 by Napoleon's engineers from Description de l'Égypte *(Panckoucke edition), Paris, 1821-29, État Moderne Volume II, Plate 84.* © A. M. Chugg

TERRANÉE

le Diamant
le Phare
Fond de Gravier
Fond de Roche
Fond de Sable
Fond de Sable
Fond de Sable
Fond de Sable

Pharillon

ORT NEUF

Côte couverte de Roc

Santon

Môle ruiné
Tour ruiné
Tour des Romains
Cimetière de
Montagne des Juifs
Monastère Grec
Mosquée S.Athanase
D E S
ARABES
Porte de Rosette

Chemin d'Al

Vestiges d'un Canal

Chemin de Rah

Aqueduc
Souterrain

Môle ruiné

A R É O T I S

process can be observed in Melchien's map of 1699 (fig. 7.1), where Pompey's Pillar is easily recognised thrusting skywards from an eminence behind the centre of the town; to its west a string of minarets decorate the new strip of land. Another interesting panorama of the harbour area is shown in F. L. Norden's 18th-century map (fig. 7.2).[2]

By the time the French arrived with Napoleon's expedition in 1798, Alexandria had reached the nadir of her fortunes. The map made by Napoleon's engineers is shown in fig. 7.3 and fig. 7.4. The old, walled Arab city was almost deserted and even the new town on the isthmus only accommodated some 5-6,000 inhabitants. In 1806 the residents were estimated to number 6,000, but in the 1820s Mohammed Ali began to revitalise the port and the population started to rise rapidly: 12,000 in 1821;

Figure 7.4 Map of Alexandria (eastern part of the city) c. 1800 by Napoleon's engineers from Description de l'Égypte *(Panckoucke edition), Paris, 1821-29, État Moderne Volume II, Plate 84.* © A. M. Chugg

52,000 in 1835; 200,000 in 1868; and 317,000 in the census of 1897. Around 1920 the figure surpassed the Ptolemaic peak of half a million and by 1960 it had reached nearly 1,000,000. Simultaneously, of course, the urbanised area burst out of the confines of the isthmus and spilt inexorably across the ruin fields, obliterating or sealing over the great bulk of the archaeological remains as it spread.[3]

The names of the great buildings of Alexandria were well known in Europe, especially after the Renaissance when the ancient Greek and Latin writers were widely read and an obsession with the classical past prevailed. A natural consequence was that European visitors to the port sought to identify the famous sites among the scattered and anonymous ruins. One of the earliest attempts to map the layout of ancient Alexandria was made by the French traveller M. Bonamy in 1731. His technique involved locating ruined monuments among the shifting sands and associating these with the description of the ancient city given by Strabo. Unfortunately, this plan (fig. 7.5) is of little practical value, since it makes many errors, such as placing Pompey's Pillar and the Serapeum on the wrong side of the Canopic Way. However, it does serve to demonstrate that only careful excavations stood any significant chance of solving the riddles of the ruins.[4]

Scientific archaeology arrived in the eastern Mediterranean with the inauguration of the French School at Athens in 1846, followed by the German Archaeological Institute, the British School and others. Unfortunately, these august institutions largely ignored Alexandria during the brief window of a few decades between their foundation and the disappearance of the ruin field beneath the sprawling modern city. Instead, the topography of ancient Alexandria was rescued from the oblivion of urbanisation by the unlikely figure of Mahmoud Bey, the court astronomer to the Khedive Ismaïl, then ruler of Egypt. Extraordinarily, his investigations were prompted by the literary ambitions of the Emperor of France.[5]

In the early 1860s Napoleon III (r. 1852-70) had conceived an ambition to compose a history of his hero, Julius Caesar. He was the nephew of

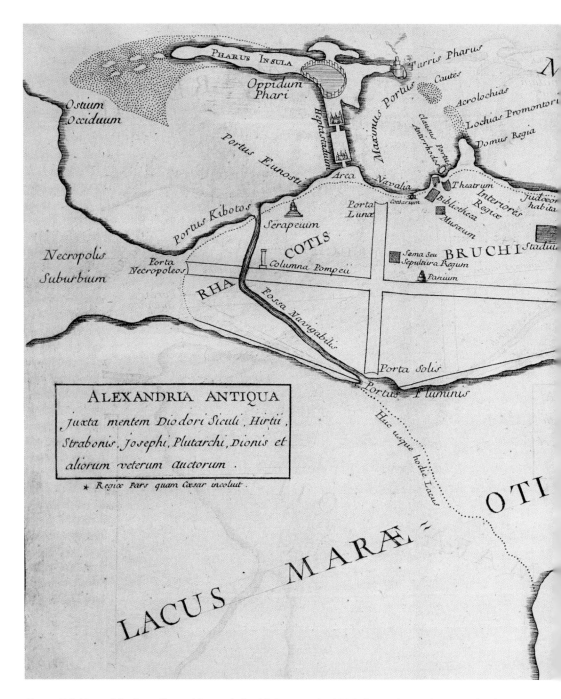

Figure 7.5 Map of Ancient Alexandria made by M. Bonamy in 1731 (Soma located just north of crossroads), from Histoire de l'Académie Royale des Inscriptions et Belles Lettres avec les Mémoires de Littérature, *Tome IX (1731-3), Paris, 1736.* © A. M. Chugg

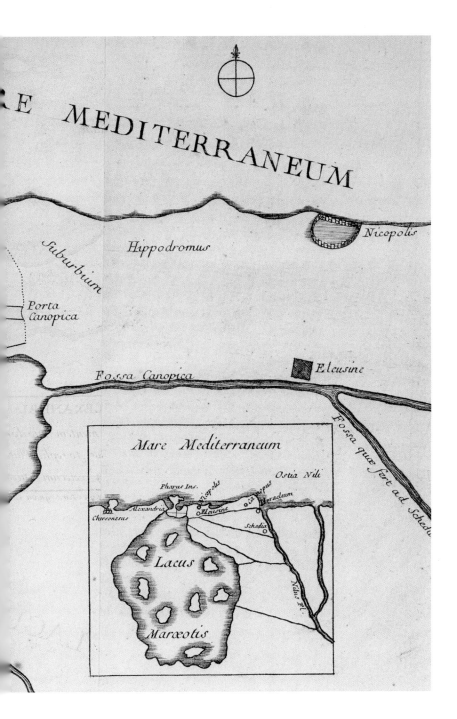

E MEDITERRANEUM

Suburbium

Hippodromus

Nicopolis

Porta
Canopica

Fossa Canopica

Eleusine

Fossa quæ fert ad Schedi

Mare Mediterraneum

Ostia Nili

Pharus Ins.

Nicopolis

Alexandria

Chersonesus

Eleusine

Vadium

Schedia

Lacus

Nilus Fl.

Marœotis

Napoleon Bonaparte and, after becoming president of the French Republic in 1848, he proclaimed himself emperor in 1852. Among the key problems Napoleon hoped to address in his biography was the detailed explanation of Caesar's Alexandrine War. To this end he asked his friend the Khedive, as a personal favour, to furnish him with a plan of the layout of ancient Alexandria. Ismaïl Pacha was naturally delighted to have an opportunity to be of service to so powerful and useful an ally. Fortunately, in 1865 he appointed an extremely competent member of his staff to undertake this research.[6]

Mahmoud Bey held the title 'El-Falaki', literally 'the Astronomer', but this was just a traditional epithet for an official operating in a scientific or technical capacity at an Ottoman court, rather than our modern understanding of this occupation. He was an engineer and cartographer by training, and had been sent in his youth to study in Paris at the École des Arts et Métiers for seven years by Viceroy Mohammed Ali as part of a modernisation programme. The quality of this training is amply attested by the outcome of his investigations: a superbly detailed and accurate chart showing the walls and street plan of ancient Alexandria (see fig. 3.1).

Mahmoud Bey's map also reflects the generous allocation of resources to this project by the Khedive. Several hundred excavations were undertaken across the ruin field by around 200 workers, yielding a great wealth of information about the line of the defensive walls and the spacing and orientation of the street grid. Despite El-Falaki's lack of archaeological training and inability reliably to assess the date of monuments, there is little reason to doubt his version of the city's layout, given his expertise as a cartographer and engineer. Only in cases where he relied on local rumours and traditions is his recording flawed, such as locating the Soma beneath the Nabi Daniel Mosque.

The exact course of the Ptolemaic walls of Alexandria is still disputed, but there are good reasons to believe that Mahmoud Bey's version is not far from the truth. The Astronomer and his team found stone foundations 5m wide running along the shore just east of the Lochias peninsula (point A on his map). He describes them as comprising rubble stones fixed with a mortar of lime and ground brick. After a few hundred metres (point B) these foundations became buried beneath loose rubble to a depth of 3 or 4m. Mahmoud Bey says he spoke to someone who had been involved in the demolition of this section of the wall to provide building material for the expanding city. He traced the foundations beneath the rubble for 2km (point C), where they descended beneath the modern water table. This provides good evidence that they were ancient, since most of Ptolemaic Alexandria is known to have subsided by around 5–6m relative to sea level since its construction (and the sea-level has risen by between 1–1.5m since antiquity). Some of the ancient catacombs have therefore flooded in their lower courses as they have sunk beneath the level of freshwater seepage.[7]

The stone robbers furnished further testimony of similar foundations near a mosque at the end of a tongue of rubble (point D). Unfortunately, in the southern sections of their course the presence of modern houses and their gardens inhibited continuous excavations. Mahmoud Bey resorted to searching for the foundations by seeking their intersections with eight paths running across their general line. In five cases he was successful in locating large tracts of masonry 5m wide (points E to I), but with mortar of a slightly different composition to that in the north-eastern sector. He also noted the presence of extensive ancient building foundations on the north side of these remains at a depth of 3 or 4m, but they were absent on the southern side. From the Serapeum to the port of Eunostos excavation was impossible, but Mahmoud Bey was able to infer the line of the wall from the condition of the soil and the general topography, probably supported by Strabo's description.[8]

Mahmoud Bey supposed the section along the sea front to have taken the form of a quay. Under the guidance of local fishermen, he used a boat on a very calm day to search the seabed from the Lochias peninsula to the Caesareum, and discovered foundations at a depth of 2 to 3m (points a–i, k and l). In the remaining stretch across the isthmus, he based his plan on knowledge of discoveries made during the construction of the foundations of modern houses some years beforehand (points m and n) and upon inspection of the soil.

The key issue in the location of the ancient wall circuit for the siting of the Soma is the extent of the ancient city to the east of the Lochias peninsula, because this has implications for identifying the centre of the Ptolemaic capital. If the eastern walls are supposed to lie further west than Mahmoud Bey's location, then the centre of the ancient city, where Alexander's tomb was situated, would have to be further west than the intersection of R1 with L1. It has been argued that the ancient cemeteries of Hadra and Chatby may lie just outside the Ptolemaic walls, because Roman graveyards had to be dug outside towns. Both places in fact are located just inside the eastern stretch of Mahmoud Bey's walls.

Interestingly, there is a fine fragment of a major Ptolemaic wall about 200m north of the eastern (Rosetta) gateway in the Tulunid walls in the northern section of the modern Shallalat Gardens (fig. 8.4). This has led some to speculate that the early Ptolemaic city may have extended no further east than road R1. Against these considerations there is a strong implication in the testimony of Josephus (1st century AD) that the Jewish quarter, known as 'Delta' and comprising up to a fifth of the entire city, lay entirely to the east of Lochias. Josephus also writes that the Jews were granted a district within Alexandria by Alexander. Tacitus records that the walls of Alexandria were constructed by Ptolemy I Soter, while Ammianus states, 'Alexandria herself, not gradually like other cities, but at her very origin, attained her wide extent'.[9]

Mahmoud Bey's walls agree well with the accounts of the nine ancient writers who give values for the physical size of the city (table 7.1). Excepting Diodorus' value, which probably includes suburbs, there is a good level of agreement for the length of the city at around 30 Alexandrian *stades*, and a breadth of about 10 *stades* at the centre and eight at the extremities. If the city is approximated as a rectangle, then it has a perimeter of about 80 *stades*, but if the sinuosities of the wall are followed, then the circuit increases to about 96 *stades*. Taking into account the fact that the length of the *stade* seems to have varied between about 145m and 185m at different places and times, there is a general consistency between Mahmoud Bey and the ancient authorities.

Pococke observed wall foundations not far from those described by Mahmoud in 1737-8:[10]

The old walls of the city seem to have been built on the height, which extends from Cape Lochias towards the east, the remains of a grand gateway being to be seen in the road to Rosetto at this high ground; and the foundations of the walls may from thence be traced to the canal.

This height seems to be the low ridge a few hundred metres inside Mahmoud Bey's location for the Canopic Gate, so Pococke's observations suggest a marginally shorter east-west dimension for the ancient city.

Judith McKenzie has plausibly argued that the faint grid marked on a map of Alexandria made in 1806 by Henry Salt (fig. 7.6), British Consul-General in Egypt, represented extant traces of Mahmoud Bey's street plan. If so, then this map also supports Pococke's version of the location of the easternmost gateway. In fact it is possible that the line of the eastern walls shifted at some time in the ancient era, so Pococke and Mahmoud Bey could both be correct.[11]

One additional piece of previously unrecognised evidence on the eastern line of the ancient walls has been brought to light in the course of the research for this book. A detailed engraving of a panoramic view of Alexandria from the east was published in 1803 to illustrate an account of the campaign of the British army against Napoleon's expeditionary force in Egypt (fig. 7.7). This is taken from a drawing, probably made at the time of the Battle of Alexandria in 1801, by an artist standing in the vicinity of the

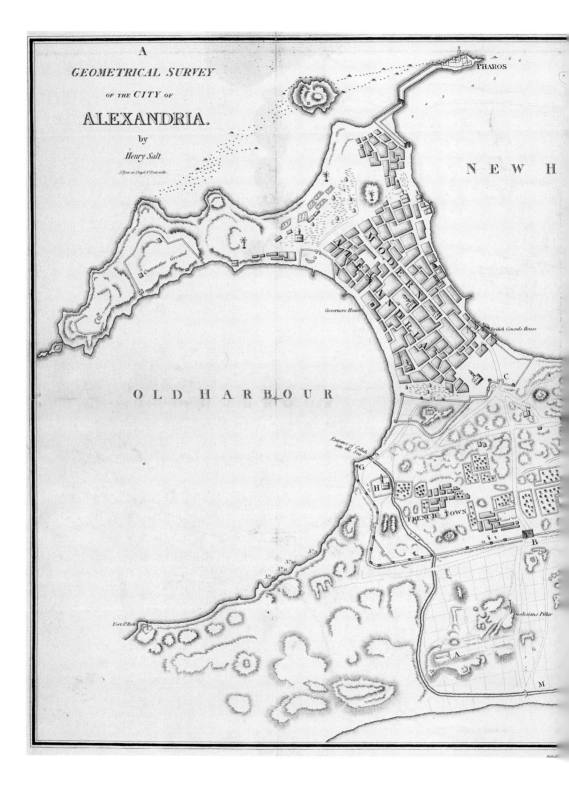

A

GEOMETRICAL SURVEY

OF THE CITY OF

ALEXANDRIA.

by

Henry Salt

PHAROS

N E W H

Quarantine Ground

Governors House

British Consuls House

C

O L D   H A R B O U R

Entrance of Calish into the Sea

G

H

FRENCH TOWN

B

N°3

N°1

N°2

Fort St Rock

Dioclesians Pillar

A

M

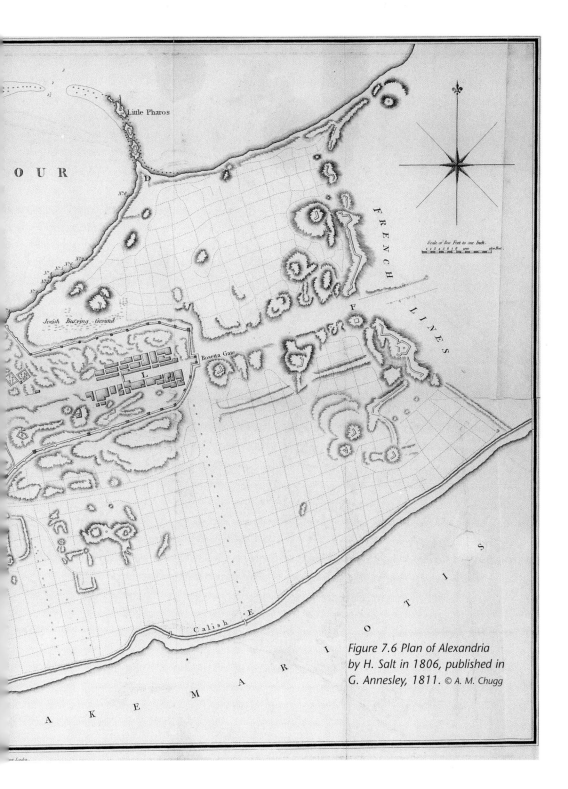

Little Pharos

O U R

D

Nº2

Nº5 Nº6

Jewish Burying Ground

Rosetta Gate

L

F R E N C H   L I N E S

F

Scale of 800 Feet to one Inch.
1 2 3 4 5 6 7 8   1000   1600 Feet.

Calish   E

O   T   I   S

A   K   E   M   A   R

*Figure 7.6 Plan of Alexandria
by H. Salt in 1806, published in
G. Annesley, 1811.* © A. M. Chugg

Figure 7.7 View of the heights fortified by the French to the east of Alexandria in 1801, from T. Walsh and T. Cadell et al, Journal of the Late Campaign in Egypt, *London, 1803.* © A. M. Chugg

compass rose in fig. 7.6 looking west towards the French lines and the city behind them. The ruined walls in the middle distance in the left and centre are located approximately on the line of Mahmoud Bey's eastern wall. Interestingly, these ruins incorporate a large archway in the approximate line of the road to Rosetta, probably an ancient gateway. Perhaps these are also the ruins described by Pococke and he simply wrote a little loosely in describing their relationship with the rising ground immediately behind them.[12]

A final line of argument in Mahmoud Bey's favour is the estimated population figure given by Diodorus in the 1st century BC of '300,000 free

Figure 7.8 Engraving of ancient granite columns along the line of the Canopic Way opposite the Attarine Mosque, from Description de l'Égypte *(Panckoucke edition), Paris, 1821-29, Antiquités Volume V, plate 35.* © A. M. Chugg

citizens', which implies a total approaching half a million, when slaves are included. The population density is uncertain, but what scant evidence there is from archaeology reveals relatively low-density housing (perhaps 200 persons per hectare). This suggests that the populace could barely be accommodated by Mahmoud's city of around 1,000 hectares, let alone a smaller area.[13]

Mahmoud Bey's survey of the ancient street grid was even more extensive than his investigation of the circuit of the defensive walls. He identified the road passing by the Attarine Mosque and through the eastern gate of the Arab city, with the Canopic Way, the main *decumanus* (east–west street) of ancient Alexandria. Six excavations were undertaken to confirm this hypothesis. One in front of the mosque, another 10m west of the gate and the rest spread over half a kilometre east of the gate. Mahmoud Bey discovered paving stones of black or greyish stone, 20cm thick and from 30cm to 50cm in length and width. The paving was well preserved in many places, 14m wide and lay 2.5m to 3m beneath the soil inside the Arab city, and 1.5m deep outside the Tulunid walls. Large pieces of masonry and broken columns were recorded when laying the foundations of houses at the time. These accord with earlier illustrations from Luigi Mayer and Bonaparte's expedition that show a few columns still standing (fig. 7.8, fig. 7.9).[14]

On his plan of the city the Astronomer referenced the Canopic Way as longitudinal street L1. He made further excavations in the lines of three additional *decumani* north of the Canopic Way (L2, L3, L4) and 3 more to the south (L'2, L'3, L'4) at a standard interval of about 278m. He also found superficial traces of two more *decumani* in the southern margins of the city, but marked them with dashed lines to distinguish them as unexcavated. The paving stones of the other *decumani* formed a band 7m wide, where they were sufficiently preserved to be measured.

At right angles to the *decumani*, Mahmoud Bey discovered 12 major *cardines* (transverse roads) at a regular spacing of 330m and traces of five intermediate streets. This interval he calculated probably represented 2 *stades* of 165m. In the Greek measurement system a *stade* comprises 6 *plethrons*, so this estimate also made the standard spacing of the longitudinal avenues equal to almost exactly 10 *plethrons*. The transverse road running from the Lochias peninsula down through the central declivity was double the width of the others, matching the Canopic Way with a breadth of 14m, but split into two carriageways of equal width separated by a metre-wide band of earth. The eastern lane was paved as elsewhere, but the surface of the western lane was composed of lime, earth, small pebbles and bits of rubble stone. A subterranean aqueduct ran parallel on its eastern side, and a sewer ran along its western edge. Mahmoud Bey found very large numbers of columns along this highway, which he labelled as the main *cardo* R1. He also labelled those to the east of it, R2^{bis} to R4^{bis} and those to the west, R2 to R8, the last being the main approach road to the Serapeum temple.

The Salt map is also important for the identification of the main *cardo*, because it seems to give special significance to the line of Mahmoud Bey's street R1 by indicating a distinctive gap in the street grid along a line of probable water cisterns spaced along the course of the subterranean aqueduct running from the *Calish* canal. In this way, Salt supports the idea that R1 was the main north–south road in the Ptolemaic and early Roman periods.

Strabo described the main *cardo* and *decumanus* of Alexandria as intersecting at right angles and being over a *plethron* wide (30m). Although El-Falaki's paving was only half this width, the streets he labelled L1 and R1 were over twice as wide as any other he excavated, so they are very likely to be Strabo's main thoroughfares. In any case, the street surfaces uncovered by Mahmoud Bey were probably Late Roman in date and therefore reflect the situation several centuries after Strabo wrote. They lay at a depth of just 2 or 3m, whereas the oldest levels are often found to lie 7 to 10m below the current surface and close to the water table. Mahmoud Bey observed that the pavings discovered could not have been Ptolemaic, since they were

Figure 7.9 Aquatint of ancient granite columns along the line of the Canopic Way opposite the Attarine Mosque by L. Mayer, Views in Egypt: from the original drawings, in the possession of Sir Robert Ainslie, *London, 1805.*

underlain by at least a metre of older debris. Intriguingly, he also noted that these sub-strata were thicker towards the north-eastern districts, possibly due to destruction by warfare, but the tidal wave of AD 365 might have inflicted similar consequences.[15]

The relatively late date of the street grid excavated by Mahmoud Bey prompts the question of whether the original Ptolemaic layout might have had a different orientation. Crucially, evidence provided by more recent excavations seems to uphold the validity of the grid back to the origins of the metropolis, subject to a few minor deviations. Three sections of the transverse street labelled R4 have been excavated at intervals spread over a kilometre of its length and Adriani has investigated the longitudinal road L2. Although one street pattern on a different alignment has been uncovered, it is confined to part of the palace area. A team of geophysicists has recently shown that the Heptastadion (causeway) was aligned with one of Mahmoud Bey's transverse streets (R9), so his oblique alignment must now be rejected. Nonetheless, Mahmoud emerges in the very latest survey by Judith McKenzie relatively unscathed from the torrent of criticism unleashed upon him by scholars such as Hogarth:[16]

Anyone, however, who attempts to write a topographical memoir on the city will have to appraise, and, I think, condemn in the main, the work of Ismail's Court Astronomer. Mahmud Bey had, it is true, facilities in 1870 which exist no longer in 1895: not only was an autocratic Khedive behind him, but the site was far more open… Mahmud Bey had had, however, no sort of training for the work he was set to do; not only did he not know any classical language, but I am given to understand that this was his first essay in excavation.

This was neither the wisest nor the most accurate judgement Hogarth ever made, for even the date is wrong.

If the broad accuracy of Mahmoud Bey's map is accepted and the extrapolation of the Roman layout back to the Ptolemaic era is considered legitimate, then there are several implications for the location of the Soma. Most obviously, the map precisely locates the central crossroads of ancient Alexandria, which seems to be the site best favoured by the ancient sources. In addition, both the large size of Mahmoud Bey's city and the near coincidence of the crossroads with the later Tulunid eastern gateway will prove significant for the location of Alexander's tomb in later arguments.

The vastness of the area within the circuit of the ancient walls suggests that the Royal Quarter Strabo described as occupying between a quarter and a third of the entire city, must have been enormous. He locates the royal palaces on the Lochias peninsula extending along the front of the Great Harbour as far as Mahmoud's Timonium. Beyond this lay the Caesareum, the Emporium and associated commercial districts. To the east of Lochias, the Royal District was bounded by Delta, the Jewish quarter, implying that Strabo's Royal Quarter must have extended a long way to the south of Lochias, possibly even beyond the Canopic Way. The location of the Soma near the main crossroads may therefore be reconciled with the Royal Quarter defined by Strabo.[17]

The association of the crossroads with the Arab gateway recalls Ibn Abdel Hakim's record of a Mosque of Dulkarnein (Alexander) situated adjacent to the gate of 9th-century Alexandria. It also prompts the question of why Sultan Ahmed Ibn Tulun chose to place the main Arab gateway at this point. Might the preserved adjacent fragment of a Ptolemaic wall mark some prior significance for this spot?[18]

The main rival to Mahmoud Bey's central crossroads as the location of the centre of the ancient city is the intersection of his transverse street R5 with the Canopic Way. This substitution of R5 for R1 as the main transverse highway remains common in published plans even today. Curiously enough, this theory also seems to have its origins in Mahmoud Bey's work, for it was he (more than any other) who transformed a mixture of legend and local gossip into a serious argument that the Soma lay beneath the Nabi Daniel Mosque. This building lies on street R5 not far south of the Canopic

Way and the reasoning runs that, if the Soma lay at the centre of town, then the centre of town must be adjacent to the supposed site of the Soma. This idea has been bolstered by evidence that the centre of Alexandria probably drifted westwards in the Late Roman period. There is no evidential basis for the Nabi Daniel hypothesis capable of withstanding scrutiny, so it remains preferable to pursue the more tangible evidence from Mahmoud Bey's excavations.[19]

The crucial issue of this chapter is the apparent veracity of Mahmoud Bey's location for the central crossroads. Although not quite certain, the intersection of R1 and L1 is supported by a preponderance of tangible evidence. By contrast, the arguments for other intersections, such as R5 and L1, seem insubstantial or circular, though they may reflect the consequences of the contraction of Alexandria into its western districts in the Late Roman period.

Table 7.1. Sources for the dimensions of ancient Alexandria.

Author	Reference	Era	Length	Breadth	Circuit
Diodorus Siculus	17.52	mid-1st century BC	40 stades	—	—
Strabo	17.1.8	25 BC	30 stades	7 or 8 stades	—
Philo	In Flaccum 92	1st half of 1st century AD	—	10 stades	—
Curtius	4.8.2	AD 50	—	—	80 stades
Josephus	The Jewish War 2.16.4	2nd half of 1st century AD	30 stades	10 stades	—
Pliny the Elder	5.11	AD 77	—	—	15 Roman miles
Pseudo-Callisthenes (Julius Valerius)	1.31.10 Alexander Romance (Kroll)	3rd century AD	—	16 stades & 395 feet	—
Stephanus Byzantius	Alexandreia	early 6th century AD	34 stades	8 stades	110 stades
Michael bar Elias	Chronicle*…v, ch.3	late 12th century (3rd century original?)	14987 feet (4.57km or 27.7 Alex stades?)	—	—
Mahmoud Bey	L'Antique Alexandrie	1865	31 Alexandrian stades	10 Alexandrian stades	96 Alexandrian stades

96 Alexandrian stades

Alexandrian stade = 165m

Typical Greek stade = 180m

Roman stade (Pliny) = 148m

Roman mile = 1,480m

*See P. M. Fraser, 'A Syriac Notitia Urbis Alexandrinae', 1951, pp. 103-8.

1 Diodorus, 18.52.6, gives 300,000 free citizens, a total around 500,000 when slaves are added in. For a comprehensive study of the population issue, D. Delia, 1988, 275-92. For issues relating to the decline of Alexandria, Haas, 1997, 45-7.
2 Empereur, 1998, 248, note 2 to ch. 1.
3 Breccia, 1922, 30; M. F. Awad, 1987, 4.
4 M. Bonamy, 1736, 416-31 (and associated map).
5 Mahmoud Bey el-Falaki, *Memoire sur L'Antique Alexandrie*, 1872, 12-28. The general accuracy of Mahmoud Bey's work has been confirmed by more recent archaeology and is analysed in detail by J.-L. Arnaud, 1997, 721-737.
6 Empereur, 1998, 25.
7 F. Goddio, 1998, 58; Fraser, 1972, vol. 2, 18-9, note 32.
8 Strabo, *Geography*, 17.1.
9 Josephus, *Contra Apion*, 2.33, 2.36; Tacitus, *Histories*, 4.83; Ammianus Marcellinus, *Res Gestae*, 22.16.15.
10 Pococke, 1743, I, 3.
11 G. Valentia, 1811, first foldout map; J. McKenzie, 1996, 111-2.
12 T. Walsh, 1803, plate 25.
13 Haas, 1997, 46; Empereur, 1998, 61.
14 Plate 35 in vol. 5 of the *Antiquités* section of the *Description de l'Égypte*, 1821-9 (Panckoucke); engraving by L.-F. Cassas showing standing columns along the Canopic Way in 1784, Empereur, 1998, 46; L. Mayer, 1804, aquatints showing columns near the Attarine Mosque.
15 The interpretation of R1 remains in dispute, but 'the reliability of little Mahmoud's street plan has in general been verified by our excavations', F. Noack, 1900, 215-79.
16 Excavations have discovered remains of R4 at the Rio Cinema, Kom el-Dikka, and at the site of the Diana Theatre, Empereur, 1998, 56-7; Haas, 1997, 30; Rodziewicz, 1995, 227-35; Empereur, 1998, 57; J. McKenzie, 2003, 35-63. Hogarth and Benson, 1895, 17, note 1.
17 Strabo, *Geography*, 17.1.8; Josephus, *Contra Apion*, 2.33, places Delta near the Royal Palaces on a harbourless stretch of the coast.
18 Fraser, 1972, vol. 2, 36-7, note 86, section 1.
19 Botti (on eccentric grounds) placed the crossroads at the intersection of R2 with L'3; Haas, 1997, 2.

8. The Latin Cemeteries and the Shallalat Gardens

Softly sweet, in Lydian measures,
Soon he soothed his soul to pleasures:
War, he sung, is toil and trouble;
Honour, but an empty bubble;
Never ending, still beginning,
Fighting still, and still destroying:
If the world be worth thy winning,
Think, O think it worth enjoying…
Now strike the golden lyre again;
A louder yet, and yet a louder strain.
Break his bands of sleep asunder,
And rouse him, like a rattling peal of thunder
Hark, hark! the horrid sound
Has raised up his head;
As awaked from the dead,
And amazed, he stares around…

John Dryden, *Excerpts from Alexander's Feast*

Sadly, the search for the Soma has acquired a faint aura of disrepute in academic circles, not just on account of the rogues' gallery of fraudsters, charlatans and crackpots who have dabbled in the subject, but also because of the otherwise distinguished scholars who have sacrificed their reputations on the altar of Alexander's tomb. Heinrich Schliemann, the famous excavator of Troy and Mycenae, visited Alexandria in 1888 with the specific objective of finding the tomb. Having declared his infallible

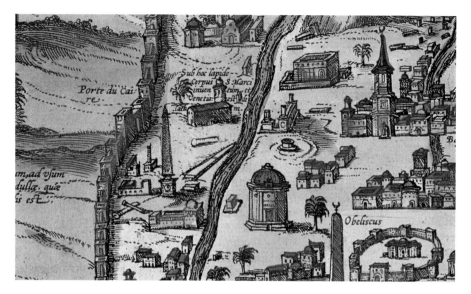

Figure 8.1. Detail of the Braun and Hogenberg map showing the site inside the Cairo (Rosetta) Gate from which the supposed body of St Mark was removed by the Venetians. The Latin reads 'Beneath this stone the corpse of St Mark was discovered and Venice is possessed of it from the rock prison.' © A. M. Chugg

conviction that its remains lay beneath the Nabi Daniel Mosque, his plans to quarry the vicinity were frustrated by the local religious authorities, who refused to grant him permission to dig. In the 20th century the Italian archaeologist Evaristo Breccia, director of the Graeco-Roman Museum in Alexandria between 1904-1932, also embraced the Nabi Daniel theory with equally misplaced enthusiasm:[1]

> *But in any case we may consider it as established that the Sema, and consequently also the Mausoleums of the Ptolemies, were near the Mosque Nabi Danial.*

These eminent archaeologists accepted an old misconception, which caused the Nabi Daniel Mosque to be linked incorrectly with the 16th-century account of the tomb of Alexander by Marmol, who was probably referring to the shrine at the Attarine Mosque. Marmol also mentioned a Church of St Mark in the city, where the body of the saint was supposed to have lain. Although Marmol's own account did not associate the church with the tomb, James Bruce, writing in 1790, mistakenly quoted him as saying that the tomb lay near the church. By the late 19th century the Church of St Mark had been razed, but a new Coptic Church of St Mark had been built about 300m north-west of the Nabi Daniel Mosque.[2]

It was assumed that the new church stood on the foundations of the old, thus linking the 16th-century accounts and the Nabi Daniel Mosque. In fact Braun and Hogenberg's 16th-century map of Alexandria depicts a stone by the Arab east gate of the city, under which the body of St Mark was believed to have been discovered, and there is a church-like building drawn beside the spot (fig. 8.1). Especially since both the map legend and Marmol mention the Venetians, who kidnapped St Mark's supposed remains in AD 828, it seems probable that it was this building beside the east gate that Marmol was describing. It is unlikely that the stolen mummified corpse was really that of St Mark, since the evangelist had died whilst the Christians were still a very minor sect, and several early Christian sources indicate that Mark's body was burnt. Perhaps the Late Roman Church recognised another mummy as that of St Mark for want of the original.[3]

Other more or less dubious theories concerning the location of the Soma abound. One of the most blatant forgeries was perpetrated by M. Joannides in 1893, who, after discovering a Ptolemaic necropolis at Chatby, east of the Lochias peninsula, reported in the *Egyptian Gazette* of 20 June 1893:[4]

Mr Joannides asserts that he has discovered the tombs of Alexander the Great and of Cleopatra. The former is at a depth of 16 metres from the surface and the latter is at a depth of 12 metres. He says the doors of the tombs are of bronze on which there are inscriptions in Greek and that the name of the occupant of the tomb is sculptured over the doorway. The bronze is eaten through in parts and with the aid of magnesium light, Mr. Joannides says that he was able to distinguish marble sarcophagi that had feet like lions' feet. He also says that he saw something like parchments or skins in these vaults. This is only part of what Mr. Joannides asserts to be in the vaults in question for it appears he found much jewellery and some beautiful Greek vases. This differs very much from the statements of the Conservator of the Alexandria Museum but we feel it our duty to our readers to place before them the statement of the original discoverer of these antiquities. In due time we shall know the real truth of the affair.

In recent years the most famous graduate of the eccentric school of tomb-hunters was the dauntless Stelios Komoutsos, a waiter in L'Élite café-bar in Alexandria, who used to fritter away his carefully hoarded tips in financing a long series of ineffectual and frequently unauthorised excavations across the city. On at least two occasions he identified locations that were underwater in antiquity and the official dossier kept by the Egyptian authorities contains 322 permit applications and excavation reports dating from 1956, when he commenced his endeavours.[5]

Komoutsos was also the proud owner of the so-called '*Alexander Book*'. This relic depicts various temple buildings in a Greek style, lining a highway and plastered with crude Greek legends enlivened by the odd Coptic character and the evocative names 'Alexander' and 'King Ptolemy'. P. M. Fraser, a well-known expert on ancient Alexandria, was shown this book by Komoutsos in June 1961 and immediately recognised that the legends were mainly poor quality reproductions of two genuine inscriptions in the Graeco-Roman Museum. Another poor quality stone forgery of one of these inscriptions was known to exist. Fraser also discovered that the two inscriptions had been acquired by the museum in 1912, having been found close to the village of Abu el-Matamir on the western edge of the Nile

Delta. From this he reasoned that the forgeries had been made in a workshop in the village in about 1912, although he was convinced that Komoutsos had no knowledge of these forgeries. Indeed, he writes that he felt too sorry for the waiter to deprive him of his fantasies. Komoutsos died in 1991, but he is still fondly remembered in Alexandria as one of the city's most colourful characters.[6]

Komoutsos' torch was kept alight in the 1990s by the boisterous Liana Souvaltzi, who began a series of widely publicised excavations at the Siwa Oasis in 1989. The object of her enthusiasm was a reputed tomb of Alexander at a small Doric Greek temple of Ptolemaic date in a place called El-Maraqi Bilad el-Rum. The structure was described when intact by Frederic Cailliaud (1822-4), Heinrich Minutoli (1826) and Gerhard Rohlfs (1869). Its interior has an unusual plan, comprising five chambers in a row. The Egyptian authorities ordered the suspension of the excavations in October 1996 for lack of tangible proof of Souvaltzi's claims.[7]

Experts are understandably dismissive of her conclusions, but it is important to be clear why her claims seem dubious: mainly because the best dating evidence for the temple suggests it was constructed at least a century after Alexander's death, when his body certainly lay at Alexandria, and the inscriptions discovered at the site provide evidence that the structure was dedicated to the goddess Isis. Claims that other inscriptions found there refer to the poisoning theory of Alexander's death appear to be incorrect. Also, the 'rays' sculpted on to stone fragments, identified by Souvaltzi as parts of a Macedonian star symbol, were misaligned with one another. Moreover, anecdotal evidence gleaned from the local people by the excavator, and the use of star designs in their clothing, are hardly reliable indications for a tomb of Alexander. It is only to be expected that Alexander's visit, and the ensuing three centuries of Ptolemaic rule, should have left some traces at the oasis and in the traditions of its inhabitants.[8]

Given the mass of contrary evidence, it is virtually impossible that Alexander was originally buried at Siwa. When the ancient writers speak of

Alexander's corpse being transported to Ammon, they do not necessarily mean the Siwa oasis. All too often it is overlooked that there were shrines to this god in virtually all the cities of Ptolemaic Egypt. There is, of course, evidence for a Ptolemaic temple dedicated to Ammon at Memphis, which was still the capital when Ptolemy I Soter brought Alexander's body there, and the main cult centre was always located at Thebes. Having gone to so much trouble to secure the corpse of the king, it is unlikely that Ptolemy would have considered sending it to a remote oasis, separated from civilisation by hundreds of kilometres of blistering desert.[9]

Nonetheless, the relocation of Alexander's body to Siwa by pagans in the 4th or 5th century AD is possible. Conceivably, Alexander's remaining worshippers may have sought to protect his remains from the ravages of Christian fanaticism, although this is pure speculation. There are many places to which the corpse may plausibly have been sent: to Palmyra by Zenobia; or to Augila, where Procopius mentions the continuing worship of Alexander in the 6th century AD; Thebes, the centre of Ammon's cult; Ethiopia, a traditional haven for Egyptian exiles; Macedon, Alexander's homeland; or to Rome, the imperial capital – the list could be extended indefinitely. In the absence of any record of its removal, or of any evidence of its presence elsewhere, it is reasonable to conclude that Alexander's body probably remained at Alexandria at that time.

Perhaps the only serious candidate for a tomb of Alexander to emerge in the 20th century is the 'Alabaster Tomb' situated in the Terra Santa section of the Latin Cemeteries around 600m north-east of the central crossroads of ancient Alexandria (fig. 8.2). This tomb was first published by Breccia in 1907, and identified as the antechamber of a possible tomb of Alexander by Achille Adriani, who succeeded Breccia as the director of the Graeco-Roman Museum before the Second World War. The structure is constructed from monumental blocks of rosy alabaster, cut perfectly flat on their interior faces, revealing the beautiful natural veining of the stone. In contrast, the external faces are roughly cut, suggestive of an earth covering,

Figure 8.2. The Alabaster Tomb in the Terra Santa Cemetery, an antechamber of an early Ptolemaic tumulus tomb, and thought by some to be the tomb of Alexander.
© Archives CEAlex/CNRS

in the tradition of a Macedonian tumulus tomb. The simple moulding over the surviving entranceway has parallels in other Ptolemaic period tombs (such as the Moustafa Pacha Tomb 2), providing firm evidence for a Ptolemaic date. Adriani has also argued that the relative proximity of its site to the central crossroads of ancient Alexandria is consistent with the central location of the Soma suggested by ancient writers.[10]

In support of Adriani's hypothesis it should be observed that the royal tombs at Vergina in Macedonia (including that of Alexander's father) were also made of stone chambers covered by large mounds of earth. The Alabaster Tomb is undeniably part of a monument of the very highest quality and magnificence. Nevertheless, there is no specific evidence to link it with Alexander and there were other individuals who died within its date range and who were of a sufficient status to merit such a fine sepulchre: for instance, members of the royal family and certain top officials and generals. Adriani is undoubtedly correct in emphasising the significance of the central crossroads located by Mahmoud Bey, but the Alabaster Tomb is not significantly close to them.

Supposing that the Alabaster Tomb was part of a tomb of Alexander, then it is more likely to have been the first Alexandrian tomb constructed by Ptolemy II Philadelphus, rather than the Soma mausoleum built by Ptolemy IV Philopator. Macedonian influence in tomb design was probably more pronounced under the earlier Ptolemies, and an earth tumulus fits ill with Lucan's description of the Soma as an imposing mausoleum surmounted by a pyramid. If the first Alexandrian tomb was a Macedonian-style tumulus (and the existence of the Alabaster Tomb bolsters this idea), then the Paneum, described by Strabo as a large, conical, artificial hill near the middle of the city, could be an equally good candidate. The tumulus over the Alabaster Tomb was possibly the Paneum, but it is more likely that this lay further west.[11]

Late in 2002, at the invitation of Professor Fakharany of Alexandria University, the Centre d'Études Alexandrines (CEA) began an excavation in the Latin Cemeteries next to the Alabaster Tomb (Terra Santa no. 2). The site is currently a plant nursery and belongs to the Governorate and the Faculty of Agriculture. The CEA followed up the research of a team of German geophysicists, whose investigations detected anomalies in the subsoil hinting at the existence of cavities in the bedrock some 6m to 10m down. The CEA opened three trenches in order to locate and access these underground chambers, but there has been no news as yet of any significant discoveries at the site.

Any book about the Soma would be incomplete should it fail to propose a new theory concerning the building's location. Of course the ambiguous evidence means there is a risk of any new ideas proving as dubious as their predecessors, although the following hypothesis is rooted firmly in a fertile and diverse mix of the best evidence currently available.[12]

The accounts of Strabo and Diodorus describe the Soma as a walled enclosure or *temenos*, and Achilles Tatius and Zenobius locate it in the middle of the city, probably straddling or adjacent to the central crossroads. If Mahmoud Bey is correct in placing this crossroads at the closest approach of the Canopic Way to the Lochias peninsula, then the Soma enclosure may well have been contiguous with the royal palaces. This is consistent with Strabo's description of the Soma being part of an expansive Royal Quarter. What would this enclosure have looked like and how large was it? Diodorus, who certainly saw it, says it was 'worthy of the glory of Alexander in size and construction', so he must have considered it immense. It is possible to gain some idea of its architectural form by considering some *temenos* structures in other cities, especially those which may have inspired Alexander, the early Ptolemies and their architects.[13]

The Mausoleum of Halicarnassus stood in a walled enclosure measuring 240m x 100m, and reconstructions suggest its walls were at least 5m high (fig. 3.5). Halicarnassus was besieged by Alexander for several months in 333 BC and formed part of the Ptolemaic Empire in the 3rd century BC. There are some striking parallels with Alexandria. Not only did the Mausoleum lie at the centre of this city, but the royal palace was located on a promontory next to the harbour, rather like a smaller version of the Lochias peninsula. It seems unlikely that the Soma enclosure was smaller than that of the Mausoleum, since it was built for a far more important king in a much larger city.[14]

The layout of Memphis would naturally have been a more immediate influence upon Alexandria's architects and their patrons. It was dominated by two gigantic, quadrilateral temple enclosures, both nearly half a kilometre square. They had roads running straight through them, entering and exiting via gates in opposite walls. One was situated in the middle of the southern half of the city (fig. 8.3) and the other lay correspondingly in the middle of the northern districts. If the builders of the Soma drew any inspiration from the sacred precincts at Memphis, then the Alexandrian enclosure may well have measured hundreds of metres square.[15]

The notion that the Soma enclosure may have been extensive is interesting because it could help to make sense of inconsistencies in the evidence for ancient Alexandria. Achilles Tatius gives a rather curious description of walking westwards down the Canopic Way through an 'open' part of the city, then entering into a 'second city', named after Alexander, where he sees the central crossroads lined with magnificent colonnades. If the Soma enclosure was extensive and straddled the central crossroads, then this makes sense, because the second city could be the Soma enclosure. Perhaps it was the walls of the Soma enclosure, rather than the defences of the city, that Caesar did not stop to admire on his way to visit Alexander's tomb in Lucan's *Pharsalia*.[16]

Achilles Tatius may be corroborated by an intriguing testimony some 600 years later of a passage by the Arab writer Suyuti (or Sujuti), apparently quoting the 9th-century Arab, Ibn Abdel Hakim. This has long puzzled historians of Alexandria:[17]

Alexandria consists of three towns, one beside the other, each surrounded by its own wall. All three are enclosed by an outer, fortified wall.

Perhaps there is a way of understanding this enigmatic report if the Soma enclosure was a first town, the Bruchion a second (albeit largely razed) and the rest of the city the third town, roughly within the remaining area enclosed by the Tulunid walls.

This hypothesis seems to identify the Soma enclosure, and perhaps its immediate vicinity, with the Alpha quarter named after Alexander, and

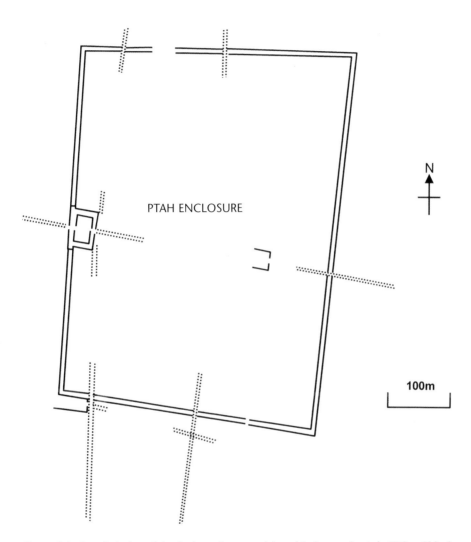

Figure 8.3. Detailed plan of the Ptah enclosure at Memphis (approximately 550 x 400m), dating from the New Kingdom, based on a plan by Dr D. G. Jeffreys, The Survey of Memphis, *reproduced courtesy of the* Egypt Exploration Society, London 1985, Fig. 63.

mentioned by the *Alexander Romance*. The obvious objection would be Strabo's inclusion of the Soma in the Royal Quarter, although he does not mention the division of the city into five quarters and, as a foreigner, he may be partitioning it according to logic rather than tradition. The official Royal Quarter (Beta) may not have extended much beyond the area Strabo calls the 'inner palaces', which apparently corresponded with the Bruchion in the Roman era.[18]

Figure 8.4. A ptolemaic wall fragment with medieval additions, 200m north of the site of the Rosetta Gate in the Shallalat Gardens. © *Archives CEAlex/CNRS*

An intriguing piece of evidence is a substantial fragment of a Ptolemaic wall of superlative quality 200m north of the site of the eastern (Rosetta) gateway of the Arab city in the modern Shallalat Gardens (fig. 8.4), less than 100m east of where Mahmoud Bey located the central crossroads. It is difficult to associate this fragment with the defensive walls of Alexandria, since it is located near the centre of the ancient city. The magnificence of its masonry, and its location beside the city's main north–south thoroughfare, must make it the boundary of a very high status area of the metropolis. Perhaps the possibility should be considered that it is the last remaining portion of the enclosure wall of the Soma.[19]

The last ruins of the rest of the Tulunid wall circuit were destroyed around 100 years ago. Fortunately, these walls and their massive towers were recorded magnificently in the *Description de l'Égypte* by Napoleon's coterie of savants (fig. 8.5). Their map of the city (fig.7.3) clearly indicates a double wall circuit for most of its extent, preserved especially well in the eastern sectors. There are good reasons to believe that the circuits were not contemporary constructions and that the outer wall may be Late Roman or earlier in parts. In the Late Roman period the population may have shrunk to the point where some reduction in the wall perimeter would have been a natural development. Interestingly, both the style and type of stone used for the surviving fragment in the Shallalat Gardens appear to be Ptolemaic, though this is also a vestige of the outer wall of the Arab city.[20]

Some illustrations of the walls in the *Description de l'Égypte* depict stonework, of an apparently ancient character, rather than of an Arab date. An engraving of an ancient portal in the Rosetta Gate (the Arab East Gate), drawn by Luigi Mayer in the late 18th century (fig. 8.8), depicts a statue niche adjacent to the gateway. This suggests a date before the Arab conquest due to the Islamic prohibition of graven images, and stylistically it is Late Roman or earlier. An exterior view of the Rosetta Gate from a drawing made by Louis-François Cassas in 1785 is shown in figure 8.7.[21]

In the Napoleonic map (fig. 7.4), a curious zigzag is marked in the course of the outer wall precisely where Mahmoud Bey's ancient street R3 would have cut this wall on the northern side. Given this coincidence, this zigzag may indicate a gateway in the outer wall, but it is not echoed by the inner wall. Pococke, who paced around the walls in 1737, made some pertinent observations:[22]

> *The outer walls around the old city are very beautifully built of hewn stone, and seem to be antient [sic]; all the arches being true, and the workmanship very good… The inner walls of the old city, which seem to be of the middle ages, are much stronger and higher than the others and defended by large high towers.*

The map by Cassas (fig. 8.6) also states that the inner and outer walls were built in different eras.

In 1895 Hogarth observed that the defensive ditch associated with the Tulunid walls running beside Mahmoud Bey's street L2 in their eastern sector had 'been cut to a depth of about 15 feet', and showed 'no indications of having pierced large buildings'. This indicates that the line of the Tulunid walls in this sector may be far older than the Arab period, since it is certain that the ancient city existed on both sides of these walls.[23]

It may also be relevant that Mahmoud Bey shows the southern and eastern sectors of the Tulunid walls coinciding with the ancient street grid to a notable degree (fig. 3.1). In fact, the whole eastern section of these walls from Mahmoud Bey's street R1, west to R3, encloses an area about 800m x 600m on three sides, and the Late Roman (and subsequently the Arab) walls possibly incorporated the remnants of the *temenos* of the Soma at this point.

Figure 8.5 View of walls and interiors of towers in the Tulunid defenses (built in the second half of the 9th century AD) from the Description de l'Égypte *(Panckoucke edition), Paris, 1821–29, État Moderne Volume II, plates 89 and 90. © A. M. Chugg*

MER MÉDITERRANÉE

le Pharillon

le Phare

le Château

Mouillages des Vaisseaux Francs

Poivre

Cometiere

Chemin Mosquée

Mouillage des Caravelles

Port vieux

Cimetere Mosquée

Ruines d'un Temple de Serapis

Aqueduc

Mosquée des mille et une Colonne

Citernes

Jardins

Jardins de Palmiers

Ruines d'anciens Tombeaux

Khachabe (ou Colonne d'Al

Bains de Ptine

Catacombes

Chemin des Karavanes de Dernèh

ou mou ou Colonne d

ou Canal d'Al

Birket Maryouth
Lac Mareotis

Levé par L. F. Cassas.

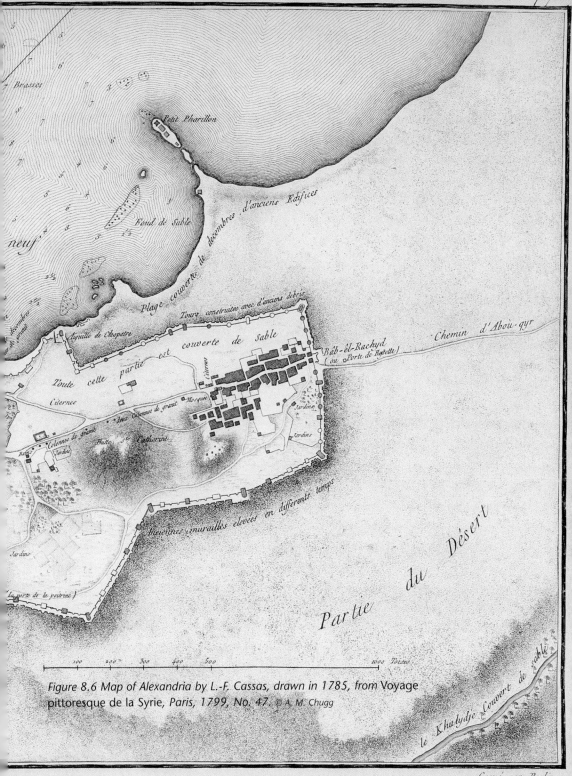

Figure 8.6 Map of Alexandria by L.-F. Cassas, drawn in 1785, from Voyage
pittoresque de la Syrie, Paris, 1799, No. 47. © A. M. Chugg

A 'New Plan of Ancient Alexandria' with the Soma shown in this location is given in fig. 8.9. Little excavation has been undertaken within the proposed area of the Soma enclosure, but Hogarth found traces of 'a massive structure' just north of Canopic Way near its intersection with the transverse street labelled R2. Mahmoud Bey also offered a tantalising description of finds in this vicinity in the early to mid-19th century:[24]

In fact, the excavations which were made by Gallis Bey (and those which were executed later) discovered some enormous foundation walls on Canopic Way on the west side between the two transverse streets R1 and R2 together with a great number of fallen columns. Beside Canopic Way and R1 we ourselves have discovered several of them beneath the rubble: one can still today see some overthrown in the area around the first bastion. The extent of these monumental foundations is greater than 150 metres on each side. In conclusion, everything on this site shows us that this was the finest monument in the city of Alexandria…

Records of almost all ancient Alexandrian portrait-sculptures of Alexander only state that they were found somewhere within the general vicinity of the ancient city. Only one example has an exact provenance: it was found at the intersection of Mahmoud's streets L1 and R2, near the centre of the proposed Soma enclosure.[25]

Despite sporadic excavations throughout the 20th century at numerous sites within the walls of the ancient city, the exact locations of most of the major buildings of Ptolemaic Alexandria are still unclear. In particular, the 'centre' of the city either side of the Canopic Way is said to have contained the Gymnasium, tribunal (*dicasterion*), groves, and the artificial mound of the Paneum as well as the Soma. These monuments remain largely a mystery: although around 140 investigations have focussed on discovering Alexander's tomb, no identifiable trace has been found.

In the 1990s the most spectacular archaeological investigations were

Figure 8.7 Exterior view of the Rosetta Gate by L.-F. Cassas, drawn in 1785, from
Voyage pittoresque de la Syrie, *de la Phoenicie, de la Palestine, et de la Basse-Égypte,*
Paris, 1799. © A. M. Chugg

performed by divers in the Great Harbour. In the sea around the base of the
Qait Bey fortress, known to have been built on the site of the Pharos
lighthouse, a team led by Jean–Yves Empereur discovered nearly 3,000 large
blocks of ancient masonry and some statuary, including column fragments,
obelisks and 26 sphinxes. Hieroglyphic inscriptions show that much of this
material was probably transported to Alexandria from Heliopolis to
decorate the Ptolemaic city. Most of this stonework may have been
deposited across part of the harbour entrance by the Mameluke rulers in an

Overleaf: figure 8.8 Aquatint depicting an ancient portal of pink granite in the Rosetta
Gate drawn in the late 18th century by L. Mayer, Views in Egypt: from the original
drawings, in the possession of Sir Robert Ainslie, *London, 1805.*

attempt to make the city more readily defensible after a major raid in 1365 by the King of Cyprus, Pierre de Lusignan. It is possible that a few pieces might be from the Pharos itself, cast into the sea as the tower disintegrated during one of the medieval earthquakes. When this debris was observed in 1980 by a team of Italian film-makers, they considered it so impressive that they published an article suggesting that Alexander's tomb had lain at the foot of the Pharos.

On the landward side of the harbour an area of submerged coastline in the vicinity of the ancient Royal Quarter has been investigated with similar success. A team led by Franck Goddio mapped in great detail the sunken foundations of the ancient quays, previously glimpsed by Mahmoud Bey. In 1998 the wreck of a ship was found nearby with artefacts including rigging, ceramics, remains of food, shards of glass and jewellery. Radiocarbon analysis of wood samples dates the ship to between 90 BC and AD 130. Further ancient wrecks have been discovered in the approaches to the harbour, but none of these discoveries has so far cast any light on the Soma problem.[26]

In the city itself archaeology mainly proceeds as built-up sites become available between demolition and redevelopment. This is a slow and erratic means of rediscovering the past, but much good work has been achieved. The archaeological institutes are so pressed for funding that they are sometimes unable to exploit all of these occasional opportunities. Much effort has concentrated on particular districts in the hope of eventually building up a reasonably complete picture of parts of the city. Relatively little attention has been paid to the areas immediately west of the Shallalat Gardens, which appear from the analysis presented here to be most relevant for the discovery of Alexander's tomb. Another of the virtues of the new theory is that it clarifies why 140 previous efforts have proven fruitless.

If Alexandria's well documented Arab walls were built on the same line as the Late Roman circuit, and this had incorporated the *temenos* of the Soma in its eastern sector, then this provides a fixed framework for interpreting the layout of the ancient city. The final irony of this convoluted story is that, in seeking an answer to the mystery of the Soma by investigating the plan of ancient Alexandria, we find that the location of the Soma enclosure may instead prove to be the key to understanding the rest of the city.

A few pages before his famous description of the *peribolos* (walled enclosure) of the Soma, Strabo refers to the foundation of Alexandria by Alexander: [27]

> *When the architects were marking the lines of the* peribolos *with white earth* [chalk?], *the supply gave out; and when the King arrived, his stewards furnished a part of the barley-meal which had been prepared for the workmen, and by means of this the streets also, to a larger number than before, were laid out.*

If, as suggested, the *peribolos* of the Soma was of such a size meriting its description by Achilles Tatius as a second city, then the two walled enclosures mentioned by Strabo were possibly the same. In proposing a location for Alexander's tomb, the plan of Alexander's original city early in 331 BC may also have been revealed.

Figure 8.9 Map of Alexandria in the Graeco-Roman period showing the location of the Soma and combining details from several ancient maps.

© A. M. Chugg

1. Antonine Gate of the Moon
2. Mosque of a Thousand Columns
3. Kibotos Harbour
4. Medieval walls
5. Pompey's Pillar
6. Stadium
7. Serapeum
8. Subterranean aquaduct
9. Attarine Mosque
10. Nabi Daniel Mosque
11. Gymnasium?
12. Church of St Mark?
13. Rosetta Gate
14. Extant ancient wall fragment
15. Alabaster Tomb
16. Canopic Gate
17. Antonine Gate of the Sun
18. Cleopatra's Needles
19. Caesareum
20. Library?

PHAROS LIGHTHOUSE

PHAROS ISLAND

HEPTASTADION

EUNOSTOS HARBOUR

NECROPOLIS

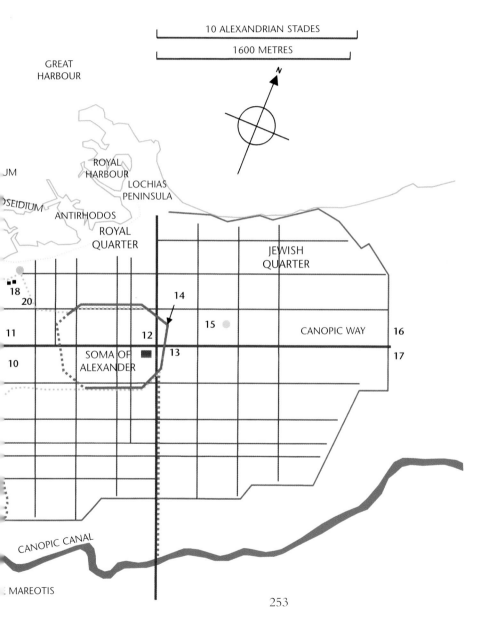

MEDITERRANEAN

GREAT
HARBOUR

10 ALEXANDRIAN STADES

1600 METRES

N

ROYAL
HARBOUR

JM

LOCHIAS
PENINSULA

OSEIDIUM

ANTIRHODOS

ROYAL
QUARTER

JEWISH
QUARTER

18
20

14

11

15

CANOPIC WAY

16

12

SOMA OF
ALEXANDER

13

17

10

CANOPIC CANAL

MAREOTIS

1   Fraser, 1972, vol. I, 16, 'The actual location of the "tomb of Alexander" has been much debated, but… the unending search for it, rather than for the Mausoleum of the Ptolemies, must be regarded as misdirected and pointless. Nevertheless a brief account of the mixture of legend and surmise is necessary…' L. Deuel, 1977; Breccia, 1922, 99.

2   Bruce, 1790, 13,' Marmol… says he saw it [Alexander's tomb] in the year 1546. It was, according to him, a small house in form of a chapel, in the middle of the city, near the church of St. Mark, and was called Escander.' For a clear explanation of this confusing issue, P. Fraser, 1972, vol. 2, note 86.

3   G. Wilkinson, 1851, 258-63. See *Patrologia Graeca*, 86, col. 59, note, which cites Dorotheus of Tyre's *Synopsis of the Apostles*; Chronicon Paschale, 252, in *Patrologia Graeca* 92, cols. 608-609; Eutychius 336 in *Patrologia Graeca* 111, col. 983.

4   Fraser, 1962, 1, note 2.

5   Empereur, 1998, 148.

6   Fraser, 1962, 244-5.

7   R. S. Bianchi, 1993, 54-5.

8   T. Spawforth, 1996.

9   C. Préaux, 1939, 299; A. Deleage, 1934, 85.

10 Breccia, 1907, 7; N. Bonacasa, 1991, 5-19.

11 Ammianus Marcellinus, *Res Gestae*, 22.11.7; Zenobius, *Proverbia*, 3.94, describes the construction of a memorial house, which does not sound at all like a description of a tumulus tomb. Strabo, *Geography*, 17.1.10.

12 For a detailed account of this hypothesis, Chugg, (2002) [2003], 75-108.

13 Diodorus Siculus, 18.28.

14 K. Jeppesen, 1992, 61 and plate 21.

15 D. Jeffreys, 1985, fig. 63.

16 Achilles Tatius, *Clitiphon and Leucippe*, 5.1; Lucan, *Pharsalia*, 10.14-20.

17 Butler, [1902] 1978, 370; Breccia, 1922, 70.

18 Stoneman, 1991, 65.

19 Identified as Hellenistic (Ptolemaic) by Empereur, 1998, 51-3.

20 Galice Bey undertook a massive program of reconstruction of the medieval wall circuit in 1826 at the behest of the Viceroy Mohammed Ali, so later maps differ in many details from that in the *Description de l'Égypte*.

21 The pink coloration is original and probably indicates the polished pink granite, which was widely used in the public architecture of ancient Alexandria. Fragments of another ancient portico in pink granite are on display at Pompey's Pillar (site of the Serapeum) in modern Alexandria. For a discussion of graven images in early Islamic frescoes, mosaics and sculpture, M. W. Merrony, 2004, 36-9.

22 Pococke, 1743, I, 3-4; Cassas, 1799, plate 47, plan of Alexandria.

23 Hogarth, 1895, 8 and 13.

24 Hogarth, 1895, 8. This is probably Galice Bey during his reconstruction of the Tulunid defences in 1826; Empereur, 1998, 50; Mahmoud Bey, 1872, 56-7.
25 B. Tkaczow, 1993, 193, Item 19.
26 Franck Goddio et alii, 1998, 1-53.
27 Strabo, Geography, 17.1.6.

9.   A Candidate for the Corpse

Hamlet: *To what base use we may return, Horatio! Why may not imagination trace the noble dust of Alexander, till he find it stopping a bung-hole?*

Horatio: *'Twere to consider too curiously, to consider so.*

Hamlet: *No, faith, not a jot; but to follow him thither with modesty enough, and likelihood to lead it: as thus; Alexander died, Alexander was buried, Alexander returneth into dust; the dust is earth; of earth we make loam; and why of that loam, whereto he was converted, might they not stop a beer-barrel?*

William Shakespeare, *Hamlet*, Act V, Scene I

The ultimate question in this enigma must be the fate of Alexander's actual body. The evidence suggests that we should be especially interested in any ancient mummified corpses that appeared within the immediate vicinity of Mahmoud Bey's central crossroads of Alexandria at the end of the 4th century AD. These seem like stringent criteria, yet there exists a unique set of human remains, which appears to satisfy them.

According to various Christian sources, the earliest of them being Clement of Alexandria in about AD 200, the Church in Alexandria was founded by St Mark the Evangelist in the mid-first century AD.[1] In the Late Roman period a church and tomb of St Mark became one of the key religious sites in the city.[2] The oldest reliable historical reference is found in the *Lausiac History* of Palladius, who wrote in the early 5th century AD of a pilgrimage 'to the Martyrion of Mark at Alexandria', which took place at the end of the 4th century.[3] Although the second half of a *Passio of St Peter* claims to describe a tomb of St Mark in Alexandria in AD 311, William Telfer has shown that this part of the manuscript was the invention of a 6th century hagiographer, who seems to have been inspired by the most influential Christian account of the Evangelist's career, the *Acts of St Mark*.[4] This is an apocryphal account of the martyrdom and entombment of the saint, which may well have been composed in Alexandria in the late 4th century. According to the *Acts*, the pagans attempted to burn St Mark's body, but a miraculous storm intervened and doused the flames, allowing the Christians to snatch back the corpse and convey it to their church beside the sea in a district of Alexandria called Boukolia. The oldest versions of the *Acts* mention that the Christians subsequently entombed the body in an eminent location in the east of the city. Although later writers have often assumed that the location of St Mark's tomb (and the associated Late Roman Church of St Mark) was at the site of the church in Boukolia, the *Acts* did not explicitly state this.[5] An alternative Christian tradition in Dorotheus, Eutychius and the *Chronicon Paschale* states that St Mark's body was actually burnt. Dorotheus observes:

> *It is said that the Apostle St Mark was led from the place called Boukolou to that referred to by the name of Angelion and he was burnt there.*[6]

So it may be wondered whether the miracle in the *Acts* was contrived at the end of the 4th century to explain a newly fabricated tomb of the saint.

The most remarkable event in the history of the Church of St Mark transpired in AD 828: the abduction of the saint's remains by the Venetians. A pair of Venetian merchant captains, Buono of Malamocco and Rustico of Torcello, sailed their vessels into the port of Alexandria, where they visited the Church of St Mark the Evangelist. The Alexandrian clergy were at that time concerned for the safety of their most sacred relics, especially the saint's corpse, owing to the antagonistic rule of their Islamic governors. Some accounts suggest that the Arabs were appropriating rich stones from the church to construct a palace. The Venetians persuaded (or bribed) the guardians of the remains to allow them to be taken away. Next, the shroud was slit up the back and the corpse of St Claudian (close at hand) was substituted for that of St Mark in order to conceal the theft. The Evangelist's remains were then carried down to the waiting ships in a large basket. However, the aroma of the embalming spices was so overpowering that it ran the risk of arousing the suspicions of the local authorities; but an inspection by port officials was foiled by covering the remains with pork (anathema to Moslems). The inspectors fled with cries of 'Kanzir! Kanzir!' (pig). The body was then wrapped in canvas and hoisted up to the yard-arm. It is alleged that a visitation from St Mark's ghost subsequently saved the ship from some peril (a reef or storm) in the course of the journey back to Venice.[7]

This story is preserved in a set of mosaics in the Basilica of St Mark in Venice (fig. 9.1) dated by Gardner Wilkinson to the 11th century on the grounds that they are an original feature, but they may date to the 12th century.[8] The mosaics cover the interior of the arch between the presbytery and the Chapel of St Clement. This tale has also been related by several early Venetian chroniclers, such as Martino da Canale in *La Cronique des Véniciens* (1275), who asserts that the aroma of the corpse was so strong that, 'If all the spices of the world had been gathered together in Alexandria, they could not have so perfumed the city.' P. Daru adds that the corpse was sealed in linen.[9]

The evidence of special interest for our story is the short legend in the Braun and Hogenberg map of Alexandria, which identifies the location of a stone just inside the Cairo Gate (later known as the Rosetta Gate) of Alexandria beneath which the Venetians are stated to have discovered St Mark's body (fig. 8.1).[10]

There is a reference to the Church of St Mark lying close by a gate on the eastern side of the city in the *Chronicle of John of Nikiu* (c. AD 670) in AD 609:

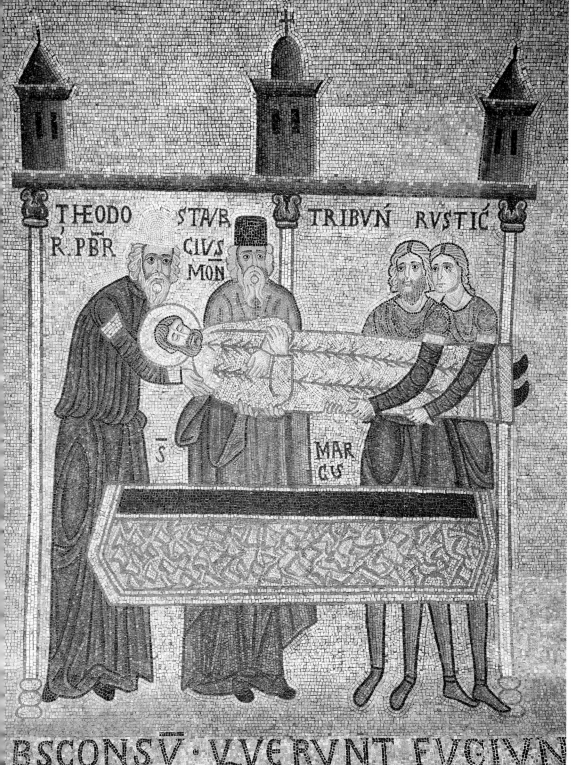

THEODO
R. PBR
STAVR
CIVS
MON
TRIBVN   RVSTIC

S

MAR
CVS

BSCONSV · VLVERVNT FVGIVN

And Nicetas opened the second gate, which was close to the church of St Mark the Evangelist, and he issued forth with his barbarian auxiliaries, and they went in pursuit of the fleeing troops and put some of them to the sword…[11]

The association of St Mark with a gateway of Alexandria at this time is also supported by a 7th-century ivory from the city, depicting the Evangelist enthroned before a monumental gateway and surrounded by his successors as patriarch (fig. 9.2).

There survives an account of a pilgrimage to Alexandria by Arculfus around AD 680, which also seems to locate the Church of St Mark just inside this gate:

Item de parte Aegipti aduentantibus et urbem intrantibus Alexandrinam (alexandriam) ab aquilonali [propinquo] latere occurrit grandis ecclesia structurae, in qua Marcus euangelista in terra humatus iacet; cuius sepulchrum ante altare in orientali eiusdem quadrangulae loco ecclesiae memoria superposita marmoreis lapidibus constructa monstratur.[12]

Approaching from the direction of Egypt as one enters the city of Alexandria on (almost) the north side a large church presents itself, in which Mark the Evangelist lies buried in the ground. His tomb is on view before the altar in the east end of this square church and a memorial to him has been built of marble stones on top of it.

The Latin contains some ambiguities preserved in the translation, especially concerning whether Arculfus approached Alexandria from the north or alternatively saw the church on his north side on entering the city. It is feasible that he thought he was entering Alexandria from the north, even though the Mediterranean shore lies on the northern side. The Rosetta Gate faced 20° north of east and we know from other clues in the text that the morning sun, by which Arculfus would have defined east, may

Figure 9.1 Mosaic of polychrome glass in the vault of the Chapel of St Clement within the Basilica of St Mark in Venice, produced by Byzantine craftsmen (11th or 12th century AD). © akg-images

Figure 9.2 Ivory relief from Alexandria depicting St Mark enthroned amongst the patriarchs (archbishops) of Alexandria (7th century AD), Louvre, Paris.

© Photo RMN – J. G. Berizzi

have been about 50° south of due east at the time Arculfus passed into Alexandria.

Around a century after Arculfus (*c.* AD 750–800) the monk Epiphanius confirmed the continuing presence of the remains:

To the west, four days away, is the city of Alexandria. There Saint Mark the Apostle and Evangelist lies buried…[13]

A medieval poem recounting the capture of Alexandria by the King of Cyprus in AD 1365 indicates that the Gate of St Mark was then an alternative name for the Cairo Gate.[14] In lines 3182-4:

Saint Marc est la porte nommée,	*This gate is called St Mark's,*
Et pluseurs, qui nommer la veulent,	*And some, who wished to name it,*
La porte dou Poivre l'appellent.	*They called it the Pepper Gate.*

Lines 3214-7:

En Alexandre a une rue	*In Alexandria is a street*
Qu'on claimme la rue dou Poivre.	*Known as the Pepper Street.*
Des autres forment se desoivre,	*It differs much from the others*
Car c'est la grant rue, à droit dire.	*For it's the main street, rightly speaking.*

Lines 3002-4:

Ceste porte estoit appellé	*This gate was called*
La porte dou Poivre, & s'estoit	*The Pepper Gate, and it was*
Li chemins qui au Quaire aloit.	*The road that led to Cairo.*

Bernard, a French monk who visited Alexandria *c.* AD 870, verified the abduction of the corpse by the Venetians and noted that the Church of St Mark lay close by a monastery dedicated to St Mark, which was located just outside the Eastern/Cairo Gate.

Haec Alexandria mari adjacet, in qua praedicans sanctus Marcus Evangelium, gessit pontificale officium. Extra cujus portam orientalem est monasterium praedicti sancti, in quo sunt monachi apud ecclesiam, in qua prius ipse requievit. Venientes vero Venetii navigio tulerunt furtim corpus a custode ejus, et deportarunt ad suam insulam.[15]

This Alexandria, in which St Mark the Evangelist preached and bore the Patriarchal office, is adjacent to the sea. Outside its eastern gate is the monastery of the saint, in which there are monks close by the church, in which he himself formerly lay at rest. But the Venetians coming by sea secretly took his body into their keeping, and bore it away to their own island.

The earliest surviving map of Alexandria, drawn by Ugo Comminelli in AD 1472, also depicts some kind of religious establishment dedicated to St Mark outside the eastern gate (fig. 9.3).[16] Nevertheless, Bernard's testimony does not exclude the possibility that the church lay just within the gate, whilst the later monastery lay just outside it, so the location specified by the Braun and Hogenberg map may well be correct.

Leo Africanus seems to have been among the last eyewitnesses of the ancient church of St Mark in Alexandria, mentioning it at the time of his visits to the city in around AD 1517:

At this present there are amongst the ancient inhabitants of Alexandria many Christians called Jacobites [Copts], being all of them artisans and merchants: these Jacobites have a church of their own to resort unto, wherein the body of S. Mark the Evangelist lay in times past interred, which hath since been privily stolen by the Venetians, & carried unto Venice. And the said Jacobites pay tribute unto the Governor of Cairo.[17]

Figure 9.3 Map of Alexandria from the Codex of Ugo Comminelli, *detailing 'St Mark's' (ecclesiastical building to the left in front of the city wall) dating from AD 1472, from G. Jondet,* L'Atlas Historique de la Ville et des ports d'Alexandrie, Tome II, *Cairo, 1921, Plate I. Bibliothèque Nationale, Paris.* © Sonia Halliday Photographs

Pompei sepulcr

In hac turri interfectus fuit

Hoc ponte transit Calicut exercitu

Cornesienus

Hec fludebant in maxi Alexandri

Porta principales

Dauid Dauid Arfenal

S. Caterina

S. marcus

Moschea

Pharus

AMC 1/8/04

Figure 9.4 Possible ancient funerary monument found beneath the main apse of the Basilica of St Mark in Venice, carved with a circular shield decorated with the 'Star of Macedon', the chief symbol of the dynasty of Alexander the Great. Drawn by A. M. Chugg

Perhaps Leo's St Mark's is the small church-like building next to the site of the discovery of St Mark's corpse, which was found just inside the St Mark/Pepper/Cairo/Rosetta Gate of medieval Alexandria in Braun and Hogenberg's map. This was not necessarily the original Roman church, because there is evidence that the building was damaged or destroyed and rebuilt several times during its long history. If these cartographers are to be believed, then the tomb of St Mark was located very close to Mahmoud Bey's central crossroads of ancient Alexandria – the likely location of Alexander's mausoleum. Libanius states that Alexander's corpse was on display in

Alexandria just before the outlawing of paganism in AD 391, but it is not heard of afterwards, whereas St Mark's tomb first appears at about this time.

Is it possible that some late 4th-century patriarch or high officer of the Alexandrian church recognised an opportunity through a small act of deception to preserve the corpse of the city's founder from the most fanatical of his own followers and to furnish Christianity with a potent relic to encourage the devotion of the faithful? There are precedents demonstrating that the Church authorities in 4th-century Alexandria were in the habit of adapting pagan relics to Christian purposes: for example, a bronze idol of Saturn in the Caesareum was melted down to cast a cross by the patriarch Alexander in the time of Constantine, and the Caesareum itself became a Christian cathedral.[18] Might a similar metamorphosis have been contrived in the case of Alexander's mummy?

Ferdinando Forlati has recorded the discovery of a supposed 'Roman funerary monument' in the ancient foundations of the main apse of the Basilica of St Mark in Venice.[19] This takes the form of a sculpted life-size round shield with a large central starburst symbol (fig. 9.4). Such a starburst on a circular shield recalls the so-called 'Star of Macedon', chief symbol of Alexander's dynasty. An elaborated version decorates the gold larnax of the tomb of Alexander's father found at Aegae (modern Vergina) and closely related eight-point versions were present on gold mini-discs in the same tomb. The starburst has also been found in a pebble mosaic in the city founded by Alexander at Ai Khanum in Bactria. It is the central decoration of a shield in a wall painting in the 2nd century BC Macedonian tomb of Lyson and Callicles between Beroia and Edessa (fig. 9.5) and it occurs on many Macedonian coins.

It should be borne in mind that the starburst also appears on a shield on a red-figure vase made in Lucania *c.* 420 BC, so it was not an exclusively Macedonian motif. One small discrepancy with the Macedonian starburst would be the roundels, which terminate each star-point in the St Mark's piece. Nevertheless, it is a startling coincidence to come across so famous a

Figure 9.5. Macedonian mural from the 2nd century BC depicting a shield with the starburst (or sunburst) symbol of Alexander's family in the tomb of Lyson and Callicles (located between Beroia and Edessa). © *Archaeological Receipts Fund*

symbol of Alexander's family in an ancient sculpture embedded in the oldest part of the foundations of the Basilica of St Mark in view of the possible connections of this context with the fate of Alexander's remains.

The evidence is largely circumstantial in that it simply defines a close coincidence in time and place between the disappearance of Alexander's corpse and the entry of St Mark's remains onto the historical stage. It extends no further than to establish an intriguing and not insignificant possibility that the two mummified bodies are one and the same.

Fortunately this need not be the end of the story, for it seems that the corpse of St Mark survives to this day beneath the high altar of the Basilica of St Mark in Venice, where it was transferred from the crypt in 1811 to preserve it from the threat posed by the city's continual floods.[20] We are fortunate also that the science of forensic archaeology has recently achieved such a degree of proficiency that a detailed investigation of the remains would be expected to reveal their true provenance (such as, carbon dating, wound evidence, facial reconstruction, tomography, examination of stomach contents, pollen grains in wrappings, DNA analysis, dentine isotope studies).

'It is a consummation devoutly to be wished', for, as a reviewer once told me, the story of Alexander's tomb without the body is like Hamlet without the Prince… 'The rest is silence.'

1   M. Smith, 1973; Eusebius, *Ecclesiastical History*, 2.16; B.A. Pearson, 1986.

2   M. Chaîne, 1924.

3   Palladius, *Lausiac History*, Section 45 on Philoromus of Galatia.

4   W. Telfer, 1949; Lipsius, *Apostelgeschichten*, 2/2:338-39.

5   J.-P. Migne (ed.), *Patrologia Graeca*, Vol. 115; Getatchew Haile, 1981; Severus, *History of the Patriarchs*.

6   *Patrologia Graeca*, 86, col. 59, note; 92, cols 608-609; 111, col. 983.

7   J. J. Norwich, 1977, 52-3.

8   G. Wilkinson, 1851; O. Demus, 1988, 28-38.

9   P. Daru, 1826, 56.

10 Braun and Hogenberg, 1572; F. L. Norden, 1755, shows the Attarine Mosque as St Mark's, but this must be an error.

11 John of Nikiu, CVIII.8-9.

12 Adamnan, *de locis sanctis* 2.30.25, where 'alexandriam' is an alternative and 'propinquo' an addition in a second manuscript (B); J. H. Bernard, 1894.

13 Epiphanius the Monk, *Description of Palestine*, v.

14 G. de Machaut, 2002.

15 Bernardus Monachus Francus, Itinerarium 6, *Patrologia Latina* Vol 121.

16 G. Jondet, 1921, Map 1.

17 Leo Africanus, 1896.

18 A. Butler, 1902, footnote to Chapter 24, *Alexandria at the Conquest*.

19 F. Forlati, 1975, 80-83.

20 E. Vio, 2000; some remains associated with St Mark's tomb were returned to Egypt by the Pope in 1968.

Conclusion

In the course of this narrative a number of arguments have been put forward that may be summarised as follows. These inferences are significant because they provide indications of where both the Memphis tomb and the Alexandrian Soma are most probably to be found and provide a basis on which to identify their archaeological remains and contents.

Alexander the Great probably died of *P. falciparum* cerebral malaria contracted from mosquito bites during a boating trip among the marshes south of Babylon about four weeks before his death.

The evidence suggests that Alexander was entombed at Memphis in 321 BC, where his body remained for at least several decades. His tomb was possibly closely associated with a temple dedicated to Ammon, but more probably to Serapis, and it is likely that Ptolemy commissioned a cult statue of Alexander for this tomb. In this sculpture Alexander may have worn an elephant scalp and the ram's horns of Ammon. Ptolemy used the same design in his original series of silver tetradrachm coins first issued about 320-18 BC. There was a temple of Ammon and Thoth in the Hellenion (Greek) quarter of Memphis in the Ptolemaic period and this is a possible candidate for the location of Alexander's tomb at Memphis. The Hellenion may have been situated in the north-western sector of the modern ruin field. However, the temple built by Nectanebo II at the Memphite Serapeum is a much better option, since its entrance was guarded by a group of Greek statues of philosophers and poets dating to the reign of the first Ptolemy and because of other associations between Alexander and Nectanebo. A chamber appended to the Nectanebo temple is likely to be the first tomb of Alexander. This site could be re-excavated to seek further archaeological evidence to confirm or reject this hypothesis.

273

The sarcophagus sculpted for the pharaoh Nectanebo II in the British Museum has a much better claim to having been used for Alexander's body than has previously been recognised. If this is true, then the Nectanebo temple at the Serapeum in North Saqqara (Memphis) was the site of Alexander's first tomb in Egypt.

The famous tomb of Alexander at Alexandria was built around 215 BC by Ptolemy IV Philopator. It lay in a mausoleum within an enclosure known as the Soma and its architecture was probably modelled on that of the Mausoleum of Halicarnassus. It was tall and splendid with a pyramidal roof probably supported by an elevated porticus. There was a subterranean funeral chamber beneath the building, sealed by Septimius Severus and probably resealed by his son, Caracalla, the last known visitor to the chamber in AD 215.

The mausoleum building overlying the funeral chamber was probably destroyed between AD 262 and 365. The revolt of Aemilianus, the Romano-Palmyrene wars between Aurelian and Zenobia, the uprising of Firmus, and the sack of the city by Diocletian, are all plausible causes of its destruction; but the most likely cause is the earthquake and tidal wave of AD 365. The collapsed masonry might have protected the burial chamber and its contents from immediate rediscovery, but a newly recognised reference by Libanius suggests that it had been excavated and the body had been placed on display by AD 390. At the end of the 4th century AD, the Bishop of Constantinople believed its location to be unknown, so suspicion falls upon the rioting of the Christian mob, when paganism was finally outlawed in AD 391, as the reason for its disappearance.

The Soma mausoleum in Alexandria was located in a walled sacred precinct (*temenos* or *peribolos*) probably on a scale of half a kilometre square, sited at or near the central crossroads south of the Lochias peninsula, straddling the Canopic Way. According to the 19th-century excavations of Mahmoud Bey, this locates the building and enclosure on the western side of the modern Shallalat Gardens. The surviving Ptolemaic wall fragment in the Shallalat Gardens and the ancient Rosetta Gate drawn by Mayer in 1792 are probably parts of the *temenos* enclosure of the Soma and it is likely that the entire eastern sector of the Arab walls of Alexandria were built on the same line as the walls of the Soma enclosure. This theory could be investigated by excavating at carefully chosen sites within modern Alexandria in an attempt to locate the foundations of the lost western wall of this enclosure.

The tomb and body of St Mark seem to have appeared at approximately the same site within Alexandria as the location of Alexander's tomb. St Mark's body appeared at the end of the 4th century AD, at about the time that Alexander's body disappeared. The Alexandrian corpse of St Mark is described as having been mummified like Alexander's, but several Christian texts state that St Mark's body was burnt, so his Alexandrian tomb was probably a forgery. These fascinating circumstances make it imperative to analyse the corpse of St Mark scientifically. This currently rests beneath the high altar of the Basilica of St Mark in Venice. There is a significant possibility, though not a probability, that it is actually the corpse of Alexander.

There are those who regard the hunt for the Soma as hopeless and see no point in its pursuit. They point to a lack of evidence and stress that there are many more appropriate projects for research funding in Egypt.[1] Yet if this book has revealed anything about Alexander's tombs, it is that there are a great variety of relevant clues from a range of archaeological and historical sources. It is the inaccessibility of the most interesting sites, sealed deep beneath a modern metropolis, which permits some lingering optimism regarding the preservation of the foundations of the Soma mausoleum.

Perhaps a more credible explanation for the reluctance of some to become involved in the search is that it is intrinsically risky to do so, for on this subject there has always been a much greater chance of being proved wrong than right. Nevertheless, others will undoubtedly consider that the magnitude of the prize is a sufficient incentive to enter the competition.

Maybe the last word on the matter should be left to the hero of this epic tale:

> *Toil and risk are the price of glory, but it is a lovely thing to live with courage and die leaving an everlasting fame.*

Alexander the Great, *Address at the Beas*[2]

---

[1] Hogarth, 1895, 1-33.
[2] Arrian, *Anabasis Alexandri*, V, 26.4.

Bibliography

Ancient Sources

Achilles Tatius, *Clitophon and Leucippe*, S. Gaselee (trans.), Loeb, Harvard, 1917.

Acts of St Mark, *in Patrologia Graeca*, Vol. 115, J.-P. Migne (ed.), Paris, 1899.

Adamnan, *de locis sanctis*, D. Meehan (ed.), *Scriptores Latini Hiberniae*, Vol. 3, Dublin, 1958.

Aelian, *Varia Historia*, N. G. Wilson (trans.), Loeb, Harvard, 1997.

Ammianus Marcellinus, *Res Gestae*, J. C. Rolfe (trans.), Vol. 2, Loeb, Harvard, 1935-9.

Arabic Synaxary of the Coptic Church, J. Forget (trans.), *Corpus scriptorum christianorum orientalium, scriptores arabici*, third series, Vols I and II, Louvain, 1905-26.

Arrian, *Anabasis Alexandri* and *Indica*, P. A. Brunt (trans.), Vols 1 and 2, Loeb, Harvard, 1976 and 1983; *Epitome of History of Events After Alexander, Photius 92, Photius Bibliothèque*, Vol. 2, René Henry, Paris, 1960.

Athenaeus, *Deipnosophistae* [fragments of Ephippus, Nicobule and Callixinus], C. Burton Gulick (trans.), Vols 1 to 7, Loeb, Harvard, 1927-41.

Bernardus Monachus Francus, *Itinerarium 6, in Patrologia Latina*, Vol. 121, J.-P. Migne (ed.), Paris, 1880.

Caesar, *The Civil Wars*, A. G. Peskett (trans.), Loeb, Harvard, 1914; *The Alexandrine War* [ghostwritten by Hirtius], A. G. Way (trans.), Loeb, Harvard, 1955.

Chronicon Paschale, 252, columns 608-609 in *Patrologia Graeca*, Vol. 92, J.-P. Migne (ed.), Paris, 1865.

Cicero, *The Speech Against Piso*, N. H. Watts (trans.), Vol. 14, Loeb, Harvard, 1931.

Clement of Alexandria, *Exhortation to the Greeks*, G. W. Butterworth (trans.), Loeb, Harvard, 1919.

Curtius, *The History of Alexander*, J. C. Rolfe (trans.), Vols 1 and 2, Loeb, Harvard, 1946; Dio Cassius, *Roman History*, E. Cary (trans.), Loeb, Harvard, 1914-27.

Diodorus Siculus, *Library of History*, Vol. 7, C. L. Sherman (trans.), Loeb, Harvard, 1952; Vol. 8, C. B. Welles (trans.), Loeb, Harvard, 1963; Vol. 9, Russel M. Geer (trans.), Loeb, Harvard, 1947.

Diogenes Laertius, *Lives of Eminent Philosophers*, Vol. 2, R. D. Hicks (trans.), Loeb, Harvard, 1925.

Epiphanius Constantiensis, *On Weights and Measures*, columns 237-94, *Patrologia Graeca*, Vol. 43, J.-P. Migne (ed.), Paris, 1864.

Epiphanius the Monk, *Description of Palestine*, columns 259-72 *in Patrologia Graeca*, Vol. 120, J.-P. Migne (ed.), Paris, 1880.

Eusebius, *Ecclesiastical History*, Vol. 1, K. Lake (trans.), Loeb, Harvard, 1926; Vol. 2, J. E. L. Oulton, Loeb, Harvard, 1932.

Eutychius, *Patrologia Graeca*, Vol. 111, J.-P. Migne (ed.), Paris, 1863.

Herodian, *History of the Empire*, Books 1 to 4, Vol. 1, C. R. Whittaker (trans.), Loeb, Harvard, 1969.

John Chrysostom, *Homilies on 2nd Corinthians*, XXVI, columns 575-84, *in Patrologia Graeca*, Vol. 61, J.-P. Migne (ed.), Paris, 1862; J. H. Parker (trans.), *The Homilies of S. John Chrysostom Archbishop of Constantinople on the Second Epistle of St. Paul the Apostle to the Corinthians*, Oxford, 1848.

John of Nikiu, *Chronicle*, R. H. Charles (trans.), Text and Translation Society Vol. 3, Amsterdam, reprint of London edition of 1916.

Josephus, *Jewish Antiquities*, H. St J. Thackeray *et al.* (trans), Vols 4 to 9, Loeb, Harvard, 1930-63; *The Jewish War*, H. St J. Thackeray, Vols 2 and 3, Loeb, Harvard, 1927-8; *Contra Apion*, H. St J. Thackeray, Vol. 1, Loeb, Harvard, 1926.

Justin, *Epitome of the Philippic History of Pompeius Trogus*, Books 11–12, J. C. Yardley and W. Heckel (trans.), Oxford, 1997; *Justin, Cornelius Nepos and Eutropius*, J. S. Watson (trans.), London, 1897.

The Koran, Surah 18, The Cave, N. J. Dawood (trans.), London, 1956.

Libanius, *Oration* XLIX, A. F. Norman (trans.), Selected Works II, Loeb, Harvard, 1977.

Lucan, *Pharsalia*, J. D. Duff (trans.), Loeb, Harvard, 1928.

Lucian, *Dialogues of the Dead*, XIII, Vol. 7, M. D. MacLeod (trans.), Loeb, Harvard, 1961; *Essay on How to Write History*, Vol. 6, K. Kilburn (trans.), Loeb, Harvard, 1959.

Nepos, *Eumenes in Justin, Cornelius Nepos and Eutropius*, John Selby Watson (trans.), London, 1897.

Palladius, *Lausiac History*, R. T. Meyer (trans.), London, 1965.

Pausanius, *Description of Greece*, Vol. 1, W. H. S. Jones (trans.), Loeb, Harvard, 1918.

Philo, *In Flaccum*, Vol. 9, F. H. Colson (trans.), Loeb, Harvard, 1941.

Pliny the Elder, *Natural History*, H. Rackham (trans.), Vols 1 to 10, W. H. S. Jones, D. E. Eichholz, Loeb, Harvard, 1938-62.

Plutarch, *Alexander, Lives*, Vol. 7, B. Perrin (trans.), Loeb, Harvard, 1919; *Eumenes, Lives*, Vol. 8, B. Perrin (trans.), Loeb, Harvard, 1919; *Demetrius, Antony, Lives* Vol. 9, B. Perrin (trans.), Loeb, Harvard, 1920; *Moralia*, Vols 3 and 4, F. C. Babbitt (trans.) Loeb, Harvard, 1931 and 1936.

Polybius, *The Histories*, W. R. Paton (trans.), Vols 1 to 6, Harvard, 1922-7.

Procopius, *On Buildings*, H. B. Dewing and G. Downey (trans.), Vol. 7, Loeb, Harvard, 1940.

Pseudo-Callisthenes, *Alexander Romance*, G. Kroll (trans.), *Historia Alexandri Magni*, Vol. 1, Weidmann, 1926; *The Greek Alexander Romance*, R. Stoneman (trans.), Penguin, London, 1991; A. M. Wolohojian, *The Romance of Alexander the Great by Pseudo-Callisthenes*, Columbia, New York and London, 1969.

Quintus Curtius Rufus, *The History of Alexander*, J. C. Yardley (trans.) with an introduction and notes by W. Heckel, Penguin Classics, Harmondsworth, 1984.

Severus, Bishop of Al-Ushmunain, *History of the Patriarchs*, B. Evetts (trans.), *Patrologia Orientalis*, Vol. 2, 4, Paris, 1907.

Socrates Scholasticus, *Ecclesiastical History, in Patrologia Graeca*, Vol. 67, J.-P. Migne (ed.), Paris, 1964; H. Wace and P. Schaff, *A Select Library of Nicene and Post-Nicene Fathers of the Christian Church*, Vol. 2, Oxford and New York, 1891.

Sozomenos, *Ecclesiastical History*, in *Patrologia Graeca*, Vol. 67, J.-P. Migne (ed.), Paris, 1964; H. Wace and P. Schaff, *A Select Library of Nicene and Post-Nicene Fathers of the Christian Church*, Vol. 2, Oxford and New York, 1891.

Stephanus Byzantinus, A. Meineke (trans.), *S. Byzantii, Ethnicorum*, Berlin, 1849.

Strabo, *Geography*, H. L. Jones (trans.), Vols 1 to 8, Loeb, Harvard, 1917–32.

Suetonius, *Lives of the Caesars; Life of Lucan*, J. C. Rolfe (trans.), Vols 1 and 2, Loeb, Harvard, 1913–14.

Tacitus, *Histories*, C. H. Moore (trans.), Vols 1 to 2, Loeb, Harvard, 1925-31; *Annals*, J. Jackson (trans.), Loeb, Vols 2 to 5, Harvard, 1931-7.

Theocritus, *Idyll XVII, Encomium to Ptolemy*, J. M. Edmonds (trans.), *Greek Bucolic Poets*, Loeb, Harvard, 1919.

Theodoret, *Graecarum Affectionum Curatio, in Patrologia Graeca,* Vol. 83, J.-P. Migne (trans.), Paris, 1864.

Vitruvius, *De Architectura*, F. Granger (trans.), Vols 1 & 2, Harvard, 1934.

Zenobius, *Proverbia*, E. L. von Leutsch and F. G. Schneidewin (eds), *in Corpus Paroemiographorum Graecorum*, 1, Göttingen, 1839.

Modern References

Adriani, A., *Repertorio d'Arte del'Egitto Greco-Romano*, Serie C, Vol. I–II, Palermo, 1963.

Adriani, A., (posthumously), *La Tomba di Alessandro*, Rome, 2000.

Africanus, L. *in* G. B. Ramusio (ed.), *Descrizione dell'Africa, 1550,* J. Pory (trans.), *Description of Africa*, (AD 1600), Vol. 3, Hakluyt Society 94, London, 1896.

Annesley, G., *Voyages & Travels to India, Ceylon, the Red Sea, Abyssinia and Egypt in the Years 1802–1806*, Vol. 4, London, 1811.

Anson, E., 'Macedonia's Alleged Constitutionalism', *Classical Journal* 80, 1985, 303-16.

Arnaud, J.-L., 'Nouvelles Données sur la Topographie d'Alexandrie Antique', *Bulletin de Correspondance Hellénique* 121, 1997, 721-37.

Austin, M. M., *The Hellenistic World from Alexander to the Roman Conquest*, Cambridge, 1981.

Awad, M. F., *La revue de l'Occident Musulman et de la Méditerranée* 46, 1987, 4.

Bailey, D. M., 'Alexandria, Carthage and Ostia (Not to Mention Naples)', *Alessandria e il Mondo Ellenistico-Romano, Studi in onore di Achille Adriani*, Vol. II, Rome, 1984, 265-72.

Balil, A., 'Una nueva representación de la tumba de Alejandro,' *Archivo Español de Arqueologia* 35, 1962, 1023.

Balil, A., 'Monumentos Alejandrinos y Paisajes Egipcios en un Mosaico Romano de Toledo (España)', *Alessandria e il Mondo Ellenistico-Romano, Studi in Onore di Achille Adriani*, Vol. III, Rome, 1984, 433-9.

Barbier de Meynard, C. and Pavet de Courteille, A., *al-Mas'udi, Les prairies d'or,* Paris, 1861-1917.

Benwell, G. and Waugh, A., *Sea Enchantress: The Tale of The Mermaid and Her Kin*, London, 1961.

Bernand, A., *Alexandrie la Grande*, Paris, 1966.

Bernard, J. H. (trans.), *Expliciunt peregrinations totius terre sancta, Guide-Book to Palestine*, Palestine Pilgrim Text Society, London, 1894, 33.

Bevan, E., *A History of Egypt under the Ptolemaic Dynasty*, London, 1927.

Bianchi, R. S., 'Hunting Alexander's Tomb', *Archaeology* 4, 1993, 54-5.

Bonacasa, N., 'Un Inedito di Achille Adriani Sulla Tomba di Alessandro', *Studi Miscellanei*, University of Rome, Vol. 28, 1991, 5-19.

Bonamy, M., 'Description de la Ville d'Alexandrie, telle qu'elle estoit du temps de Strabon', *Histoire de l'Académie des Inscriptions et Belles Lettres*, Tome 9, 1736, 416-32.

Bosworth, A. B., *Conquest and Empire: The Reign of Alexander The Great*, Cambridge, 1988.

Bosworth, A. B., *Alexander and the East: the Tragedy of Triumph*, Oxford, 1996.

Botti, G., *Plan d'Alexandrie à l'époque Ptolémaïque*, Alexandria, 1898.

Bowman, A. K., *Egypt After the Pharaohs*, London, 1986.

Braun, G. and Hogenberg, F., *Civitates Orbis Terrarum*, Cologne, 1572.

Breccia, E., *Rapport du Musée Gréco-Romain*, Alexandria, 1907.

Breccia, E., *Alexandrea ad Aegyptum*, Bergamo, 1922.

Brown, D. M. (ed.), *Greece: Temples, Tombs and Treasures*, Richmond, 1994.

Browne, W. G., *Travels in Africa, Egypt and Syria*, London, 1799.

Bruce, J., *Travels*, Vol. I, London, 1790.

Brunt, P. A., *Arrian, Anabasis Alexandri and Indica*, Vols I and II, Loeb, Harvard, 1976 and 1983.

Budge, E. A. W., *The Life and Exploits of Alexander the Great*, London, 1896.

Bury, J. B., Cook, S. A. and Adcock, F. E. (eds), *The Cambridge Ancient History. Volume VI. Macedon, 401-301 BC*, Cambridge, 1927.

Butler, A. J., *The Arab Conquest of Egypt and the Last Thirty Years of the Roman Dominion*, 2nd edition, revised by P. M. Fraser, Oxford, [1902] 1978.

Cassas, L.-F., *Voyage pittoresque de la Syrie, de la Phénicie, de la Palestine et de la Basse Égypte*, Paris, 1799.

Chaîne, M., 'L'Église de Saint-Marc à Alexandrie', *Revue de l'Orient Chrétien*, Vol. 24, 1924, 372386.

Chauveau, M., *L'Égypte au temps de Cléopâtre*, Paris, 1997.

Christiansen, E., *The Roman Coins of Alexandria*, Aarhus, 1988.

Chugg, A. M., 'An Unrecognised Representation of Alexander the Great on Hadrian's Egyptian Coinage', *The Celator Journal* 2, Vol. 15, 2001, 6-16.

Chugg, A. M., 'The Sarcophagus of Alexander the Great?', *Greece and Rome*, Vol. 49, No. 1, 2002, 8-26.

Chugg, A. M., 'The Sarcophagus of Alexander the Great', *Minerva* 13.5, 2002, 33-6.

Chugg, A. M., 'The Tomb of Alexander the Great in Alexandria', *American Journal of Ancient History, New Series* 1.2, (2002) [2003], 75-108.

Chugg, A. M., 'A Double Entendre in the Alexandrian Bigas of Triptolemos', *The Celator Journal* 8, Vol. 17, 2003, 6-16.

Chugg, A. M., 'Alexander's Final Resting Place', *History Today* 7, 2004, 17-23.

Claridge, A., *Oxford Archaeological Guide: Rome*, Oxford, 1998.

Clarke, E. D., *The Tomb of Alexander, a dissertation on the sarcophagus from Alexandria and now in the British Museum*, Cambridge, 1805.

Clarke, P. D. and Bryceson, A., *The Medical Protection Society, Casebook (GP) no. 4*, London, 1994, 4-5.

Clarysse, W. and van der Veken, G., *The Eponymous Priests of Ptolemaic Egypt*, Leiden, 1983.

Colange (de), L. (ed.), *Voyages and Travels or Scenes in Many Lands, with 850 Illustrations on Wood and Steel; View from All Parts of the World comprising Mountains, Lakes, Rivers, Palaces, Cathedrals, Castles, Abbeys and Ruins, with Original Descriptions by the Best Authors*, New York, *c.* 1887

Cuntz, O., *Itineraria Romana*, Rome, 1929.

Daru, P., *Histoire de Venise*, 3rd edition, Tome 1, Paris, 1826.

Décobert, C. and Empereur, J.-Y. (eds), *Alexandrie Médiévale 1,* Institut Français d'Archéologie Orientale, Cairo, 1998.

Déléage, A., *Etudes Papyrologiques 2*, 1934.

Delia, D., 'The Population of Roman Alexandria', *Transactions of the American Philological Association* 118, 1988, 275-92.

Demus, O., *The Mosaic Decoration of San Marco Venice*, Chicago, 1988.

Denon, D.V., *Travels in Upper and Lower Egypt*, London, 1802.

Deuel, L., *The Memoirs of Heinrich Schliemann*, New York, 1977.

Dodson, A., *After the Pyramids*, London, 2000.

van Egmont J. A. and Heyman, J., *Travels Through Part of Europe, Asia Minor, the Islands of the Archipelago, Syria, Palestine, Egypt, Mount Sinai*, London, 1759.

Empereur, J.-Y., *Alexandria Rediscovered,* London, 1998.

Empereur, J.-Y. *et al., The Tombs of Alexander the Great (Hoi Taphoi tou Megalou Alexandrou)*, Athens, 1997.

Engels, D. W., 'A note on Alexander's death', *Classical Philology* 73, 1978, 224-8.

Erskine, A., 'Life After Death: Alexandria and the Body of Alexander', *Greece and Rome*, Vol. 49, No. 2, 2002, 163-79.

Fedak, J., *Monumental Tombs of the Hellenistic Age*, Toronto, 1990.

Ferrill, A., *Caligula, Emperor of Rome*, London and New York, 1991.

Ferron, J. and Pinard, M., 'Un Fragment de Verre Gravé du Musée Lavigerie', *Cahiers de Byrsa* 8, 1958-9, 103-9.

Forlati, F., *La Basilica Di San Marco Attraverso I Suoi Restauri*, Trieste, 1975.

Lane Fox, R., *Alexander the Great*, London, 1973.

Fraser, P. M., 'A Syriac Notitia Urbis Alexandrinae', *Journal of Egyptian Archaeology* 37, 1951, 103-8.

Fraser, P. M., 'Some Alexandrian Forgeries', *Proceedings of the British Academy* 47, 1962, 243-50.

Fraser, P. M., *Ptolemaic Alexandria*, Oxford, 1972.

Geer, R. M., *Diodorus Siculus*, Vol. IX, Loeb, Harvard, 1947.

Gibbon, E., *The Decline and Fall of the Roman Empire*, Vol. I, London, 1782 (revised 1845).

Goddio *et al.*, *Alexandria: The Submerged Royal Quarters*, London, 1998.

Goralski, W. J., 'Arrian's Events After Alexander', *Ancient World* 19, 1989, 81-108.

Grant, M., *Cleopatra*, London, 1972.

Grimal, N., *A History of Ancient Egypt*, Oxford, 1994.

Haas, C., *Alexandria in Late Antiquity*, Baltimore, 1997.

Haile, G., 'A New Ethiopic Version of the Acts of St Mark', *Analecta Bollandiana* 99, 1981, 117-34.

Hammond, N. G. L., *Alexander The Great*, London, 1981.

Hammond, N. G. L., *Three Historians of Alexander the Great*, Cambridge, 1983.

Hammond, N. G. L., *Philip of Macedon*, London, 1994.

Hauben, H., 'The First War of the Successors – Chronological and Historical Problems', *Ancient Society* 8, 1977, 85-120.

Hogarth, D. G. and Benson, E. F., 'Report on Prospects of Research in Alexandria', *Egypt Exploration Fund* 1895, 1-33.

Ingrassia, A. M. B., 'Influenze Alessandrine Sull'Arte Punica: Una Messa A Punto', *Alessandria e il Mondo Ellenistico-Romano, Studi in onore di Achille Adriani,* Vol. III, Rome, 1984, 835-42.

Irwin, E., *A Series Of Adventures In The Course Of A Voyage Up The Red-Sea, On The Coasts Of Arabia And Egypt And Of A Route Through The Deserts Of Thebais Hither To Unknown To The European Traveller In The Year 1777,* Vol. I, London, 1780.

Jacoby, F., *Die Fragmente der griechischen Historiker*, Berlin, 1923-30, Leiden, 1940-58.

Jeffreys, D., *The Survey of Memphis*, London, 1985.

Jeppesen, K., 'Tot Operum Opus, Ergebnisse der Dänischen Forschungen zum Maussolleion von Halikarnass seit 1966', *Jahrbuch des Deutschen Archäologischen Instituts*, Bd. 107, 1992, 59-102.

Jondet, G., *Atlas historique de la ville et des ports d'Alexandrie*, Mémoires de la Société Sultanieh de Géographie, Vol. 2, Cairo, 1921.

Koldewey, R., *Das wieder erstehende Babylon*, Leipzig, 1913.

Kroll, G., *Historia Alexandri Magni (Pseudo-Callisthenes)*, Germany, 1926.

Lambert, R., *Beloved and God*, London, 1984.

Lauer, J.-P. and Picard, C., *Les Statues Ptolémaiques du Sarapieion de Memphis*, Paris, 1955.

Lavery, B., *Nelson and The Nile*, London, 1998.

Lipsius, R. A., *Die Apokryphen Apostelgeschichten Und Apostellegenden*, Braunschweig, 2.2, 1883-90, 338-39.

Littré, E., 'On Alexander's Death', *Médecine et Médecins*, Paris, 1872, 406-415.

Luigi, G. and Filibeck, G., *Il Porto di Roma Imperiale*, 1931.

Machaut (de), G., *La Prise d'Alixandre (1369)*, R. Barton Palmer (trans.), New York and London, 2002.

Mahmoud Bey el-Falaki, *Mémoire sur l'antique Alexandrie, ses faubourgs et environs découverts*, Copenhagen, 1872.

Mariette, A., *Choix de monuments et de dessins découverts ou exécutés pendant le déblaiement du Sérapéum de Memphis*, Paris, 1856.

Mariette, A. *in* G. Maspero (ed.), *Le Sérapéum de Memphis*, Paris, 1882.

Marlowe, J., *The Golden Age of Alexandria*, London, 1971.

Matz, F., 'Review of Lauer and Picard; Les Statues Ptolémaiques du Sarapieion de Memphis', *Gnomon* 29, 1957, 84-93.

Mayer, L., *Views in Egypt,* London, 1804.

McKenzie, J., 'Alexandria and the Origins of Baroque Architecture', *Alexandria and Alexandrianism*, Malibu, 1996, 109-25.

McKenzie, J., 'Glimpsing Alexandria from Archaeological Evidence', *Journal of Roman Archaeology*, 2003, 35-63.

Meinardus, O., *Christian Egypt Ancient and Modern*, 2nd ed., Cairo, 1977.

Merrony, M. W., 'The Graven Image in Early Islamic Floor Mosaics: Contradiction or Convention?' *Minerva* 15.1, 2004, 36-9.

Milns, R. D., *Alexander the Great*, London, 1968.

Montevecchi, O., 'Adriano e la fondazione di Antinoopolis', *Neronia IV, Alejandro Magno, modelo de los emperadores romanos, Collection Latomus,* Vol. 209, 1990, 183-95.

Mørkholm, O., *Early Hellenistic Coinage*, Cambridge, 1991.

Müller, C., *Fragmenta Historicorum Graecorum*, Paris, 1868.

Neroutsos-Bey, T., *L'ancienne Alexandrie*, Paris, 1888.

Noack, F., 'Neue Untersuchungen in Alexandrien', *Mittheilungen des Kaiserlich Deutschen Archäeologischen Instituts, Athenische Abtheilung*, Vol. XXV, 1900, 215-79.

Norden, F. L. *Voyage d'Égypte et de Nubie*, Paris, 1755.

Norwich, J. J. *Venice: the Rise to Empire*, London, 1977.

Norwich, O. (ed. Stone, J.), *Norwich's Maps of Africa*, Norwich (Vermont), 1997.

Oates, J., *Babylon*, London, 1979.

O'Brien, J. M., *Alexander the Great: the Invisible Enemy*, London and New York, 1992.

Oldach, D. W. and Richard, R. E., 'A Mysterious Death', *The New England Journal of Medicine* 24, Vol. 338, 1998, 1764-9.

Pearson, B. A., 'Some Observations in The Roots of Egyptian Christianity', *in* B. Pearson and J. Goehring (eds), *Earliest Christianity in Egypt*, Philadelphia, 1986, 132-59.

Pearson, L., *The Lost Histories of Alexander the Great*, New York and Oxford, 1960.

Le Père, G. *et al., Description de l'Égypte*, Paris, 1829.

Perrot, N. (trans.), *L'Afrique de Marmol*, Paris, 1667.

Picard, C., 'Quelques représentations nouvelles du Phare d'Alexandrie', *Bulletin de Correspondance Hellénique* 76, 1952, 61-95.

Pococke, R., *Description of the East*, London, 1743-5.

Pory, J., *The History and Description of Africa written by Leo Africanus*, London, 1896.

Préaux, C., *L'economie royale des Lagides*, New York, 1939.

Sierotka, M. R., *Hierosolymitana peregrinatio illustrissimi domini Nicolai Christopheri Radzivilli,…Ex idiomate Polonica in latinum linguam translate… Thorma trelere interprete*, Brunsbergae, 1601 and Krakow, 1925.

Rea, J. R., 'A New Version of P. Yale inv. 299', *Zeitschrift für Papyrologie und Epigraphik* 27, 1977, 151-6.

Renault, M., *The Nature of Alexander*, London, 1975.

Rhomiopoulou, K., 'An Outline of Macedonian History and Art' *in The Search for Alexander: an Exhibition*, New York, 1980, 21-5.

Richardson, L., *A New Topographical Dictionary of Ancient Rome*, Baltimore, 1992.

Rodziewicz, M., *Les habitations romaines tardives d'Alexandrie*, Warsaw, 1984.

Rodziewicz, M., 'Ptolemaic street directions in Basilea', *Alessandria e il Mondo Ellenistico-Romano, Congrès Alexandrie, 1992*, Rome, 1995, 227-35.

Rolfe, J. C., *Ammianus Marcellinus*, Vol. II, Loeb, Harvard, 1937

Sallares, R., *Malaria and Rome*, Oxford, 2002.

Samuel, A. E., *Ptolemaic Chronology*, Munich, 1962.

Sandys, G., *Relation of a Journey begun in AD 1610*, London, 1617.

Schachermeyr, F., *Alexander der Grosse*, Vienna, 1973.

Shotter, D., *Augustus Caesar*, London and New York, 1991.

Sly, D., *Philo's Alexandria*, London and New York, 1996, 44-7.

Smith, M., *Clement of Alexandria and a Secret Gospel of Mark*, Harvard, 1973.

Sonnini, C. S., *Travels in Upper and Lower Egypt*, Vol. I, 67, London, 1800.

Stevenson, S. W., Roach Smith, C. and Madden, F. W., *Dictionary of Roman Coins*, London, 1889.

Stewart, A., *Faces of Power: Alexander's Image and Hellenistic Politics*, California, 1993.

Stoneman, R., *Alexander the Great*, London, 1997.

Tarn, W. W., *Cambridge Ancient History, Vol. 6, Macedon 401–301 BC,* Cambridge, 1927.

Tarn, W. W., 'The Hellenistic Ruler Cult and the Daemon', *Journal of Hellenistic Studies* 48, 1928, 206-19.

Taylor, L. R., 'The Cult of Alexander at Alexandria', *Classical Philology* 22, 1927, 162-9.

Telfer, W., 'St Peter of Alexandria and Arius', *Analecta Bollandiana 67*, 1949, 117-30.

Thiersch, H., 'Die Alexandrinische Königsnecropole', *Jahrbuch des Kaiserlich Deutschen Archäeologischen Instituts,* XXV, 1910, 55-97.

Thompson, D., *Memphis under the Ptolemies*, Princeton, 1988.

Tkaczow, B., *Topography of Ancient Alexandria (An Archaeological Map),* Warsaw, 1993.

Trigger, B. G. *et al., Ancient Egypt: A Social History*, Cambridge, 1983.

Turner, E. G., *Greek Papyri*, Oxford, 1980.

Valentia, G., *Voyages and Travels to India, Ceylon, the Red Sea, Abyssinia and Egypt in the Years 1802 – 1806,* Vol. 4, London, 1811.

Vio, E., *St Mark's Basilica in Venice*, London, 2000.

Wace, A. J. B., 'The Sarcophagus of Alexander the Great', *Farouk I University, Bulletin of the Faculty of Arts* 4, 1948, 1-11.

Walsh, T., *Journal of The Late Campaign in Egypt: Including Descriptions of that Country and of Gibraltar, Minorca, Malta, Marmorice and Macri*, London, 1803.

Welles, C. B., *Diodorus Siculus, Library of History*, Vol. VIII, Loeb, Harvard, 1963.

Wilcken, U., 'Hypomnematismoi', *Philologus*, 1894, 84-126.

Wilcken, U., 'Die griechischen Denkmäler vom Dromos des Serapeums von Memphis', *Jahrbuch des Deutschen Archäologischen Instituts 32*, 1917, 149-203.

Wilkinson, G., 'On an Early Mosaic in St Mark's Representing the Removal of the Body of the Evangelist to Venice', *Journal of the British Archaeological Association*, Vol. VII, 1851, 258-63.

Williams, S., *Diocletian and The Roman Recovery*, London and New York, 1985.

Williams, S. and Friell, G., *Theodosius: The Empire At Bay*, London, 1994.

Wolohojian, A. M., *The Romance of Alexander the Great by Pseudo-Callisthenes*, Columbia, New York and London, 1969.

Wood, M., *In The Footsteps of Alexander The Great*, London, 1997.

Zogheb (de), A. M., *Études sur l'ancienne Alexandrie*, Paris, 1909.

Index

A

Achilles **Tatius**
xiii, 30, 81, 82, 100, 189, 237, 238, 251, 254

Achilleus
(Corrector of Egypt) 149

Adriani, Achille
xix, 78, 100, 193, 222, 234, 235, 236

Aegae
39, 40, 42, 57, 120, 267

Aelian (Claudius Aelianus)
xiii, xvi, 18, 30, 31, 34, 42, 43, 45, 46, 47, 66

Aemilianus (Marcus Julius)
145, 274

Agathos **Daimon** (=Agathodaimon)
155, 156, 157

Alexander IV
36, 50

Alexander Romance
17, 20, 30, 37, 41, 47, 54, 62, 66, 74, 77, 79, 82, 100, 141, 181, 225, 240

Alpha (Quarter)
74, 238

Ammianus Marcellinus
xiv, 148, 150, 154, 155, 157, 159, 164, 212, 226, 254

Ammon
10, 13, 28, 35, 36, 39, 46, 47, 51, 53, 54, 55, 57, 63, 64, 67, 168, 234, 273

'**Amr**
203

Antigonus
16, 49, 50

Antinous
124, 125, 129, 130, 138, 143

B

D

H

Hadrian
xiv, xviii, 121, 123, 124, 125, 126, 127, 128, 129, 130, 138, 143, 155

Halicarnassus (Mausoleum)
85, 86, 87, 88, 89, 91, 93, 97, 114, 132, 237, 274

Hanging Gardens
1, 7, 12, 15

hellebore
19

Hellenion
57, 273

hepatitis
19

Hephaistion
xxiv, 5, 6, 7, 8, 9, 10, 11, 26, 35

Heptastadion
74, 96, 203, 222

Heracles
12, 27, 52, 55

Heraclius
203

Herodian
xvi, 81, 100, 135, 138, 139, 142

Heyman, Johannes
174, 196

Hieronymus
35, 36, 47

Hogarth, David George
xx, 164, 193, 197, 222, 226, 242, 246, 254, 255, 276

Hogenberg
90

Homer
9, 25, 43, 59, 62

Hypereides
16

K

Khabbash
182

Kom el-Dikka
76, 163, 186, 189, 193, 226

Komoutsos, Stelios
232, 233

L

Latin Cemeteries
229, 231, 233, 234, 235, 236, 237, 239, 241, 247, 251, 255

Lauer, Jean-Philippe
xxi, 61, 65, 67

Leo Africanus
xix, 169, 173, 178, 196, 264, 270

leukaemia
19

Libanius
xvi, 159, 160, 161, 164, 184, 186, 266, 274

Lochias
159, 211, 212, 213, 219, 223, 231, 237, 274

Lochias peninsula
74

Lucan (Marcus Annaeus Lucanus)
xvii, 83, 84, 85, 86, 88, 93, 100, 105, 138, 236, 238, 254

Lucian
27, 35, 51, 53, 66, 164

Lysimachus
55, 66, 168

Lyskirchen
172, 196

M

Mahmoud Bey el-Falaki
xx, 70, 100

N

S